THE
BELONGING
HEART

THE BELONGING HEART

THE ATONEMENT AND RELATIONSHIPS WITH GOD AND FAMILY

BRUCE C. HAFEN
AND
MARIE K. HAFEN

Deseret Book Company
Salt Lake City, Utah

Chapters 6, 12, 13, 17, 18, and 19 first published in the *Ensign* magazine. © LDS Church. Used by permission.

"Father and Son" from *The Poems of Stanley Kunitz 1928–1978* © 1944, 1979 by Stanley Kunitz. Permission granted on the author's behalf by Darhansoff & Verrill Literary Agency.

Quotation on page 63 from *The Prophet,* by Kahlil Gibran. Copyright 1923 by Kahlil Gibran and renewed 1951 by Administrators C.T.A. of Kahlil Gibran Estate and Mary G. Gibran. Reprinted by permission of Alfred A. Knopf, Inc.

Library of Congress Cataloging-in-Publication Data

Hafen, Bruce C.
    The belonging heart / by Bruce C. and Marie K. Hafen.
      p.   cm.
    Includes bibliographical references and index.
    ISBN 0-87579-827-6
    1. Family—Religious life. 2. Atonement. 3. Spiritual life—
Church of Jesus Christ of Latter-day Saints. 4. Mormon Church—
Membership. 5. Church of Jesus Christ of Latter-day Saints—
Membership. I. Hafen, Marie K. II. Title.
BX8643.F3H34   1994
248.4'89332—dc20   93-40451
                                               CIP

Printed in the United States of America

10 9 8 7 6 5 4 3 2

*For Jon, David, Tom, Emily,
Sarah, Mark, and Rachel*

Contents

PART I

Introduction: The Longing to Belong

PART II

The Atonement and Belonging to God

CONTENTS

Preface

The preface to *The Believing Heart*[1] tells the story of our attempt over the past fifteen years to write a three-volume "Trilogy of the Heart." The heart of this trilogy is the Atonement of Jesus Christ. The three books focus on three dimensions of the Atonement: (1) Faith prepares us to receive the Atonement. (2) When our faith brings us to the Savior with a broken heart and a contrite spirit, the Atonement purifies, mellows, and strengthens us. (3) The Atonement then blesses our relationships with the Lord and with others, especially family members. In a general way, this developmental sequence reflects the three spiritual gifts described so eloquently by both Paul and Moroni: faith, hope, and charity. (See 1 Corinthians 13 and Moroni 7.) After *The Believing Heart* in 1986 came *The Broken Heart*, published in 1989. The present work, *The Belonging Heart*, completes the trilogy.

This book continues the application of Atonement doctrines that was undertaken in *The Broken Heart*, but it does so primarily in the context of a central theme about relationships. For example, the previous book discussed how "the Atonement is not just for sinners," meaning that the doctrines of the Atonement can help us deal with all earthly sorrow and pain—traumas we suffer not only because of our sins but also because of unavoidable adversity or because of personal misjudgments arising from our ignorance or carelessness. We further explore these issues in this book, especially as they are affected by our relationships with other people or with the Lord.

Thus one chapter discusses how the Atonement can help us when we are harmed by the sins of others. Another chapter treats the Atonement's developmental nature, which lets us learn from our experience without being condemned by that experience. Other chapters summarize the doctrinal foundation that makes the Atonement's broad reach possible, a foundation located primarily in our covenant relationship with Jesus Christ.

As was the case in *The Broken Heart*, "the doctrines of the Atonement are relevant to [all of the book's] chapters but are not always on center stage. At times the Atonement acts here only as a backdrop, a source of quiet but sure perspective."[2] For instance, our attitude toward the idea of "belonging" profoundly affects our ability to enter into the relationship of being "at one" with the Lord, because a crowning blessing of the Savior's Atonement is that we will fully belong to him as children of Christ. Similarly, the Atonement blesses the belonging we find in marriage and family life, because the gift of charity toward others is a fruit of the Atonement, and because the Atonement makes it even possible that "families can be together forever."[3]

With the Atonement thus acting as a backdrop, this volume's core theme about relationships revolves around two general concepts that are introduced in part I: *the longing to belong* and *the waning of belonging.*

In the modern world, these two opposing concepts are locked in a growing struggle, a kind of war for our souls. We all carry deep inside ourselves an inborn longing to belong that naturally draws us toward certain people, beginning with our mother and our father, then extending to others as we grow older, including especially our spouses, our children, and ultimately our Father in Heaven. The fulfillment of this longing leads to the achievement of humankind's deepest aspirations.

Running counter to this instinctive desire to belong is the waning of belonging, a growing assumption in American culture that we should hold ourselves apart from other people and from God. This is a major theme of twentieth-century life that draws on the historic decline of community and on the emergence of the lonely individual as the symbol of our age.

None of us today can completely escape the tension between these two forces. As we face that tension, the current momentum throughout society and sometimes among Church members seems to favor the forces of individualism.

Our life experiences tell the two of us that the teachings of the gospel of Jesus Christ offer the best—often the only—answers to this complex dilemma. Only the gospel explains how we can find personal freedom and meaning for our own lives as we lose our lives in belonging to others and to the Lord. Only the gospel can help us understand the true nature of man-woman relationships in this time of the sexual revolution and the radical feminist critique of society. Only the gospel can teach us how entering into the Atonement-based relationship of belonging to Christ will unlock the most potent blessings of heaven and apply them like healing balm to the most disturbing problems of our lives.

Our work on this book has raised many more questions for us than we can possibly address in these pages. Some disclaimers are therefore needed. For example, we emphasize here the blessings of a good marriage and a secure family life. Yet some of our closest and most admired friends have been denied the blessings of marriage, or they have found themselves in marriages or child-parent relationships with which they must struggle every day, even to survive. Our awareness of these realities makes us want to qualify many of our general observations or to argue for exceptions to general principles.

But we also believe that one of the forces that now hasten the waning of belonging is that American society, often with good intentions, has made so many allowances for exceptional cases that we have retreated from the expectations that should be our cultural norms. We are paying too dearly for that retreat. In the national White House Conference on Families a few years ago, for example, the delegates could not even agree on the meaning of the word *family*.[4] This impasse arose from an understandable desire to make everyone feel included; but the effect of the impasse was to signal that the nation is no longer sure whether relationships based on marriage and kinship are more worth striving for than any other relationship.

If at times we seem idealistic, that is only because we believe that striving for ideal relationships will lead to greater long-term growth and blessings, even when we fall short of the ideal. Some tension between the ideal and the real is not only normal but also healthy,[5] so long as we can refrain from harshly judging each other (and ourselves) when that tension stretches us beyond our limits.

We next acknowledge that this volume might have sought a more obvious balance between the need for personal identity and the need to identify with God and with other people. By emphasizing belonging in these pages, we do not wish to minimize either theologically or practically the critical importance of individual development and the quest for self-fulfillment. Chapter 4 speaks directly to this issue. Moreover, while most of this volume stresses our ties with God and with others, the two earlier books emphasized the individual: *The Believing Heart* treated themes showing the importance of individual initiative, and *The Broken Heart* was primarily concerned with the process of personal religious development in the crucible of mortal experience. Thus the balance we hope to convey between allegiance to self and allegiance to others is best seen by viewing all three volumes as part of a conceptual, developing whole.

Moreover, the sequence that progresses from a believing heart to a broken heart to a belonging heart generally reflects the normal three-stage process of human development, and this volume addresses primarily the third stage. As psychologist Erik Erikson puts it, healthy maturation in the three stages of our life span (childhood, adolescence, and adulthood) moves from hope to fidelity to care. We begin our lives as children, having an unavoidably self-centered focus. This focus is best channeled toward growth by a hope-oriented environment of trust and safety. As we move into adolescence, our self-focus intensifies, creating a heightened awareness of our personal freedom and our autonomy. When wisely worked through, the adolescent preoccupation with self can actually help orient our sense of personal identity toward future altruism. Our maintaining a strong "fidelity to that identity"[6] then helps propel us into a successful adulthood.

Erikson believes that the primary task of those in the third (the adult) stage of the life span is "learning to care for and nurture the next generation."[7] Thus, as we continue along the path toward adult maturity, we typically assume new forms of responsibility for others as we become missionaries, spouses, parents, leaders, and teachers. As we assume such duties, we have experiences that often lead us to be as concerned about others as we are about ourselves. Furthermore, our involvement in others' needs also adds "wisdom"—wise self-understanding—to the development of our own identity.[8] Those who do not experience this normal process of growth may end up "pursuing false forms of intimacy, self-absorption, and isolation."[9] We see the waning of belonging as a broad and recent cultural trend that results from arrested personal development of this kind all across American society.

In an inviting parallel to the three concepts involved in our Trilogy of the Heart, Erikson has compared his "three major life-span developmental tasks" to the three "Christian virtues of hope, faith, and charity."[10] It is natural, then, that this third volume might address itself primarily to the relationships of care that express our sense of charity.

A related disclaimer: this is more of a "why" book than a "how to" book—even though we still believe, as stated in the prologue to *The Broken Heart*, that nothing is more practical than a good theory. We are concerned essentially with the foundations of attitude and orientation that develop the root idea of belonging. This leaves much room for discussion about what we can and should do once our belonging hearts are right. In an important sense, our belonging is a means to larger ends. Belonging is a fundamental need, but once it is being met, we are then simply in a better position to thrive, to contribute, and to grow toward the perfection of our higher nature. We have not here extensively considered where and how one might travel the growth path "beyond belonging."

We also realize that society offers many forms of belonging, and some of them are destructive counterfeits of the gospel's authentic pattern—such as the youth gangs that now haunt the nation's streets and neighborhoods. It would be a valuable exercise to compare authentic forms with imitative forms of belonging, but we have done only some of that here.

In addition, the subject of belonging raises important questions that extend beyond our two areas of primary focus—relationships with family members and with the Lord. We might have considered the broader matter of relationships within society and among Church members, including the need to strengthen the community interests of our culture, now that Americans' recent emphasis on individualism has malnourished our sense of community. We could also productively explore the problems of individuality vs. conformity in the Church. We believe, for example, that belonging to the Church and to the Lord should lead not only to stronger family and institutional bonds but also to richer individual development. Our belonging should not lead primarily to pinched attitudes of shallow compliance. But for the most part, these issues, like the others noted above, must remain for other authors on other days.

Finally, we live in a day of too much contention, frustration, mistrust, and anger. We see all around us too much loneliness, aimlessness, and hopelessness. In all of this, we sense an advanced state of decay on both sides of the natural structure of belonging—both the giving side and the receiving side. On the giving side, we need more charity so that we may genuinely nourish, guide, and support those we love. On the receiving side, we need greater trust, greater willingness to submit to legitimate authority, more patience to remain vulnerable. It is our conviction that the Atonement and the teachings of the Savior will bring these needs together in ways that lead all of us—those who love and those who are loved—to greater freedom and to full satisfaction of the soul. This is the way of the belonging heart.

Acknowledgments

We express appreciation to Jon Hafen, Daniel H. Ludlow, LuAnn Snyder, and Lynn D. Wardle for reading earlier manuscript drafts and making many helpful suggestions. We are also grateful to other family members and friends for valuable editing and stimulating consultation. Additionally, we thank Dillon K. and Jeanne B. Inouye for their insights on chapters 1 and 7. We offer special thanks to Professor Akira Morita of Toyo University in Japan for introducing us to the concept of *amae*, and to Professor Van Gessel of the Brigham Young University Department of Asian and Near Eastern Languages for validating our impressions of the significance of Dr. Takeo Doi's work.

We also wish to thank The Church of Jesus Christ of Latter-day Saints for permission to publish chapters 6, 12, 13, 17, 18, and 19, earlier versions of which appeared in the *Ensign;* to Brigham Young University for permission to publish chapter 11, one version of which appeared in *Brigham Young Magazine* and a still earlier version of which was published as the 1985 Harman Lecture sponsored by the Division of Continuing Education; to the administration of Religious Education at BYU for the opportunity to present the material in chapter 6 to the 1990 Sperry Symposium; and to the BYU Women's Conference for the opportunity to present earlier versions of chapters 5 and 14 at the 1985 and 1993 conferences.

Finally, the opinions expressed here are our own. These should not be construed as representing Brigham Young University or its Board of Trustees.

Part I

INTRODUCTION: THE LONGING TO BELONG

CHAPTER ONE

The Longing to Belong

On some days, our dealings with other people might prompt us to think that the greatest reward in the life after death should be that God, and everyone else, will just leave us alone, unencumbered by the needs and demands of others.

However, Jesus Christ came to accomplish the great at-one-ment,[1] not the great alone-ment. He came to overcome our separation from God and from one another. He seeks to bring us to his Father, to himself, and to each other, at one, through the gift and power of his Atonement. Even though we do need some space for ourselves,[2] something deep inside each of us instinctively responds to this gospel of belonging, drawing us to certain other people and to God.

We recently attended two memorial services, just weeks apart, for two three-year-old girls, Jessica and Nicole, whose fathers had both grown up in what was once our neighborhood. These little girls were the same age as our own granddaughter, whose expressive personality just melts us whenever we see her or talk to her on the phone.

Jessica had been killed in a freak automobile accident in a neighborhood driveway; Nicole had died from a sudden attack of spinal meningitis. In one moment, they were skip-

3

ping and running and squealing with delight; in the next, they were gone. And somehow, when they left, they seemed to take a piece of many hearts with them, including ours.

Just after Jessica's grave was dedicated, her five-year-old brother, Jaren, walked toward the grave holding the strings to a bevy of helium-filled pink balloons. As he looked for the last time at his sister's casket, he released the pink balloons, and they soared through the sky toward heaven, as we sensed that Jessica's spirit had done.

Something about this scene pulls at our hearts. Why does it move us as it does?

We also noticed a great sense of loss among those we saw at the services. Many felt the sadness we did. We wondered what would explain our feelings. Children who die at their age are assured of exaltation in the celestial kingdom. We therefore had cause to rejoice for them. Why did our hearts remain so heavy? Much of that sadness was empathy for our friends, their parents and grandparents. But some of it was for us. As John Donne wrote four centuries ago:

> All mankind is of one author, and is one volume; when one man dies, one chapter is not torn out of the book, but translated into a better language; . . . God's hand is in every translation, and his hand shall bind up all our scattered leaves again. . . . No man is an island entire of itself; every man is a piece of the continent, a part of the main. If a clod be washed away by the sea, Europe is the less, as well as if a promontory were, as well as if a manor of thy friend's or of thine own were. Any man's death diminishes me, because I am involved in mankind, and therefore never send to know for whom the bell tolls; it tolls for thee.[3]

If no man is an island among the generality of humankind, we are even more involved when sharing ties of close kinship. Few expressions are more tender to us than certain pages written in 1935 in the journal of Bruce's father,

Orval Hafen. Orval and his wife, Ruth Clark, had just buried their first and, at that time, their only child, a fifteen-month-old boy named Joseph. They called him Jan. Jan had died within days of contracting a respiratory illness. His death stunned his young parents.

In his private hour of grief, Orval wrote:

> We loved our boy, perhaps too much. He was the light, the life, and the joy of our lives. Everything was wrapped up in him—all our hopes, plans, aspirations, and ambitions. . . . During the night before he died, we prayed constantly that we might keep him. I prayed to God that I didn't want to keep him just because we would be grieved to have him go; that was selfish; but I did ask that he might be permitted to stay so that he could get all the development he was meant to get from life upon this earth; that he could grow into manhood; that he could become a great Christian, fighting aggressively for the right, that he could develop his talents and his character and his personality. . . .
>
> [His death] makes us more mellow, it gives us more vision, more faith. It makes us more appreciative of our friends and relatives, and of the problems and sorrows of others. It makes us want to do good, to comfort the sorrowing, to live worthy lives so when our time comes we can meet [him] without regrets and without apology. Even so, there will always be an empty place in our hearts for our little boy.

Two months later, Orval's journal records a "letter" he wrote to his little Jan "in Heaven," including:

> I'm in your little room now; it seems so empty without you. Tonight on the stairway to the basement when I switched the light on, I could almost see you there with a mischievous twinkle in those happy little eyes of yours turning the light off again just to tease your Daddy. . . . We wish you could

5

> write back to us, but you're such a little boy. . . .
> You'll always know, won't you son, that our love is
> with you to help you with your problems, just like
> we know yours is with us. We believe, little as you
> were, that you loved us, and our love for you [will]
> carry us over those years between. We will try as
> best we can to prove worthy of the heavenly little
> soul you are. So good night.

In Orval Hafen's heart was a touching desire—a long-ing—to stay close to his child. These feelings remained with him throughout the rest of his life. His longing, like the broad urge to reach out to others that John Donne described or the tenderness we felt for Jessica and Nicole, is understandable to each person who has felt closeness and love for others.

These feelings vary widely from one person and one relationship to another. They come in many shades of meaning and intensity, and they are driven by a variety of motivations. For such reasons, no single phrase or concept can begin to capture such feelings, much less explain them. Nonetheless, there is some common core of meaning in our experience with other people and with God that surfaces in many of these contexts. People simply feel a desire to be connected with others, especially in close relationships. They are feeling the longing to belong.

In *Heaven: A History*, recently published by Yale University Press, historians Colleen McDannell and Bernhard Lang trace both popular and religious beliefs about the concept of heaven throughout the centuries of Western history. They chose this subject for study because "it reflects a deep and profound longing in Christianity to move beyond this life and to experience more fully the divine. The ways in which people imagine heaven tell us how they understand themselves, their families, their society, and their God." Indeed, these authors regard their subject as "a key to [understanding] our Western culture."[4]

The McDannell and Lang study concludes by assessing beliefs about heaven in twentieth-century America. They report that 71 percent of Americans believe "there is a heaven where people who have led good lives are eternally rewarded." Significantly, the fraction of the population who hold this belief is about the same today as it was in 1952.[5] In attitudes toward topics ranging from cemeteries to love songs, people from all Christian denominations still express their instinctive belief in "the eternal nature of love and the hope for heavenly reunion," especially with their family members.[6] These popular sentiments echo Emily Dickinson's hope from a century ago that the "Life that is to be" will be "a Residence too plain/Unless in my Redeemer's Face/I recognize your own."[7]

The natural yearning to belong eternally to close friends and family also includes a longing for an eternal relationship with God. A 1983 survey reported in a prominent Catholic publication revealed that many American Catholics "want to 'hug God' when they arrive in heaven." McDannell and Lang note that this response echoes "the hopes of earlier generations: God will be a personal character willing to be hugged, individuals will retain their personalities, families will reunite, and earthly activities will continue."[8]

Sadly and ironically, as described more fully in chapter 6, these authors go on to report that mainline Christian teachings offer little support for or response to these widespread hopes and feelings. They then add that there is one major exception to this theological vacuum—the teachings of The Church of Jesus Christ of Latter-day Saints, which offer the most fully developed concept of heavenly belonging available in the modern age.

The McDannell and Lang findings verify in society what most of us have experienced individually: at times we feel an emotional or spiritual hunger, a kind of psychic emptiness. We wander to and fro, trying to satisfy this intuitive

craving, which Robert Browning called "the passionate longing of the heart for fulness."[9] The world leads us to believe
that we can fill the void with immediate pleasure, power,
and material things. In response, most of us sample these
short-term gratifications, often at great cost. Yet when we
taste them, our soul-hunger is somehow still with us. We
can't get enough of what we don't really need. So we remain
incomplete. And the philosophy and religion available to
most people today are disappointingly unresponsive to our
needs.

The good news is that the gospel of Jesus Christ answers
the heart's longing for fulness. The Father of our spirits
knows where we belong—where our core being can say, "I
was made for this." To that end, God would have us fulfill
our deepest eternal yearnings and know the meaning of our
very existence.

We do not live by bread alone, and we were not made
to *be* alone. "Happiness is the object and design of our existence," wrote Joseph Smith.[10] But the life of alienation and
distance from God and from other people leads away from
that object and design. The life of faith, hope, and charity—
the life of the belonging heart—brings us to and keeps us
within the arms of the Holy One of Israel. When in his presence, we will embrace not only him but also those we loved
and served on earth. And in all these bonds of belonging is
the fulness of our joy.

The gospel not only recognizes the longing to belong—
it offers the most complete available means of fulfilling that
longing. For example, among its greatest gifts, the gospel
offers the doctrine and the ordinances of eternal marriage.
We know from nearly universal human experience that
enduring love between a man and a woman can approach
the highest form of mortal fulfillment. There is some kind of
mysterious magnetism that draws a specific man and a specific woman toward one another, like homing pigeons look-

ing for home. And when we have paid the price of patient preparation, self-discipline, and an irrevocable commitment to another person's happiness, we can taste the sweet joy of authentic human love. The gospel's assurance that we can be encircled about *eternally* in the arms of this romantic love promises to fulfill our deepest longing for security and belonging—hopes expressed in the poetry and song of all our history.

Further, the gospel recognizes that God's children—all of us—also sense at times a particular longing for Him. Eliza R. Snow's moving "O My Father" reaches deeply into our hearts to stir within us a dim, undefinable memory of an eternal home:

> O my Father, thou that dwellest
> In the high and glorious place
> When shall I regain thy presence
> And again behold thy face?
> . . . .
> For a wise and glorious purpose
> Thou hast placed me here on earth
> And withheld the recollection
> Of my former friends and birth;
> Yet ofttimes a secret something
> Whispered, "You're a stranger here,"
> And I felt that I had wandered
> From a more exalted sphere.
>
> . . . .
> When I leave this frail existence,
> When I lay this mortal by,
> Father, Mother, may I meet you
> In your royal courts on high?
> Then, at length, when I've completed
> All you sent me forth to do,
> With your mutual approbation
> Let me come and dwell with you.[11]

The gospel teaches us that these are echoes of home, the whisperings of an unexplainable homesickness.

Children of all ages give voice to their longing for home and for heavenly parents when they sing, "Lead me, guide me, walk beside me,/Help me find the way./Teach me all that I must do/To live with him someday."[12] As we faithfully weather the mortal experience, the wondrous gift of Christ's Atonement promises the fulfillment of these desires for family and for God. Because of what He did, if we are true and faithful, we may not only return to God's presence; we may also become truly "at one" with him, belonging to him in a full spiritual sense.

The gospel defines this desire as our ultimate hope— returning to God's presence in the celestial kingdom. In that place, we will find not only him but also husbands, wives, family members, friends—all those we love most. We teach our children that we must become like God—but that too is so that we may dwell with him, and with each other, eternally. The saving ordinances reflect and enable these hopes: through baptism we enter a two-way covenant relationship with the Savior; through temple marriage a man and woman are sealed to each other eternally; and children born under temple covenants or blessed by temple ordinances are sealed to their parents. Both our theology and the feelings of our hearts make us want to *belong*, now and eternally, to the Father of our Spirits, to his Son, and to those we love on earth.

Given the existence, then, of a longing to belong, and given the gospel's basic promise to fulfill that instinct, let us consider now some possible sources that may explain where the longing comes from. Because these feelings represent universal human experiences, scholars and practitioners in many fields have written about them.

For example, psychologists commonly place the need to be loved and accepted at or near the top of any list of basic human needs. Among the most significant of the psychological descriptions is the Japanese concept of "*amae*," which

describes an inborn desire for emotional and spiritual fulfillment that can be satisfied only through close, nurturing relationships. *Amae* is essentially the desire to receive love. This
concept is important enough to warrant separate treatment
in chapter 2.

Other authors have sought to explain the human desire
to draw close to others. In a noted recent book, for instance,
philosopher James Q. Wilson analyzes the natural instincts
that cause men and women everywhere to feel fundamental
concerns and commitments toward others in "moral univer-
sals" that include the "universal attachment between child
and parent."[13] And as Alex Haley's work demonstrated a few
years ago, the search for biological, ancestral roots can capture the public imagination, echoing the commonly felt
desires of many people to know their origins and their
ancestors.[14]

One of the most provocative, even if speculative, explanations of our desire for closeness to others is illustrated by
the work of anthropologist Joseph Campbell and psychologist Carl Jung. Campbell and Jung have each identified a
kind of "collective memory" of the human race within each
person, which they believe explains why so many people,
across all times and cultures, share common moral codes,
common religious and mythical imagery, and common personal aspirations.[15]

This collective consciousness may originate in our biological make-up, which carries a human memory bank that
could explain some of our attraction toward immediate
ancestors and descendants, those who most closely share our
gene pool. Modern science, which is exploding with new
understanding of our genetic coding, seems to support such
assumptions. Recent discoveries suggest that the DNA within
each of our body cells may predispose us to exhibit certain
tendencies transmitted to us by our parents and grandparents. These discoveries confirm how each human being is a

physical, literal part of the bodies of his or her parents. In this sense, our parents live on through us, as we live on through our children.

The scriptures make it clear, of course, that each person is a free, independent, and eternal being.[16] As one friend described his seven-year-old boy, "Some of who he is comes from Mom, some comes from Dad, but some just comes from himself."[17] Still, our genetic linkage with family members often causes us naturally to feel an emotional as well as a biological kinship for them—as if the risks they face may threaten us as well.

For instance, the 1852 French story "The Corsican Brothers" describes two identical twins, Fabien and Louis, whose identities were so intertwined that when one was injured the other felt pain, regardless of the miles that separated them. As Fabien described it, "There is a strange, mysterious sympathy between us; no matter what space divides us, we are still one in body, in feeling, in soul. Any powerful impression which the one experiences is instantly conveyed by some invisible agency to the senses of the other."[18]

Joseph Campbell also theorizes that our internal memory bank may explain our attraction not only to parents and children but also to our marriage partners. He believes that this unconscious "inner mystery" carries a memory of the archetypal life patterns of those who began the human race. We may reflect this hidden instinct in our innate longing to marry, because marriage "is the reunion of the separated duad. Originally you were one. You are now two in the world, but the recognition of the spiritual identity is what marriage is. It's different from [only] a love affair." This "reunion of the self with the self, with the male or female grounding of ourselves" reflects the "Chinese image of the Tao, with the dark and light interacting," the "relationship of yang and yin, male and female." In this relationship, "The one isn't just you, it's the two together as one."[19]

While these insights help us understand some possible sources of the longing to belong, they are incomplete in comparison to the doctrines of the gospel. For example, the original oneness in marriage that Campbell describes began in the unity of Adam and Eve: "This I know now is bone of my bones, and flesh of my flesh; she shall be called Woman, because she was taken out of man. Therefore . . . they shall be one flesh." (Moses 3:23.) With such origins, even though we do not understand the full meaning of the Lord's disclosure that woman was taken out of man, the longing for marriage feels very natural.

On a broader scale, the scholars who see evidence of inborn memories and instincts toward belonging are witnesses of a truth much larger than they perceive. Consider two gospel-based illustrations that explain our general desire to be close to ancestors, descendants, and loved ones—the Spirit of Elijah and the doctrine of the premortal existence.

As chapter 12 develops more fully, both Malachi and Moroni have told us that Elijah literally "turns the hearts" of children and their fathers toward one another. Elijah creates some of this heartfelt yearning by planting "in the hearts of the children the promises made to the father, and the hearts of the children shall turn to their fathers." (D&C 2:2.) He also "shall turn the heart of the fathers to the children." (Malachi 4:6.) Drawing on this understanding, the Lord taught through Joseph Smith that we have strong ties with those who precede and follow us in our ancestral chains of being. He referred to these ties as "a welding link" that must be nourished by our performance of ordinances for our dead. These links matter so much that "we without them cannot be made perfect; neither can they without us be made perfect." (D&C 128:18.) As both parents and genealogical researchers know, Elijah's turning of children's and parents' hearts toward one another creates a moving, tangible longing.

The scriptures also verify and explain more fully the

13

source of humankind's group memory. All of us collectively shared certain experiences prior to mortality, which suggests why people might be drawn to each other and exhibit common tendencies. Our spirits were fathered by the same eternal God, who nurtured us while we were with each other prior to our birth. (See Alma 13; Abraham 3:22–28.) The conditions of premortal life were evidently not unlike the sociality that exists among us here. Each of us had a distinctive identity and gender. We possessed there "a pre-existent, spiritual personality, as the sons and daughters of the Eternal Father."[20] Therefore, our associations together in mortality and the idea of continuing our associations after death naturally sound both attractive and familiar to us.

The knowledge that we are literal, spirit children of God also reveals a stirring source of our attraction to him—the genetic-like link between ourselves and our Father in Heaven. We share with Jesus Christ the common heritage that God is the literal father of our *spirit* body, the substance that clothes our eternal essence or intelligence.[21] We are not certain how our spirit bodies were formed, but we do know from early First Presidency statements that "man [is] the direct and lineal offspring of Deity . . . formed in the divine image and endowed with divine attributes."[22] God did not father our *physical* bodies, as he did the Savior's, but of all the living things God created on the earth, only human beings were created in his own image. (See Moses 2:26–27.) Moreover, as Paul taught the Athenians, "We are the *offspring* of God;" therefore, "in him we live, and move, and have our being." (Acts 17:28–29; emphasis added.) Is there a spiritual equivalent of DNA?

Even if only by analogy to mortal genetics, it may be that, just as we carry certain genetic receptors that draw us to our parents and our children, we also carry some kind of spiritual genetic coding that is literally a part of the Father himself. This divine substance would give form to our spirits

in God's image in much the same sense as we are biologi-
cally created in the image of our natural parents. If so, it is
no mere symbolism to sing "I am a Child of God."

Given the likelihood of that nearly incomprehensible tie,
no wonder we long for God. No wonder we intuitively
desire *more* of his Spirit to be "with us." We express this
hope in virtually every prayer we utter, as we pray for guidance, inspiration, and the literal presence of his Spirit in our
lives. Yet no matter how much of his Spirit we have, it may
never be enough to satisfy fully our longing to draw closer
to him. Perhaps that eternal fulness is possible only when we
are permanently reunited with him.

This divine inheritance may also explain why we can
experience no sense of loss quite so devastating as the complete withdrawal of his Spirit, which removes the life-giving
connection between the Lord and the divine substance
within us. As the ancient Nephites learned: "When the Spirit
ceaseth to strive with man then cometh speedy destruction."
(2 Nephi 26:11.) The Savior also felt an awful emptiness
when the Lord withdrew his Spirit while Jesus hung on the
cross: "My God, My God, why hast thou forsaken me?"
(Matthew 27:46.) (See page 62.) The removal of God's Spirit
can so wound our core being that the Lord has pleaded with
us to repent. "Repent," he said, "lest you suffer [eternally]
these punishments of which I have spoken, of which in the
smallest, yea, even in the least degree you have tasted at the
time I withdrew my Spirit." (D&C 19:20.)

If the ultimate deprivation is a total severance from the
Lord's Spirit, leaving us *alone* from him in spiritual darkness,
the ultimate joy may be the blessing of being *with him*,
totally filled with that Spirit. Then "there shall be no darkness
in" us, for if our eye is single to his glory, our "whole bodies
shall be filled with light" (D&C 88:67), a light that "groweth
brighter and brighter until the perfect day" (D&C 50:24). That

perfect day is when our being permanently reunited with God eternally fulfills our yearning for him.

Having seen that the longing to belong is instilled in our very *nature*, we consider next the doctrinal sources that describe how our knowing and obeying the Lord's commandments will lead him to *nurture* within us the development of our longing toward its fulfillment. The Lord's doctrines instruct us to seek and build close relationships, both with family members and with him. As we obey his counsel, our disposition to strengthen those relationships intensifies. Ultimately, our obedience to the commandments will then fulfill our longings. The first and most significant of these doctrines and blessings is the gift of charity.

Rising above the discouragement of their personal circumstances, a family in Eastern Europe listened to the message of Latter-day Saint missionaries. They read the Book of Mormon, took to heart its message of hope, and joined the Church. Some time later, a friend asked the father, "Well, now that you have become a Mormon, what has changed most in your life?" The man could have described his initial sense of loss in giving up coffee and cigarettes. He might have compared how differently he spent his Sundays than he did before. But instead, the father replied thoughtfully, "What has changed most is the increased sense of love we all feel for one another in our family."[23]

As described in the concluding chapter on charity in *The Broken Heart*, the scriptures and the experiences of many people verify what happened to this family: after we accept the Atonement of Jesus Christ unto the forgiveness of our sins, we will naturally begin "to feel a desire for the welfare" of others (Enos 1:9), first with those closest to us—our families. This desire wells up in us partly through our initiative, as we try to obey the Savior's commandment, "That ye love one another; as I have loved you." (John 13:34.) In addition, we feel increased love for each other because God literally bestows upon us the gift of charity—the love Jesus himself has for all mankind. He bestows this gift upon "all who are true followers of his Son." (Moroni 7:48.) As the Savior taught his disciples, "By this shall all men know that ye are my disciples, if ye have love one to another." (John 13:35.)

For example, when Lehi in his dream tasted the fruit of the tree of life, he began to feel "the love of God, which sheddeth itself abroad in the hearts of the children of men." (1 Nephi 11:22.) This fruit, a symbol of the blessings of the Atonement, filled his soul "with exceedingly great joy; wherefore, he began to be desirous that his family should partake of it also." (1 Nephi 8:12.) Because of the way the gift of charity worked upon Lehi as he embraced the gospel, he longed for those he loved most.

As we begin to follow Christ, then, the Lord gives us charity—a natural impulse to extend mercy and grace to others as we receive them from him. "Because I have been given much," we sing, "I too must give."[24] As we reach our hands toward theirs, sometimes their reaching touches ours—and we somehow sense the Lord's grace coming back to us, multiplied, through them. So we sing again, "Each life that touches ours for good reflects thine own great mercy, Lord."[25] As we receive God's love, we extend it to others in a circle that brings it back to us and brings us back to him. In this kind of life, a full life of *gracious* connections with other people, we live the spirit of charity.

Charity is but one illustration of the way obedience to God's commandments both nurtures and satisfies our longing to belong. Many other core gospel doctrines instruct us to develop relationships of belonging with the Lord and with family members. For example, the commandment to accept the Savior's Atonement directs us to become "at one" with him and his Father: "Now this is the commandment: Repent, all ye ends of the earth, and come unto me." (3 Nephi 27:20.) Our embracing of Christ's gospel can lead us eventually to

embrace him, in a relationship of unity that fulfills everlastingly our longing to belong. At the very hour of his
Atonement, the Savior prayed: "For their sakes I sanctify
myself, that they also might be sanctified. . . . That they all
may be one; as thou, Father, art in me, and I in thee, that
they also may be one in us: . . . that they may be one, even
as we are one." (John 17:19–22.) The Savior's intercessory
prayer for at-one-ment expressed in words what his sacrifice
made possible.

Our accepting and living the doctrine of eternal marriage
also increases, then fulfills, the longing for eternal unity that
accompanies genuine love. From the beginning, the Lord has
taught his children the value of married love, not only for
mortal time but also for heavenly eternity. Indeed, marriage
is a *commandment* having both earthly and heavenly implications: "It [is] not good that the man should be alone."
(Moses 3:18.) Therefore, God gave Adam and Eve to each
other, and he directed that a man *shall* "leave his father and
his mother, and shall cleave unto his wife; and they shall be
one flesh." (Moses 3:24.) In addition, the Lord commanded
our first parents to bear children: "Be fruitful, and multiply,
and replenish the earth." (Moses 2:28.)

The loving attachments of marriage and family life often
develop so naturally and so deeply that it may surprise us to
learn that in modern revelation the Lord has actually commanded us to love our spouses: "*Thou shalt* love thy wife
with all thy heart, and shalt cleave unto her and none else."
(D&C 42:22; emphasis added.) And more broadly, "*Thou
shalt* live together in love, insomuch that thou shalt weep for
the loss of them that die." (D&C 42:45; emphasis added.)

Further, no individual, woman or man, has access to the
highest degree of celestial life alone: "Neither is the man
without the woman, neither the woman without the man, in
the Lord." (1 Corinthians 11:11.) To obtain exaltation, we
must receive the priesthood ordinance of eternal marriage.

(See D&C 131:1–3.) And one of exaltation's further blessings is the promise that parents sealed in the new and everlasting covenant of marriage will be joined in those eternal bonds by their worthy children.

Our children anticipate the fulfillment of this promise when they sing that through Heavenly Father's plan, "families can be together forever."[26] President Ezra Taft Benson has spoken of this joyful anticipation in describing heavenly reunions for families where there are "no empty chairs." Thus, if we keep our covenants, we may look forward with assurance to that day: "When the Savior shall appear we shall see him as he is. We shall see that he is a man like ourselves. And that same sociality which exists among us here will exist among us there, only it will be coupled with eternal glory." (D&C 130:1–2.) The ongoing enjoyment of prized relationships—"that same sociality which exists among us here"—is fundamental to our very definition of eternal life.

The eternal emptiness of choosing through disobedience to fill no family chairs at all is captured in these sobering words: "Thy sons and thy daughters shall be given unto another people, and thine eyes shall look and fail with longing for them all the day long: and there shall be no might in thine hand." (Deuteronomy 28:32.)

Not everyone, of course, is given the blessings of marriage and children in mortality, even when those blessings are what he or she most desires. But the Lord's prophets have assured us that eternal marriage awaits the faithful ones who did not choose their singlehood: "On occasions when you ache for that acceptance and affection which belong to family life on earth, please know that our Father in Heaven is aware of your anguish, and that one day he will bless you beyond your capacity to express."[27]

To summarize, we can identify the longing to belong in many common experiences—attitudes toward the death of loved ones; natural attractions toward marriage and children;

and our human yearning for heaven and for God. We carry some of these feelings with us as we leave our Father in Heaven and enter into mortality. We reflect them in our attitudes toward ancestors and descendants, and in our universal human need for psychological security and freedom—our *amae*. Our longing is stirred when it is touched by the spirit of Elijah. It expands when God gives us the gift of charity. The Lord increases and nourishes our longing, even unto fulness, as we obey his commandments. We may not know all of the sources of this longing, but we do know that the gospel is the pathway to its fulfillment.

So is it promised and so can it be: after our *believing heart* nourishes us with faith unto repentance, we offer the Lord through our faithfulness a truly *broken heart*. Then his acceptance of that sacrifice blesses us with a *belonging heart*, a heart in which the longing to belong is fully satisfied and filled with love: "Seeing ye have purified your souls in obeying the truth through the Spirit . . . see that ye love one another with a pure heart fervently." (1 Peter 1:22.) This natural, three-step pattern of happiness and holiness could be described in three books—or in three words: faith, hope, and charity.

Each of us has a heart that longs for fulness, and the gospel is designed to fill that need as nothing else can. Indeed, to be exalted is to find such fulfillment eternally. Today's waning of belonging is therefore frightening, because it can keep us from satisfying our heart's deepest hunger. But if we come to Christ and live the commandments, our longing is exponentially and simultaneously strengthened and satisfied, until it is permanently filled with the blessing of a belonging heart.

CHAPTER TWO

Amae *and the Longing to Belong*

We completed a draft of the manuscript for *The Belonging Heart* in June of 1993.[1] Only a month later, I first met Akira Morita, a Japanese law professor from Tokyo, who was making his first trip to the United States.* He had come to BYU to discuss our common interests in family law, particularly issues relating to children and juvenile courts.

During our visit, Professor Morita introduced me to the significant Japanese concept of *amae*, which, he said, bears striking resemblance to what he had heard me call "belonging." The word *amae,* for which no English equivalent exists, describes the innate need and desire within each person to depend on and feel connected to other people, especially in relationships of love and intimacy. In a sense, *amae* is the desire to *receive* love. Through the fulfillment of our *amae* we find not only security but also freedom and meaning. I found it remarkable that I could learn of this rich idea just after writing a possible introduction for this book called "The Longing to Belong."

An understanding of *amae* articulates and clarifies some

---

*Because this essay reflects Bruce's interaction with Professor Akira Morita, he writes here in first person singular.

of the unspoken premises about relationships of belonging from which I have intuitively proceeded over the past several years, not only in working on our religious "Trilogy of the Heart," but also in my professional research and writing in the field of family law. For instance, my work on children's legal rights has expressed concern about "abandoning children to their 'rights,'"[2] and I have lamented "the waning of belonging" in American law's recent approach to marriage and family obligations.[3] I'm also troubled about the deterioration of the nation's public schools, some of which I attribute to a general erosion of paternalistic authority.[4] Professor Morita's view is that recent American law tends to divide people—but he correctly perceives and shares my belief that it would be far better if the law could somehow create incentives that bring people together.

In the religious sphere, to explore the meaning of *amae* is to make more explicit the nature of our innate longing for God, which was discussed in the previous chapter. When Alma saw a vision of God and his holy angels, he exclaimed, "My soul did long to be there." (Alma 36:22.) His desire for his eternal home echoes the yearning expressed in the hymn "O My Father." *Amae* expresses a similar longing but expands it to a wide range of human feeling, beginning with infancy and extending beyond death.

The Japanese concept of *amae* reveals that our intuition to belong, both to others and to God, is "something instinctive [that is] common to all mankind."[5] Each of us possesses an inborn wish to "draw close to the other person," like the craving of a newborn child for its mother. It is a "desire to [overcome] the . . . separation that is an inevitable part of human existence, and to obliterate the pain that this separation involves."[6] *Amae* "manifests itself in a longing to merge with others." Yet, for long-standing historical and cultural reasons, the European and American societies have overlooked, ignored, and often denied the value of *amae*—which is why

"in Western societies . . . there is no . . . word correspond-
ing to *amae* and feelings of *amae* would seem not to exist."[7]
In fact, however, those natural feelings exist everywhere; but
Western traditions often suppress or divert them. The West's
propensity to neglect *amae* helps to explain why American
culture has offered so little resistance to the strong forces of
individualism that have fueled today's especially withered
sense of belonging.

Against this background, let us explore briefly the meaning and the implications of *amae*, which have been most
fully described in the work of the distinguished Japanese
psychiatrist Dr. Takeo Doi, particularly in *The Anatomy of
Dependence*, first published in 1971 and supplemented in
1981. (Unless the context indicates otherwise, the quoted
phrases in this chapter are Doi's language, and the page ref-
erences are to his book.)

Amae is a noun; its verb form is *amaeru*. It is an emotion or sense of longing, reflected in an attitude of trust that
a specific other person will nurture and fulfill one's basic
need for security and love. The prototypical example is a
baby nursing at his mother's breast. The baby, who implicitly assumes his mother's goodwill toward him, is utterly con-
tented and secure, not wanting "to be separated from the
warm mother-child circle and cast into a world of objective
'reality.'" (P. 7.) Hence, he "feel[s] *at one* with . . . his surroundings." (P. 8; emphasis added.) The nursing mother
"enfolds everything in an unconditional love. . . . Everything
is accepted without difficulties or questioning." (P. 77.) For
her part, the mother "understand(s) the infant mind and
respond(s) to its needs, so that mother and child can enjoy a
sense of commingling and identity." (P. 74.) Such a mother
thus finds her own fulfillment in fulfilling her child's *amae*.
Fulfilled *amae* for both parent and child is the chief charac-
teristic of a good child-parent relationship.

Dr. Doi's translator chooses "dependence" as the closest

one-word English equivalent for *amae*. Professor Morita tells me he finds my use of the term *belonging* to be somewhat closer. But, he says, better than either of these is the German translation of *amae*, which is *Freiheit in Geborgenheit*, literally "freedom through emotional security." The German phrase overcomes the negative connotation of *dependent* in English—a connotation that reflects American culture's traditional disdain for "dependent persons," who seem to lack self-reliance. The German use of *Freiheit* (freedom) also captures the positive nature of fulfilled *amae* as achieving a kind of boundless psychological freedom—a freedom found not *in spite* of being cradled in strong, nurturing arms but found precisely *because* of that secure cradling.

Even animals will *amaeru*, such as a cat or dog that loves being petted and played with—once the animal has established that it can trust the hand that pets it. One family we know uses the term *koochy* to describe an animal (or a person) so wrapped up in being paid attention to that it loses all self-consciousness, rolling over, shivering with delight, and coming back for more. Such an animal may often feel *Freiheit in Geborgenheit,* not despite being "owned" by a stronger human but more probably *because* of the way the owner responds to its *amae*.

The Japanese do not describe a baby's longing for his mother as *amae* until he is old enough to realize his independent existence from his mother—then his "craving for close contact" (p. 74) is very conscious and his anxiety over any separation is very real. Thus, part of *amae*'s meaning derives from the fear of its opposite—separation. *Amae's* fear of separation suggests the pain Adam and Eve felt in being "cast out" from God's presence in Eden into a "*lone* and dreary world." This primal separation from God, which we all, Adam-like, also bring upon ourselves through our own sins, is called the "spiritual death"—to be "cut off from the presence of the Lord." (Alma 42:9.) One of its consequences is that we carry throughout our mortal lives, as did Adam and Eve, a hunger to reunite with God. The gospel's most fundamental promise is the at-one-ment of Jesus Christ, which offers the assurance of returning us to unity with God in eternal satisfaction of our *amae*. In a distinct echo of this hope, to "lie in the realm beyond the anguish of unsatisfied *amae*" is the "essence of the Japanese concept of divinity." (P. 63.)

Among the Japanese people, the childlike feelings of *amae* continue into adult life, influencing attitudes toward all personal and group associations, beginning with the family and decreasing in intensity toward the outer circle of one's contacts. For example, between husband and wife: "Once two people have confessed their love for each other . . . they begin to seek indulgent love from each other—that is, they *amaeru*. . . . [True] romantic love . . . cannot come into existence unless the desire for *amae* . . . is already secretly present."[8]

The psychic satisfactions that flow from a good marriage do have an uncanny power to provide reassurance and fulfillment. In the amazing arithmetic of *amae*, no matter how much rejection and disappointment a person may encounter outside the home, the emotional nourishment provided by one loving, genuine marriage partner can be enough to sustain one's fundamental sense of well-being. For this reason, someone who is blessed to enjoy a sound husband-wife relationship is likely to be happy no matter what other problems arise. Conversely, someone who lives in a bad marriage is unlikely to find lasting happiness from successes outside the home. In other words, no external failure will outweigh *amae*'s success in the home.

Moreover, having children brings to literal fruition *amae*'s "longing to merge," as parents see in their child a literally "merged" being whose physical appearance makes visible the merger of their two beings. Perhaps the natural swell of parental pride in beholding such a being is evidence of the parents' fulfilled *amae*. And the profound, inconsolable sense of loss a family feels in losing a child in death demonstrates the utter emptiness of being suddenly deprived of *amae*.

The *amae* mentality is so deeply ingrained in the Japanese soul that Dr. Doi calls it the "leading concept" of the nation's "whole social system"; indeed, it is the "Japanese spirit." (P. 57.) In complex and subtle ways, Japanese society and customs accommodate and reflect both *amae* and the responses of those who instinctively nurture it.

For example, when Doi first visited the United States, he constantly found his hosts asking him, "Are you hungry?" (p. 11) or telling him to "help yourself" to his food—as if "nobody else will help you" (p. 13). By contrast, "Japanese sensibility would demand that . . . a host should show sensitivity in detecting what was required and should himself 'help' his guests." (P. 13.) Doi notes the religious version of this American attitude in the common English phrase, "The Lord helps those who help themselves." But he also notes that this phrase was "not originally derived from Judaism or Christianity but first appeared in George Herbert's" writings in England in 1640. (P. 87.) This observation suggests that original Christianity gave less emphasis to self-help than does modern, westernized Christianity.

The "help yourself" ethic derives from a Western tradition—and from substantial Western history—that assumes "a world where all men are each other's enemies" and "the only safe course is self-reliance and self-defense." (P. 87.) Note the complete contrast in these ideas from the world of *amae*, which depends entirely on being able to trust that certain other people will place our interests above their own. Self-reliance is a virtue, but, taken too far, American pride in self-sufficiency is "a warning against reliance on god or man" that not only ignores but rejects the spirit of *amae*. (P. 87.)

The family tradition, group solidarity, and "team player" attitudes that characterize the Japanese also reflect their subliminal acceptance of *amae*. They "like group action. It is extremely difficult for a Japanese to transcend the group and act independently [because he or she] feels vaguely that it is treacherous to act on his own without considering the group to which he belongs, and feels ashamed, even, at doing something on his own." (P. 54.) Thus, a Japanese person may resign from a prominent position in connection with an unfortunate public event, even when he or she had no personal responsibility for what happened. This is because he or she acts from a sense of responsibility to the group, not just from a sense of individual fault. And the Japanese sense of guilt is sharpest when one fears that his or her action has betrayed the group to which one belongs. Similarly, the most acute sense of "shame" comes from being ostracized by the group. Such shame arises not from concern for the opinions of others but from "feeling [oneself], his *amae* unsatisfied, exposed to the eyes of those about him when all he wants is to be wrapped warm in his surroundings." (P. 55.)

In the American tradition, on the other hand, guilt is a function of one's personal interaction with God. This idea was heavily influenced by Martin Luther's thought, which gave higher priority to one's direct relationship with God than to one's relationship with the Church or the community. But when God "faded away with the advent of the modern age," the individual awareness was left "to carry on by itself." (P. 49.) As a result, the much weaker Western sense of guilt reflects self-disappointment more than it reflects accountability to others or to God. The weak sense of guilt and shame in the Western psyche makes it difficult for Americans to understand the Japanese propensity to apologize. But because of *amae*'s deep sense of group belonging, guilt to a Japanese begins with a sense of betrayal of the group and can end only with a genuine apology to the group.

Moreover, the sense of group renders privacy a less meaningful concept in Japan than it is in America. To a Japanese, being "left alone" is far more negative than positive, in part because "without some kind of group life, it is doubtful . . . whether man could survive at all." (P. 174.) As one Japanese proverb states, "On a journey, a companion; in life, compassion." (P. 87.) Dr. Doi describes the acute pain of his patients who suffered from extended isolation from other people, a phenomenon that echoes the *amae*-like Western idea that exile, banishment, and solitary confinement are especially harsh punishments.

The breadth of "the *amae* sensibility" (p. 79) is reflected in attitudes toward aesthetic beauty and the world of nature. *Beauty* to the Japanese suggests an object so "pleasing to the senses" that the beholder is drawn to become "one with it." The Japanese tendency to be "more aesthetically inclined than other peoples" may result from living in a cultural environment where "the *amae* sensibility is subject to constant stimulation." (P. 79.) Further, "the famous Japanese fondness of nature" reflects their urge to "become one with nature . . . [indulging] in the feeling of pure *amae*."[9] Doi notes a similar appreciation for nature in some Western thought; for instance, he quotes Wordsworth—"Nature never did betray / The heart that loved her." But a sense of "total immersion . . . in nature" is "more pronounced and pervasive in Japan," which has "thousands like [Wordsworth] who gave expression to those feelings."[10]

Clearly, not everything about *amae* is positive. As Doi's English translator writes, the centrality of *amae* accounts for both the failings and the virtues of Japanese society: "Only a mentality rooted in *amae* could produce a people at once so unrealistic yet so clear-sighted as to the basic human condition; so compassionate and so self-centered; so spiritual and so materialistic; so forbearing and so wilful; so docile and so violent." (P. 9.) At the same time, the "suppression, or diversion" of *amae* into "different channels, explains much of what is most admirable and detestable in the Western tradition." (P. 10.)

In this book, we are principally concerned with the present need to understand and restore our sense of belonging in family and religious contexts. We are especially interested, therefore, in what *amae* can teach us about that process— but that does not mean we look uncritically at *amae*. Let us consider some of its limitations.

Among *amae*'s apparent weaknesses is that it relies on intuition rather than logic, sometimes to the point of being quite unrealistic. The baby in his mother's arms must eventually learn to stand on his own feet—he cannot forever remain the indulged child. Properly understood, however, *amae* is different from merely spoiling a child: "If the parent spoils the child, . . . though it may seem to be *amaeru*-ing, in fact [the child] becomes incapable of doing so." (P. 173.) A spoiled child will not have learned *jibun*, the level of self-awareness needed to keep *amae* in check. One who is wholly "at the mercy of *amae* has no *jibun*." (P. 19.) The truly nurturing parent will teach the child the proper mix of *amae* and *jibun* on the path to maturity.

On the other side of the mother-child picture of *amae* lies a different risk—the smothering mother, whose exaggerated sense of possession may lead to a suffocating sense of domination. This extreme, like the risk of the abusive partner in any relationship of belonging, underscores the fragile nature of all human interdependence. However, as we will note shortly, in the present day and in the Western mind the fear of such domination has assumed so much importance that it undermines the positive potential of *amae*.

Another limitation in Doi's description of *amae* is that he does not tell us much about the motivations of the nurturing person who allows another to *amaeru*. The picture of the nursing mother as the prototype for *amae* suggests that women may most naturally fill the nurturing role. This idea is further reinforced by Doi's suggestion that the unconditional, embracing love of "the mother . . . lies at the bottom of the Oriental nature" (p. 77), and that the ultimate symbol of lonely despair in modern society is "the infant . . . left by its mother." (P. 150.)

We saw in chapter 1 that in the gospel's sense of belonging, those who "nourish and cherish" (see Ephesians 5:29) others are most fully motivated by the spiritual gift of *charity*, which is given to all who accept the Atonement and the gospel of Jesus Christ. We may first recognize charity in the lives of mothers and other women (the women's Relief Society motto is "Charity Never Faileth"), but charity is an attitude of love for other people that fills the heart of every spirit child of Christ, man or woman.

A fully developed relationship of belonging, informed and blessed by the gospel, will have both charity and *amae*. Charity describes the giving side of belonging, and *amae* describes, at least in part, the receiving side. If so, we may at times play both roles—sometimes as the nurtured, receiving child, and other times as the giving, charitable mother or father. We do play both roles in the varying moods of marriage and in our multiple relationships with others, where we may be both givers and receivers of spiritual support.

Our relationship with the Lord also reflects both charity and *amae*. We can think of that relationship through *amae*'s prototypical metaphor of the mother and her nursing child. Here Christ is like the mother, and the one whom he has redeemed is like the child: "Zion hath said: The Lord hath forsaken me, and my Lord hath forgotten me—but he will show that he hath not. For can a woman forget her sucking child, that she should not have compassion on the son of her womb?" (1 Nephi 21:14–15; for further development of this theme, see chapter 5.) At the same time, the Savior endows those who become the children of Christ with the charity to be giving, nurturing figures for others of God's children. The unique contribution of *amae* to this understanding is that it gives expression and legitimacy to the childlike feelings we have in longing to be nurtured by and to be in unity with the Lord and with those whom we love—and who love us.

Japan has recently discovered the limitations of *amae*. The outcome of World War II had a profound effect on the Japanese mentality because it deeply shook the nation's confidence in the feelings of trusting, *amae*-based family loyalty that bound the people to their emperor. The war's devastation and embarrassment revealed to the Japanese the naive and childish side of *amae*, challenging their previously unquestioning tendency to trust authority in general. This loss of innocence raised a central question about *amae*: if our ability to *amaeru* depends on the goodwill of others, what do we do when that goodwill does not exist? How can we know whether it exists? Such questions have rippled through Japan's family-centered society since the war, until Dr. Doi worries that his society's "aim from now on, surely, [will] be to overcome *amae*." (P. 84.)

This experience is reminiscent of the entire historical pattern that has established distrust of authority as a cornerstone of the Western tradition—a tradition that has, as a by-product, discouraged *amae* in the West. Yet the West has also recently experienced its own crisis of confidence—and many people now fear that the promised pot of gold at the end of the rainbow of Western-style "individual freedom" might actually be empty—reflecting too much loneliness, alienation, and lack of meaning. The comparison between modern Japanese and American disillusionments suggests that each society might well learn from the other. This leads us to consider Doi's view of *amae* in Western society.

Takeo Doi and others regard *amae* as a conceptual key to understanding Japanese culture, but they also regard it as a "psychological phenomenon that is basically common to mankind as a whole." (P. 28.) Doi's English translator regards *amae* as a "basic human need summed up in . . . one Japanese word" that has been "strangely neglected" by the West. (P. 10.) Another American scholar says that *amae* exists under the "rubric of 'love'" and "is precisely the emotion that is concerned with having the other *belong* to one and which I, lacking the term *amae*, had to label 'desire.'" (P. 170; emphasis added.) Oddly, English has neither a word nor a concept that begins to capture the meaning of *amae:* "It is indeed uncanny that in a country where so much weight is put on individuality the most profound demands of the individual are not perceived."[11]

Doi believes this is less a limitation of language than it is a reflection of Western cultural history and values, particularly the Western idea of freedom as a *political* concept. No story is more typical of Western history than the story of liberation from political oppression. The early motifs for this story draw on the ancient prevalence of slavery, as in Greece, where *freedom* came to mean the absence of enforced obedience to another person. In the archetypal story of Hebrew history, Moses "freed" the children of Israel from bondage to the Egyptian pharaoh. The Roman Empire carried its widespread sense of political control to the Middle Ages, when the feudal era superseded it with a variety of rigid aristocratic controls and virtual caste systems. The European Renaissance and Reformation then introduced a sweeping era of revolutions that "freed" people from these fixed orders. Martin Luther regarded "freedom" as being free from sin through Jesus Christ; but "his rebellion against the political control of the Church of Rome led in time to an increasing emphasis on freedom [as] individual freedom in the face of political oppression." (Pp. 92–93.)

Drawing on these themes, many of the American colonies were founded as a place to escape political and religious persecution. The founding documents of the American

Republic were explicitly grounded on the concept of freedom from political bondage, which have given that concept the status of both a "secular religion" and a Christian "article of faith" in American thought. Since then, the Western democracies have continually fought against totalitarian governments that suppressed individual political freedom.

This rich history tells us much about freedom *from* . . . but it tells us less about freedom *for,* especially how we may use freedom to find personal significance and fulfillment within a free political climate. In many ways, political freedom in the Western mind has now, unfortunately, become an end in itself—not simply a means to larger ends. Political freedom is crucial, but it only creates a protected open structure that we must then fill with our own personal meaning. Without this filling—or fulfilling—content, freedom *from* outside interference remains an empty shell. Political freedom thus describes a different condition from *amae's Freiheit in Geborgenheit,* the psychological and spiritual "freedom" that comes through fulfillment of one's deepest inner need to find meaning and to feel wanted, loved, and encouraged.

As freedom in the Western mind has come to mean personal liberation from political bondage, with its profound skepticism toward authority, the Western mind has been relatively closed to the values of *amae.* For example, Americans "have always looked down on the type of emotional dependency" inherent in *amae.* (P. 86.) Moreover, their fear of oppression and their fierce commitment to self-reliance has made Americans innately cautious about trusting or depending on others—attitudes that are prerequisite to *amae.* The European ideas that underlie American political theory also expressly assume that people in a "state of nature" are natural enemies, and they create a government primarily to protect themselves from one another.

These suspicions have ample and persuasive foundations in centuries of bitter Western experience in which authoritarian people and organizations exploited the natural vulnerability of those who trusted them enough that they might have sought *amae*. At the same time, from the earliest days of the American Republic, our history's most astute observers worried that democracy's emphasis on personal independence—a virtue when applied to the individual's relationship with the state—was a grave risk when applied to personal relationships. So warned Alexis de Tocqueville of America's democracy in 1830:

> They owe nothing to any man, they expect nothing from any man; they acquire the habit of always considering themselves as standing alone, and they are apt to imagine that their whole destiny is in their own hands.
>
> Thus, not only does democracy make every man forget his ancestors, but it hides his descendants and separates his contemporaries from him; it throws him back forever upon himself alone, and threatens in the end to confine him entirely within the solitude of his own heart.[12]

As a result of these tendencies, Western skepticism has created serious barriers to relationships of belonging and loving interdependence—even to the point of defining freedom as the rejection of dependency on others, which may mean freedom as the rejection of *amae*. In other words, our Western sense of freedom seeks to avoid belonging.

For example, Americans have trouble understanding an idea as basic as gratitude. We feel the need to "repay" what other people do for us so we will not feel "indebted" to them. (P. 89.) "I don't want to feel beholden to them," we say, because indebtedness seems to encroach on our need to feel free from obligations to others.

In our spiritual life, this view can interfere with our unrestrained acceptance of the Savior's grace, because our Western-style self-reliance makes us reluctant to be "beholden" to anyone—even Christ. We resist feeling "indebted" to the Savior when we assume that freedom means not being subject to anyone's claim on us. Yet no attitude is more central to our relationship with the Lord than our humble awareness of our "own nothingness, and his goodness" (Mosiah 4:11) and our utter inability ever to repay him: even "if [we] should serve him with all [our] whole souls yet [we] would be unprofitable servants. And behold, all that he requires of [us] is to keep his commandments." (Mosiah 2:21–22.) We cannot fully "belong" to him as long as we cherish a view of freedom that is essentially "a warning against reliance on god or man." (P. 87.) The spirit of *amae* teaches that "if there were some being, essentially superior to mankind, [who] would bestow freedom on the individual as a gift," then no matter how overwhelmed one felt with gratitude, "there would surely be no need to feel that one's freedom had been infringed." (P. 92.)

Doi notes that among the Japanese, "the more intimate the relationship the fewer the expressions of gratitude." (P. 91.) So in relationships that draw on an understanding of *amae*, those who love intimately will freely nurture others, but not at all because they expect to be thanked or rewarded. Thus, while interdependent partners will not exploit one another's love and trust, they sense that an overemphasis on expressing gratitude runs the risk of demeaning a limitless sense of love to the level of a contract: serving others in exchange for something in return.

Given the West's victory in World War II, it is highly ironic that more and more people are now sensing that the Western view of individual freedom has "begun to deteriorate into an empty shell." (P. 94.) "The West . . . today is caught in a morass of despair and nihilism," suggesting that Western man's "attempts . . . to deny or to sidestep *amae* have not been enough to transcend it." (P. 95.) Even young people, all across the world, have "a primitive awareness" (p.

146) that something is wrong with the present flow of history. "Where man once felt pride in [modern civilization's creations of] science and technology, he has now come to fear its ever-accelerating advances." Whether from fears of economic chaos, nuclear war, or massive threats to the global environment, modern man worries "that in return for civilization he is being deprived of something irreplaceable." (P. 147.) Doi sees the ultimate origin of this contemporary alienation "in the discovery that man was mistaken in believing . . . that he could . . . be self-sufficient through reason alone." (P. 148.)

When we feel abandoned or threatened by such uncontrollable forces, the real threat is to our unidentified but latent *amae*: "When the infant is left by its mother, it feels an uneasiness, a threat to its very life; and . . . it is precisely this feeling that lies at the heart of what is described by modern man as 'human alienation.'" (P. 150.)

Thus does Takeo Doi conclude that all modern peoples are being overtaken by a sense of despair that results primarily from unfulfilled *amae*. In the West, our very idea of freedom as the abandonment of *amae* sets us up for such a fall when we are battered by the vast, impersonal forces of modernity. In Japan, the post-war disillusionment has been accompanied by an uncritical willingness to borrow the West's ideas—just at the time when Western writers were discovering the potential psychological emptiness of the West's own philosophy.

Doi captures these general feelings in his description of the contemporary global culture as "the fatherless society": All across the world, "modern youth is in violent revolt against existing society, and shows a strong mistrust of the older generation." There is "no feeling of paternal authority." (P. 144.) Doi asserts that, simultaneously, today's youth are losing trust in their elders just as the older generation has lost its own self-confidence, its authority, and its sense of values.

To the extent that this is true, we are losing both sides of the structure of *amae*—the strong parental figures who teach and nurture, and the young people who trust them. With the Western view of freedom now sweeping Japan and the entire globe, adults relieve themselves of their parental duty to nurture the young by claiming to respect children's freedom—abandoning them to their "right" to be "politically" free. So today, asks Doi, who will "be a father" and teach youth "the meaning of authority and order?" He expects little from professors, politicians, intellectuals, or "men of religion." (P. 146.) Religion seems impotent because the anarchy of our age "has come increasingly to take the absence of God for granted." (P. 156.) And our dilemma is not simply that "God is dead," but, as Nietzsche also said, "God remains dead! And we have killed him!" (P. 157.)

With the loss of paternal authority, taboos are swept aside, a sexual revolution ensues, and we are unconsciously "wallowing in a mood of [false and superficial] *amae*." (P. 158.) This is an unrestrained and therefore purely childish sense of *amae*, because adults and children alike hunger only to be indulged—but not on terms that require submission to *jibun* and to the nurturing love of strong mothers and fathers (either literal parents or stable cultural norms), who have at heart their children's best interests in developmental maturity. Thus, "the present tendency to shelve all distinctions—of adult and child, male and female, cultured and uncultured, East and West—in favor of a uniform childish *amae* can only be called a regression for mankind." (P. 165.)

One growing manifestation of this perverted sense of *amae* is that social activists see the suffering of various groups at home or abroad, and they criticize the entire social system for neglecting the victims of society's systemic weaknesses. "They conclude . . . that the root of all these evils lies in a vast and repressive social organization, on which they launch a bold assault." (P. 159.) This critique has the virtue of shaking Westerners from their individualistic self-centeredness, but Doi believes it fails when the critics, rather than actually helping the victims, essentially identify with them: "Through identifying with the victim . . . they deny their own . . . sense of guilt" and "become victims themselves and begin to abuse those who ignore the victim." (P. 162.) Thus the group identification that might be encouraged by true *amae* "is deliberately chosen for the sake of achieving a sense of community with others." (P. 162.) But this happens primarily to relieve the critics of their own guilt in a way that turns everyone against the very structures and patterns of paternalistic authority whose love and support is essential to fill the void of unfilled *amae*.

Even as the cultures of both East and West now suffer from these complex feelings of unsatisfied authentic *amae*, we find virtually no one to feed our emotional hunger, because our fear of strong parental figures—personally or socially—has led us to patricide and matricide: We have removed our "parents" by removing legal and cultural norms that once at least tried to require some sense of personal accountability for our discharge of family and other duties. For example, we have recently relaxed our view of what spouses owe each other or what parents owe their children, and we now seem far less judgmental toward the parents of children born outside marriage—formerly called "illegitimate" children.

In addition, we have begun using our most powerful legal concepts to separate ourselves further from one another. The idea of personal rights in the Constitution was established, like the root idea of Western freedom, to protect American citizens from the state. Thus the protections of the Bill of Rights are the most potent legal tools our culture knows—a fact that verifies Doi's view that "freedom" to Americans is largely a political concept, not a social or personal one. But we have in recent years applied those tools to legal conflicts involving interpersonal disputes—including such family disputes as divorce and some children's rights issues—not just to disputes between citizens and their government. As a result, American law now, literally like the proverbial bull in the china closet, powerfully invades the sacred domain of *amae*, where *Freiheit* and *Geborgenheit* (freedom and security) intertwine in a productive paradox.

American law then pries—sometimes blows—apart the connection between psychological freedom and psychological security, impairing the possibilities for sustaining either one. American law now assigns its highest priority to "the right to be let alone,"[13] and the emotional nightmare of a legally enforced *amae*-less society is beginning to come true. Yet we go on wondering why we can find no mother to answer our childish cries for help. Having forgotten that authority (despite its potential for abuse) is needed to teach and to nurture, we have abandoned not only children but adults to their "right" to be "free."

So what of *amae* today, especially for Americans? Geography and demographics alone may explain the Japanese origins of *amae* and the widely different experiences of East and West. A commitment to personal and group interdependence may inevitably reflect the psychological adaptations necessary when 124 million industrious people live together on islands so crowded as to carry some of the world's highest population densities. No wonder American ideas are fundamentally different, given the historic American image of the brave little band of colonial settlers or the independent pioneer family conquering the wilderness along a perpetual frontier. Downtown Tokyo has little in common with the plains of Kansas.

At the same time, for reasons discussed in the pages that follow, I was convinced before I ever heard of *amae* that "the waning of belonging" in American society has created very serious cultural, religious, and personal problems. Our history and our evolving social understanding have created a sense of personal isolation and loneliness that stands in stark contrast to the ethic of *amae*. If nothing else, perhaps our awareness of the Japanese perspective will expose some of those distortions and excesses, putting them in bold enough relief to help us understand them—and, where needed, correct them.

In addition, the gospel represents universal concepts, not Western or Eastern ones. And there is no question that the longing to belong is fundamental to the teachings of Jesus Christ. The heart of his personal mission is his Atonement, that unfathomable act of mercy that makes possible the fulfillment of our deepest hunger to "be with" God and with each other, in an eternity of belonging together. Surely that blessing will everlastingly fulfill our inborn *amae*.

Which picture, then, best captures the meaning of "freedom"—being held in the arms of God, or being cast out (liberated?) from God's presence? Typical modern Western instincts would choose the latter, but both *amae* and the gospel would choose the former.

CHAPTER THREE

The Waning of Belonging

M

any voices in American culture have become deeply suspicious of the serious, long-range commitments on which marriage and family ties are based. The sounds from these voices are seeping into the consciousness of the general population. More and more people seem confused about what it means to "belong" to others or to God.

For example, we see a growing and surprising willingness among people we know (both members and nonmembers of the Church) to seek divorce as the obvious solution to marital stress. The sad stories behind these decisions recount much frustration and unhappiness; but as unfortunate as the stories are, they seldom rise to the extreme forms of breakdown, abandonment, or abuse that historically explained a divorce. Today's stories only occasionally tell the tales of which we thought divorces were made. Yet these stories do offer many variations on such common attitudinal themes as "Why should I put up with this?—I don't belong to her (or him)."

The modern confusion extends beyond marriage. As one contemporary but anonymous writer put it, we are seeing today a "general transformation of our society from one that strengthens the bonds between people to one that is, at best, indifferent to them; a sense of an inevitable fraying of the net of connections between people at many critical intersections, of which the marital knot is only one."[1]

For instance, a friend's daughter came home from elementary school one day, crying and upset. "Is it true that I don't really belong to you, Mom?" she asked. Knowing this was her natural child, the startled mother asked what she meant. The girl said her teacher had told her class that everyone is free to control his or her own life and that no one *belongs* to anyone else. Children don't belong to parents, husbands don't belong to wives; nobody belongs to anybody. Then the child asked, "I *am* yours, aren't I, Mom?" Her mother hugged her close and whispered, "Of course you're mine—and I'm yours, too." As the two embraced, they both felt the love and the security of really belonging to each other.

A couple we know adopted a young child after having had other natural children. By the time the adoption became final, the child was old enough to speak a few sentences. At the conclusion of the temple sealing ceremony, the family members joyfully reached out their arms to the child in a gesture of complete acceptance. The little boy smiled broadly as he looked into his parents' eyes and exclaimed, "Now we are *ours!*" Note the possessive form: "ours."

A man and woman who love each other have traditionally felt joy and meaning in the thought that they could "belong" to each other; indeed, many phrases from the language of romantic love draw on the idea of belonging. "Be mine," invite the little candy hearts we see on Valentine's Day. "I'm yours," proclaimed a hit song of the '50s. And the opening line of another once-popular song reads, "If I give my heart to you, will you handle it with care?"

In everything from bumper stickers to billboards, a red heart has become our symbol for love. In its highest form, this symbol represents the ultimate gesture of giving our hearts to those we love. To offer our hearts is to offer our innermost selves. And if the offer is accepted, there may one day be a wedding—that ancient and sacred ritual in which a man and woman gladly give themselves to each other in the "bonds" of matrimony.

We have always known that people who offer their hearts to others take the risk of getting them banged up, and sometimes of getting them broken. One honky-tonk Western tune treated this theme with vivid simplicity: "Baby, you just sorta stomped on my aorta . . . and smashed that sucker flat!"

These days, however, a fear more bewildering than the risk of a broken heart clouds our willingness to give ourselves to one another. The teacher's comments to her class fairly remind us that family members are neither slaves nor inanimate objects. But her attitude also typifies the fears of a growing number in today's society who honestly wonder whether the bonds of kinship and marriage are valuable ties that bind, or are sheer bondage.

Some are confused because the sense of possession implicit in the concept of belonging can imply relationships as beautiful as romantic love—or as ugly as slavery. In earlier times, our common sense told us the obvious differences between slavery and love, which are at opposite ends of the spectrum of human interaction. But the spirit of the 1990s seems to tell us we are not fully free until we break loose from all relationships and commitments that tie us down. Belonging, in the modern view, seems to enslave rather than to enrich. Yet those who break loose from the arms and bonds that hold them often replace their previous sense of belonging only with a sense of longing, as this age of liberation becomes more and more the age of isolation and loneliness. Ours is the age of the waning of belonging.

Of course, some people do exploit and abuse the trust placed in them by marriage partners and family members.

When we express concern about a loss of belonging, we are fully aware of the harm inflicted by abusive parents and spouses or by insensitive authority figures who take advantage of those who are dependent on them. Still, the fact that some have used the vulnerability of intimate relationships to harm others is no reason to suppose that sustained intimacy itself is the problem.

We can also see the modern ambivalence about belonging in attitudes toward God and religion, including the Church. The Enemy of faith and love is attacking the very idea of belonging, urging us to flee from any arms that would hold us close, whether the arms of mortal loved ones or the arms of God.

For example, if a Latter-day Saint says, "I belong to the Church," is that good news or bad news? Does it mean I have surrendered control of my life and my mind to the point of being "owned" by the Church?

An academic dean at BYU recently invited us to speak at a fireside for his students. When we asked what subject he would suggest, he reported a growing uneasiness among some LDS college students about the "institutional authority" of the Church. "We need to reconnect these young people with priesthood authority," he said, "so they can claim their rightful blessings." These students' attitudes reminded us of something another person told us, to our surprise: "BYU should distance itself from the Church," she said, "so it can protect Mormons who find the institutional Church to be oppressive and intrusive."

We realize that "authority" can be abused, and we believe deeply that college students must generally be skeptical about authoritarianism if they are to develop the crucial qualities of intellectual independence and personal self-reliance. However, we also know, as does every missionary who preaches the restoration of the gospel, that our very salvation depends on our giving heed to—even submitting to—

proper "authority," even "as a child doth submit to his father." (Mosiah 3:19.) As the Lord said to Joseph Smith in Liberty Jail, "The ends of the earth shall inquire after thy name, and fools shall have thee in derision, and hell shall rage against thee; while the pure in heart, and the wise, and the noble, and the virtuous, shall seek counsel, and *author-ity*, and blessings constantly from under thy hand." (D&C 122:1–2; emphasis added.)

A friend felt that the Lord and his servants were intervening in his life in ways that felt very confining, even disturbing. He said to himself one day in frustration, "The Lord won't leave me alone!" Almost as the words left his tongue, he realized their double meaning. As soon as he regained his perspective, he said once more, this time in humble gratitude, "The Lord won't leave me alone."

He won't leave me alone. Good news or bad news? That probably depends on whether one sees divinely inspired intervention as confining or liberating. Most of us at one time or another are likely to find some request of the Lord or his Church at least inconvenient and perhaps even disturbing. But when "the inconvenient Messiah"[2] stands by us in our hours of most acute need, we will sing, "When other helpers fail and comforts flee,/Help of the helpless, oh, abide with me!"[3] In such moments, all our hope may come from knowing that the Lord won't leave us alone.

A related modern urge is that we don't want anyone to tell us what to do. Once we accept this premise, what could more plainly define our idea of a "free country" than a place where nobody tells us what to do with our lives? But some reflection on this idea will suggest its direct contrast with the question the rich young ruler asked Jesus: "Good Master, *what shall I do* that I may inherit eternal life?" (Mark 10:17; emphasis added.) The young man yearned for guidance—so he sincerely asked the Lord what he should do with his life. Where would this young man turn in a society so free and democratic that no one will tell him what he should do to find purpose and happiness?

The *advantage* of democracy is that no one will tell us what to do. But the *disadvantage* of democracy is that no one will tell us what to do.

The Apostle Peter knew how lost he would be without the teachings of him who "taught . . . as one having authority." (Matthew 7:29.) After Jesus had taught some hard doctrine, "many of his disciples went back, and walked no more with him. Then said Jesus unto the twelve, Will ye also go away? Then Simon Peter answered him, Lord, *to whom shall we go? thou hast the words of eternal life.*" (John 6:66–68; emphasis added.)

The words of eternal life, including the commandments, can be precious secrets to those who have discovered that knowing and obeying these words and laws will unlock the secrets of life's meaning: "I am a stranger in the earth: hide not thy commandments from me. My soul breaketh for the longing that it hath unto thy judgments at all times." (Psalm 119:19–20.)

Consider also the way the young ruler addressed the Lord: "Master," he called him. We use the term *master* in two very different senses. One sense connotes the coercive relationship of master and slave. But at the opposite end of the spectrum of personal relationships, we find a very different sense of *master*—the liberating, learning relationship of master and apprentice. That is what *master* meant to the young ruler. But as our sense of belonging has waned, some people are now so skeptical about authority figures that they can no longer tell the difference between masters who might enslave them and masters who might teach them what to do to become truly free. When our vision becomes that blurred, our unwillingness to submit to the direction of any master can deprive us of the opportunity to learn and grow through authentic apprenticeships, including an apprenticeship with the Master of the Universe.

Alma taught us to be very cautious about blindly submitting to the authority of just any teacher: "Trust no one to be your teacher." (Mosiah 23:14.) However, when we can be taught by those who have the words of eternal life, Alma counseled submission, not skepticism: "Trust no one to be your teacher . . . , except he be a man of God." (Mosiah 23:14.)

Where does today's general uneasiness about belonging come from? There are both long-term and short-term causes. As discussed in chapter 2, a general skepticism about submitting ourselves to the control of any institution or person is part of America's historical character. One of Western history's oldest and largest themes is what social philosopher Robert Nisbet calls "the decline of community,"[4] referring to the rise of individualism and the decline of group ties over the past several centuries.[5]

In more recent years, this long-developing momentum has accelerated its pace, sometimes breathtakingly. For example, a serious antiestablishment mood has been growing rapidly in the United States over the past thirty years. This restless questioning became most visible during the late 1960s and early 1970s. The various protest movements that took root during that era have now rattled the foundations of virtually every major American institution—public or private—from government bodies and corporations to schools, families, and churches.[6] Even though most Americans understand that institutions are essential for our individual as well as our social survival, "most of the people some of the time are [now] suspicious" of their own allegiance to institutional authority. They "complain about it, distrust it," in no small part because they "fear that such *belonging* is simply serving someone else's ends."[7]

Much of this recent skepticism rejects concepts like

belonging and authority, but it does so primarily for ideological and political reasons, not because of serious, new evidence of institutional repression in American society.

For example, as discussed in chapters 11 and 12, the individual rights movements of the past generation launched a forceful attack upon the legal status of marriage, on the family's institutional authority, and on the cultural norms that nurtured and justified that authority. These developments were not primarily the result of conscious and documented dissatisfaction with existing patterns in family law; rather, the family was only one of many institutions whose authoritarian and role-oriented traditions were subjected to the withering scrutiny of a general social and political movement that viewed the family's "vital role in authoritarianism" as "entirely repugnant to the free soul in our age."[8]

Experience in the field of education illustrates the same point. The student protests on American college campuses during the 1960s and 1970s played a key role in establishing an intense anti-establishment mentality that still heavily influences many academic disciplines and American culture generally. The first such anti-university protest began at Berkeley in 1964 as a "free speech" movement. Oddly, general student attitudes on that campus only weeks before the movement began indicated high levels of satisfaction with the university. But as the spirit of protest swept across that and other campuses, greatly aggravated by public reaction against the Vietnam War, the movement's leaders were not concerned with particular institutional shortcomings at all. In fact, they told their followers, "The issue is not the issue"—meaning that challenging any campus policy or event would serve the movement's larger purpose of establishing civil disobedience toward established authority as an end in itself.[9]

This protest-oriented "counterculture" challenged "any institution attempting to assert authority over young adults. . . . With its contempt for rationality and its reverence for

48

immediacy, the counterculture openly opposed the self-discipline, order, and respect for reason that educational institutions rely on."[10] It was especially ironic that higher education became a target for protest, because "the youthful revolutionaries . . . tried to destroy the one institution in American society that provided a sanctuary for their views."[11] Over time, this trend has had disastrous effects on both academic and behavioral standards throughout American education, from which much of the nation is still reeling. It was "a shift of profound dimensions," as "adult authority [in the public schools was] increasingly defined [only] by what will stand up in court."[12]

While bumper stickers and T-shirts are not the best evidence of actual cultural norms, they do drop some hints about current student attitudes. We have recently noticed the following slogans on T-shirts worn by young people in various American and European cities: "Faith no more." "Question authority." "Put a fire under the powers that be." "Kill your idols." (The latter slogan was printed just below a picture of Christ that was surrounded by a red circle with a diagonal slash through it.)

Such sentiments are captured at a more philosophical level in the recent emergence of "personal autonomy" as a key value in modern thought. In the rights-oriented rhetoric of the day, some now describe the notion of unrestrained personal autonomy as "the right to be let alone," which they argue is "the right most valued by civilized men."[13] For many people, this includes the right to be "let alone" from any relationship or institutional obligation that seems to tie them down.

How have leading thinkers in today's society arrived at such a position? Since ancient times, people have sought for a frame of reference that gives order and meaning to "life," not only a meaning for life in general, but a meaning for one's own individual life as well—"my life." One of the

major contributions of ancient Greek thought was the idea
that the universe has a natural order, and that humankind
would fulfill its highest purpose by living in harmony with
that order. In other words, the meaning of "my life" was to
be found by reference to a surrounding natural framework
for "life" in a larger and more objective sense.

For many centuries before A.D. 1500, the dominant frame
of reference in European society was a religious view of the
world. Given that framework, the meaning of "life" as a universal construct was defined by Christian religious teachings.
The source of meaning for "*my* life" was defined as living in
harmony with those larger scale teachings about "life."

The revolutionary age that began with the Renaissance
in about A.D. 1500 emphasized at its very core the significance of individual freedom, thereby giving new meaning to
the value of "my life" for each person. This strong sense of
personal liberty was especially significant as a political concept, becoming the major premise of the American
Revolution and the U.S. Constitution. Ideas about the importance of individual choice also led to the development of a
free-market economy, which in turn hastened the coming of
the Industrial Revolution. The restoration of the gospel in
early nineteenth-century America would not have been possible without the protection of free conscience and freedom
of religion made possible by this individualistic environment.

At the same time, the triumph of individualism in the revolutionary era did not alter Western culture's basic assumption that the universe was based on ordering principles of
Nature; rather, the revolutions in science and culture simply
shifted the prevailing assumptions from a *religious* explanation of the cosmos to a *scientific* explanation. Even with so
huge a shift, Western thought continued to take for granted
that there is a large, natural, and objective order within
which each person can find a sense of harmony and purpose.

For example, with or without religious assumptions, most people during this period believed in "human nature," the notion that a basic set of inborn attitudes and moral instincts is common to all men and women. Each person's individual makeup obviously varied, but he or she still partook of this larger natural order, because people believed that humanity "belonged" to, or was simply part of, Nature—or God's creation. Each individual reflected "natural" impulses, because he or she carried some of Nature within.

Thomas Jefferson began with this assumption in writing the Declaration of Independence: "We hold these truths to be self-evident, that all men are created equal, that they are endowed by their Creator with certain unalienable Rights, that among these are Life, Liberty and the pursuit of Happiness." The German philosopher Immanuel Kant powerfully articulated the idea that each person is born with a discoverable, inner set of moral standards—a conscience. Similar ideas are found in the more recent work of the Swiss psychologist Carl Jung, who discovered what he called "the collective unconscious," a universal sense of humankind's collective "Self" reflected in the common patterns and images of world religions and mythologies.[14]

The history of Western civilization over the past hundred years, however, tells the story of a rapidly eroding confidence in the idea that there is any fixed framework, either "out there" or internally common to everyone. Many of society's leading thinkers have become skeptical not just about particular ordering principles furnished by religion, science, or some other source; rather, they are skeptical that any such thing as a set of natural, pre-existing principles exists at all. This is a very different development from the earlier shift to scientific explanations from religious ones, because the modern era doubts the very idea of a comprehensive order of meaning.

This unsettling mind-set is a major theme of twentieth-century life. As Tevye says in *Fiddler on the Roof,* "Without our traditions, our lives would be as shaky as a fiddler on the roof." And life has begun to feel just that shaky. The Austrian psychologist Viktor Frankl, who survived a German prison camp for Jews, echoes Tevye's worry: "The traditions that had buttressed man's behavior are now rapidly diminishing. No instinct tells him what he has to do, and no tradition tells him what he ought to do; soon he will not know what he wants to do."[15]

We can see this rejection of traditional patterns and assumptions in many of the expressions of twentieth-century art, music, and literature. Art forms really do mirror the society that produces them. The true, the good, and the beautiful are now less likely to be defined by traditional objective standards that most people accept; rather, the standards for judgment now tend to be in the eye of the artist, the writer, and the beholder. Many traditional patterns of rhythm, harmony, and aesthetic quality have been uprooted in favor of sometimes incomprehensible abstractions that represent only the author's own subjective "I-centeredness."

As summarized by Western historian Thomas Greer, when the German writer Nietzsche said in the late nineteenth century that "'God is dead,' he meant not only the God of the Judeo-Christian faith but the whole realm of philosophical absolutes, from Plato down to his own day."[16] We have since lived through a century of uncertainty and anxiety, fears that have been greatly aggravated by world wars, threats of economic collapse, and the risk of nuclear annihilation. These worries have been widely shared, partly because of nearly universal education and communication, which cause the philosophical problems that once bothered only the elite few now to bother almost everybody.

In the middle of this turmoil rages a central fear: if there is no objective order, no natural framework for "life" in general, then all values are relative and "my life" is without foundation or meaning. Of course, this same circumstance also produces a perverse sense of liberation: with no fixed framework, I can do as I please, without accountability.

These developments have profoundly affected our sense of belonging and connectedness to other people. As twentieth-century writers have struggled to make sense out of the uprooting of our traditions, a new form of individualism has emerged as the predominant anchor point. This is the age of "the celebration of the self."[17] However, this time the individual does not exercise his or her precious agency as part of a surrounding field of natural order. Rather, as the influential French writer Jean-Paul Sartre put it, "Man makes himself," meaning, "It is the individual who gives meaning to history, not the other way around."[18] Thus, "there is no final truth about human beings; they are what they choose to be."[19] We cannot assume that "all people everywhere are ultimately like us,"[20] because "there is no such thing as human nature."[21]

In the current "post-modern" age, many scholars see a new island of apparent certainty in the surrounding sea of turmoil, one last absolute: the sanctity of individual autonomy, which they would now isolate from and exalt above any particular social or natural context. In these scholars' view, we now need pick up only one piece from our shattered cultural consensus—the piece called "my life." Then we can reconstruct a sense of meaning, but not one that begins from a larger set of surrounding principles or human connections—because, they assume, there are no fixed principles beyond the prejudices of our local culture, and such personal connections as may exist are purely transitory. Rather, other people and the universe itself must find their meaning by reference to "my life" as the starting point.

This "celebration of the self," and the celebration's ongoing conflict with traditional values, is captured in the contemporary comic strip "Calvin and Hobbes."

[Calvin] is a little boy (implausibly given the name

53

of a stern Protestant theologian) asserting that what he wants—fame, luxury, diversion, staying out of school, hitting Susie with a snowball—is all that should matter.

I am the center of the universe, he says; values are what I say they are.

And then there is the tiger [Hobbes] (paradoxically given the name of an English philosopher [whose writings] pretty much defend [Calvin's] view), who offers the sober judgment of [traditional] mankind about this self-centeredness, all in the language of gentle irony.[22]

For example, in one recent Calvin and Hobbes feature, Calvin complains about a traditional three-tiered snowman a neighbor has built: "The soulless banality of this snowman is a sad comment on today's art world," he says. Then he shows Hobbes the unique snowman he has built—a hideous monster Calvin calls "the torment of existence weighed against the horror of nonbeing." Hobbes comments thoughtfully, "I admire your willingness to put artistic integrity before marketability." Calvin stops to think about Hobbes's remark; then in the final frame we see Calvin strenuously building a traditionally shaped snowman.[23]

James Q. Wilson, a thoughtful moral philosopher who shares our concern about this problem, believes that discovering why "Calvin is usually wrong and Hobbes is almost always right" is "the fundamental moral issue of our time," because that inquiry will reveal our basis for making any moral judgments today.[24]

We recognize that these generalizations gloss over many distinctions and issues that deserve treatment in a thorough review of recent cultural and intellectual history, but a review of that kind is beyond the scope and purpose of the present work. We must at least note that some of the questions raised in this chapter have generated raging debates in many professional fields and across nearly all university campuses.

For example, the recent "critical legal studies" movement in American law schools has challenged the foundations of not only legal education and law practice, but also the very idea of a system of law. This movement asserts that law has no objective legitimacy and is simply a euphemism for entrenched power. Other less radical but similarly individualistic currents help to explain why some of the "individual rights" of those who threaten society the most have become more important than society's collective interests, at least in some courts and contexts. And a variety of self-focused attitudes in literary criticism and the social sciences challenge every discipline they touch.

Many of these arguments have value, asking us to rethink traditional assumptions and helping us to unmask entrenched forms of discrimination and unfairness against unprotected minority groups. During some past times, the personal interests and biases of some organizations and individuals really have masqueraded as objectively fixed and neutral standards, and such forms of pretense need to be unmasked. Some current advocacy therefore appropriately urges us to examine the political motives or the cultural biases of writers or public figures, because where such people "stand" on an issue often simply reflects where they "sit" in terms of institutional interests or self-interest.

However, for present purposes, we urge only the very general point that the contemporary "preoccupation with the autonomy of the individual and the exaltation of his subjective longings" too often seems bent on "obliterating," not merely "reforming" our society.[25] Our primary concern in this book is with the effect of these extremist tendencies on the relationships we have with each other, with the Church, and with God.

Thus it is enough for us to note that the modern preoccupation with "self" is a complete reversal of the earlier assumptions by which individual meaning was determined with reference to larger spheres of meaning. Many of the prior assumptions, at least after the Renaissance, enhanced social strength as well as individual liberty, in part by anchoring ideas about personal liberty within thought systems designed to ensure long-term cultural stability. But in today's unanchored celebration of the self, we see only the lonely individual, standing atop the rubble of a disintegrating urban civilization, proclaiming not just that God is dead but also that each person is his or her own God. In a religious context, this means that "the authority of canonical scripture and apostolic tradition are [now] set aside in favor of the individual's interior divinity."[26]

This view affirms the provocative idea that each person is responsible to make of life what he or she will—an idea that draws on true principles regarding individual agency. But this view also draws too much on the false assumption that we will find our greatest meaning when we cut ourselves adrift from all institutions, traditions, and binding ties to other people. When that happens, we no longer belong to nature, to love, to each other, or to God. Having given up the idea that we really are, or should be, part of something larger than ourselves, we are at first isolated and then finally abandoned—to our unattached freedom. Ours is the age of the waning of belonging.

CHAPTER FOUR

Personal Identity, Individuality, and Belonging

Does having a belonging heart confine us or liberate us?

There is no more stirring truth in God's revealed word than the idea that each individual personality is unique, eternal, independent, and possesses free agency. And it is the gospel's high purpose to develop that personality to its utmost potential, as expressed in the doctrine of eternal progression, which can lead to ever-increasing meaning and freedom for each living soul.[1] For, "if the Son . . . shall make you free, ye shall be free indeed." (John 8:36.) Let us consider the connection between individual fulfillment and belonging to others.

The idea of belonging has ancient roots. In the very beginning, God directed Adam and Eve to undertake their earthly experience not as independent sojourners but together, as husband and wife. Further, he commanded them to have children and to live in families. Secular historical sources also make clear that in ancient times, the primary "unit" of which both society and law took account was the family, not the individual.[2] However, the doctrinal and historical prominence of marriage and family belonging does not diminish the significance of the individual personality.

On the contrary, a review of the individual's place in Latter-day Saint doctrine shows that belonging can actually enhance our potential for personal fulfillment.

One of the unique conceptual keystones of Latter-day Saint theology is the doctrine that each one of us has always existed in some essential form, and each will continue to exist forever. As the Lord revealed to Abraham, the "intelligences that were organized before the world was" (Abraham 3:22) "have no beginning; they existed before, they shall have no end, they shall exist after, for they are . . . eternal." (Abraham 3:18.) That is why the Lord said through Joseph Smith, "Man was also in the beginning with God. Intelligence, or the light of truth, was not created or made, neither indeed can be." (D&C 93:29.)[3]

No theology or philosophical system assigns the individual a status of greater dignity and promise than does the restored gospel of Jesus Christ. In addition to the unique and eternal character of each personality, our Father in Heaven also clothed each intelligence in its premortal state with a spirit body that derived literally from God himself. So when we sing "I Am a Child of God," we describe a divine heritage that is only one spiritual generation away from the great Elohim. Yet even with such parenthood, each person also enjoys the eternal gift of agency, which leaves him or her, like truth, "independent in that sphere in which God has placed it, to act for itself, as all intelligence also; otherwise there is no existence." (D&C 93:30.) Further, each individual identity represents a personality so distinct from all other creations that no two of us are exactly alike.

The gospel teaches the meaning of individual worth in many specific applications. For example, the Lord's Church has always taken great care to preach the message of the Restoration to individuals *as individuals*. We could blanket the globe with missionary messages to millions of people at once through the miracle of mass communications, then simply invite people to apply for baptism by return mail or perhaps in large groups within individual cities. But each soul is too precious for such mass treatment. Each person's quest and each person's questions, each person's testimony and each person's growth—each is a personal, private affair; and each person and each family deserve their own missionaries. So we send missionaries by the thousands to teach in one of the lowest possible student/teacher ratios—sometimes two teachers for a single student.

And to the missionaries, the Lord declares an even more awesome ratio as he teaches the value of each individual soul: "If it so be that you should labor all your days in crying repentance unto this people, and bring, save it be one soul unto me, how great shall be your joy with him in the kingdom of my Father!" (D&C 18:15.)

The same principle holds true in genealogical searches and temple work for the dead. The process of having one living individual perform temple ordinances for a single deceased person is far less efficient than having each proxy represent ten or a thousand names at a time. But whether for the living or the dead, each person's moment in the temple, truly like a moment in the sun, is too precious for mass production. We can hardly count the years required to perform the ordinances in this manner for all the dead who need them. But the temple work goes on, and will go on as long as necessary, one person spending several hours for each name. Each soul has that much personal worth.

The Savior's approach to teaching his doctrine during his mortal ministry also reflects this pattern of individual attention. For instance, he delivered some of his most sublime discourses in private conversations with individuals. He was not concerned about waiting for a large enough audience to justify expending the energy needed to teach in great depth. He gave his memorable sermon on the meaning of baptism only to Nicodemus, who came to him by night to learn. (See John

3:1–21.) He taught the lesson of the gospel's living water to a Samaritan woman alone by Jacob's well. (See John 4:1–26.) The scriptures record other examples of this pattern, such as Mormon's letter to Moroni on infant baptism (see Moroni 8) and Alma's discourse to Korihor on the challenge of agnosticism (see Alma 30). In addition, some of the most complete expositions in all scripture about repentance, justice, mercy, and the Atonement are contained in Alma's individual conversations with his sons. (See Alma 36–42.)

As with missionary service, temple work, and teaching, even the process of salvation is, to a significant degree, an individual affair. The parents of Zion are instructed to teach their children the gospel. (See D&C 68:28.) But no matter how powerfully and effectively they may teach, parents cannot simply transmit to a child the faith and testimony they have won personally through years of arduous testing and sacrifice. How often parents wish they could simply implant their own faith in a child's heart in times of spiritual stress!

The prayers and bonds of belonging have great power to support and sustain those we love, but, finally, each testimony and each spiritual battle must be won by the exercise of freely chosen agency and obedience. In some ultimate sense, as Heber C. Kimball has said, we cannot "live on borrowed light." We cannot ride to heaven on the coattails of strong and faithful relatives or friends; even those who love us most cannot enter God's presence ahead of us and "save us a seat" there.

There is, of course, one exception to this pattern. It is generally true that no one has enough "influence in high places" to compensate for our failure to qualify on our own merits to join them in those high places. However, the Savior has won the right to such influence, not only by his unique family relationship to the Father but also because of his sinless life and his Atonement. And when the merits of our case are not strong enough by themselves to return us to the highest place of all, he, having arrived there ahead of us, will plead our case before God. He will lend us his strength, "saying: Father, behold the sufferings and death of him who did no sin, in whom thou wast well pleased; behold the blood of thy Son which was shed. . . . Wherefore, Father, spare these my brethren that believe on my name." (D&C 45:4–5.) But this exception to the general pattern is not unqualified; for his advocacy, even though it does for us what we are unable to do for ourselves, is also conditioned on our individual choice to repent and to "believe on [his] name." Even his mighty influence cannot take those fundamental steps for us.

By accepting his advocacy, we gain entry to a personal relationship with him. This relationship is independent of any other relationships we may have. After being supported and even carried toward him on the shoulders or in the arms of those who nurture us, we finally enter his presence alone. Yet while this solitary path unfolds apart from our bonds of human belonging, it is the pathway to another form of belonging—our belonging to Christ. This sacred relationship is personal to him as well as to us. Even the angels, seen and unseen, who go before our face and minister God's love to us throughout our lives, recede into the background as we approach the gateway of coming unto Christ, for the keeper of that gate is the Holy One himself, "and he employeth no servant there." (2 Nephi 9:41.) It must be so, because only he paid our debt to justice with his blood; and what he did was not only for "us"; it was also most profoundly for "me."

Through this intensely personal quality of the Atonement, Jesus also learned firsthand that his belonging to the Father did not supplant *his* personal agency. His heart belonged to his Father with such completeness that he prayed in Gethsemane, "If it be possible, let this cup pass from me: nevertheless not as I will, but as thou wilt."

(Matthew 26:39.) And, "I have glorified thee on the earth: I have finished the work which thou gavest me to do. . . . Thou, Father, art in me, and I in thee." (John 17:4, 21.) Yet in the Savior's darkest hour on the cross, not only did the angels (who had comforted him in Gethsemane) withdraw, but the Father also withdrew the support of his Spirit, leaving Christ utterly alone to finish his atoning battle with the Prince of Darkness. This moment of unmitigated freedom left him fully responsible for the consequences of whatever he chose to do. But as he realized what had happened, being left alone brought him only the anguish of feeling utterly forsaken. (See Matthew 27:46.) He and his Father belonged to one another, and surely his Father vicariously shared his agony; but the final responsibility of his act of Atonement belonged only to him.

In addition to its religious meaning, the independent nature of each personality carries great meaning into our relationships of marriage. These pages contain much about "the waning of belonging" today, because the erosion of intimate ties in the modern world is a great threat to human happiness. But no true sense of belonging, religious or romantic, was ever intended to smother or submerge our sense of personal identity. Indeed, one of the most rewarding blessings of true belonging is that it can enrich so fully—even make possible—the process of each person's development toward personal fulfillment. This is partly because of the personal growth we experience in learning how to respond to the sometimes demanding needs of those we love.[4] Moreover, an exquisite spiritual and psychological freedom flows from fulfilling our inborn yearning to belong—our *amae*—a literal "freedom through belonging," *Freiheit in Geborgenheit*.[5]

Consider these lines from Kahlil Gibran on the paradoxical but liberating relationship between marital bonding and individual identity:

Then Almitra spoke again and said, And
    what of Marriage, master?
And he answered saying:
You were born together, and together you
    shall be forevermore.
You shall be together when the white
    wings of death scatter your days.
Ay, you shall be together even in the
    silent memory of God.
But let there be spaces in your togetherness,
And let the winds of the heavens dance
    between you.

Love one another, but make not a bond
    of love:
Let it rather be a moving sea between
    the shores of your souls.
Fill each other's cup but drink not from
    one cup.
Give one another of your bread but eat
    not from the same loaf.
Sing and dance together and be joyous,
    but let each one of you be alone,
Even as the strings of a lute are alone
    though they quiver with the same music.

Give your hearts, but not into each
    other's keeping.
For only the hand of Life can contain
    your hearts.
And stand together yet not too near
    together:
For the pillars of the temple stand apart,
And the oak tree and the cypress grow
    not in each other's shadow.[6]

Gibran thus concludes with the idea of personal
growth—which does not occur in the heavy shadows of personal domination. Growth is the conceptual bridge between
belonging and individual identity. Rather than depriving us
of individuality, belonging, as taught by the gospel—whether

belonging to Christ or to spouses, children, and parents—actually enhances personal freedom by developing our personal capacity for fulness. In this sense, our ties to others are actually a major source of our personal liberation. And a weakening of our commitments of belonging can therefore undermine the development of our ability eventually to function with complete, mature capacity.

This point is most vividly illustrated by the example of children. A child's sense of belonging—especially to parents—contributes enormously to the child's development of enough psychological stability to be capable of independent action. In addition, a young person is unable to act with meaningful independence until he or she develops the ability to act rationally, a power gained only through submitting to a disciplined educational process. Based on long experience with this process, society has established the *right* of children to receive an education. Children may regard the constraints of *compulsory* school laws as bondage, but those bonds are their liberation. A school is for this reason a vital mediating institution between a child and a free society, if society is to be composed of free and autonomous individuals.

For example, a child can appear to be at liberty to act autonomously, but if the child is not given developmental opportunities, he or she cannot become really free to act autonomously. Sometimes, ironically, parents or teachers believe they are respecting a child's right to autonomy by leaving the child alone. But leaving a child alone can also amount to abandonment, depriving him or her of the growth experiences needed to gain true autonomy.

Similarly, I am not free to play the piano just because no one is physically restraining me from walking to the piano bench. I am free to play the piano only when I have submitted to the discipline—the bondage as some see it—of many "slavish" hours of practice, following a teacher's demanding directions. Further on this theme, a school child does not enjoy "freedom of expression" by being left alone to write whatever he or she pleases on a blank sheet of paper. Freedom of expression has two meanings: freedom *from* restraints on expression, and freedom *for* expression—that is, having the *capacity* for self-expression and, obviously, having something worth saying. Until one has developed freedom "*for* expression" in this sense, being free from restraints has little meaning. For this reason, a child's most fundamental interest in self-expression is developed only through the growth process of effective education.

That is also why the waning of belonging described in chapter 3 has the long-range effect of reducing meaningful individuality and actual personal autonomy. When the search for personal liberty is divorced from commitments to discipline and duty, that separation only increases the likelihood that our lives will lack meaning. In their best sense, liberty and duty exist in a rich paradox as two poles at opposite ends of a single construct. Neither is meaningful without the other. When we sever the link between them, we face two unhappy options: being dominated by others, or being abandoned by others.

The liberty/duty paradox echoes the paradox of *amae*—the truth found in the apparent contradiction that we can find freedom (*Freiheit*) in belonging (*Geborgenheit*), in love, to another person. These two puzzles further echo the central gospel paradox embodied in the Savior's statement, "Whosoever will save his life shall lose it: and whosoever will lose his life for my sake shall find it." (Matthew 16:25.) Jesus here warned his listeners against focusing only on themselves. He taught uncompromisingly: "If any man will come after me, let him deny himself, and take up his cross, and follow me." (Matthew 16:24.)

Yet in the very act of denying self on the Lord's terms and "for [the Lord's] sake," those who find Christ will also *find themselves*. The gospel asks not for mere self-renunciation but rather for self-sacrificing acts of obedience and service that, paradoxically, develop the self to its fullest potential.

We become more willing to submit to the need for such sacrifices as we become "older"—that is, more mature—in our understanding that the Lord does have our interests deeply at heart, even when his requests of us may not be what we would choose for ourselves. As Christ said to Peter near the end of his ministry: "When thou wast young, thou girdest thyself, and walkedst whither thou wouldest: but when thou shalt be old, thou shalt stretch forth thy hands, and another shall gird thee, and carry thee whither thou wouldest not." (John 21:18.) As we have more experience with the Good Shepherd, we come to know that wherever he carries us will increase our capacity for joy—even if, at first, he proposes to carry us where we, of ourselves, may not choose to go.

Recognized authorities in the psychological and sociological literature confirm the idea that subordinating one's own needs in order to serve others' needs actually enhances, rather than extinguishes, one's quest for personal meaning and autonomy. For example, Erik Erikson's theory of human development holds that "a person must develop three fundamental characteristics to become psychologically healthy and mature: hope, fidelity, and care. The development of each of these characteristics takes center stage at one of the major periods of the life-span: childhood, adolescence, and adulthood, respectively."[7]

Children can best discover hope when they resolve the infant's basic conflict that arises from the inner contradiction of sensing both "basic trust" and "basic mistrust" toward others.[8] The healthy child will conclude that "the world is a safe, good place to live."[9] This attitude carries children into the adolescent stage, where they "need to develop a sense of their own identity and a fidelity to that identity."[10] The success of this stage depends on the adolescent's resolving the basic conflict between "identity" and "identity confusion," not only to renew one's trust in self but also to trust others enough to "commit one's loyalty . . . to a cause."[11] Erikson here implicitly recognizes that self-confident identity actually enhances one's ability eventually to "belong" to a cause or a group larger than oneself.

Continued healthy development into the adult stage then requires "sustained nurturing involvement" in the lives of others. The experience of being a father or a mother, for example, contributes to adult psychological health because "children have a way of making people around them grow up and become less self-centered. They deflate the adolescent preoccupation with self that is often carried into adulthood in a self-centered culture."[12] Erikson describes care as "the instinctual impulse to 'cherish' and to 'caress' that which in its helplessness emits signals of despair."[13] This sounds very much like the capacity to nurture to fulfillment another person's *amae*.

As with children and adolescents, adults must also resolve natural conflicts as they develop the capacity to care. These include the conflict between "intimacy" and "isolation" in learning to love; the conflict between "generativity" (nurturing the next generation) and "self-absorption" in learning to care; and the conflict between "integrity" and "despair" in learning wisdom.[14] Erikson's view that caring develops integrity and wisdom in the caregiver illustrates how losing oneself for the sake of others can naturally lead to finding oneself in the sense of having developed a mature, adult self-identity evidenced by wisdom and integrity. He thus defines integrity as "a sense of coherence and wholeness."[15]

Sociologist Robert N. Bellah has described a similar pattern in explaining how an individual's "autonomy" will flourish to maturity only through adult forms of self-forgetting:

I would certainly regard autonomy as a positive good, but not a self-sufficient good. My doubt about autonomy is that it is not really a fully adult virtue. It is the critically important virtue of late adolescence, when an individual needs to be freed from parental and other authority in order to find a form of fidelity to one's self. This is the normal outcome of the adolescent identity crisis. It is a working out of needs for individuation and separation that have begun as early as the second year of life. But it is a moment which must be included and surpassed in a return in later adulthood to a larger sense of social responsibility and spiritual sensitivity based on a recognition of dependence and interdependence as forming a polar complementarity to autonomy. . . .

The point can be illustrated with the example of social roles. To the adolescent just come of age, roles may appear to be oppressive, masks that inhibit the 'true self.' . . . [But young people who have effective role models will] begin to see roles not as external encumbrances but as the very forms through which one becomes an authentic and responsible adult.

What all this suggests is that the hard-won autonomy of the young adult needs to be supplemented by the conscious choice of roles, the conscious acceptance of the degree to which we are always 'implicated' . . . with other people. Thus as we come to accept the fact that we are fathers and mothers, teachers and community leaders, we more fully understand the virtues that go with those roles[—] virtues of responsibility, care and wisdom, that do not subvert but enrich the virtue of autonomy.[16]

The self-discovery that can result from self-sacrifice occurs not only in our psychological development but also in the course of our natural spiritual development. Just as children must learn from experience, we can learn much from our mistakes when we commit a transgression or engage in some act of thoughtless, adolescent-style indepen-

68

dence. The roots of such learning draw nourishment from the rich soil of repentance.

> Adam and Eve are the prototypes who teach us this lesson. Because of their transgression, they were cast out of their garden of innocence into the lone and dreary world. . . . They began to suffer pain as a consequence of their independent action. In humility and childlike faith they called upon God for help. They offered sacrifices as instructed by an angel, even though they had no idea why they should. Through the symbol of sacrifice they were then taught about the Savior and were shown how they could return to God's presence through his Atonement. . . .
>
> What did Adam and Eve know after they returned to God's presence that they hadn't known when they were originally with him in the Garden?[17]

Their years of mortal experience with repentance, humility, sorrow, and faithful striving became the Lord's course of instruction to help Adam and Eve develop the capacity to live a meaningful celestial life, which included at its center the flowering of their own individuality: "finding" their own lives.

When we deny ourselves and follow Christ, submitting ourselves in dependence to commandments that direct us to love our neighbors as ourselves, we will also develop greater personal independence. This occurs because we cannot return to God's presence without "an understanding of who we are, who God is, and what our lives mean." And "this understanding is impossible without the experiences that teach us, sometimes painfully, about our own agency and independence. Paradoxically, it is only in discovering our independence from God that we understand our utter dependence on him."[18]

In our eventual union of being "at-one" with God, we will thus be both more dependent and more independent than at present, because our experience in applying the Atonement to the sorrows and disappointments of our lives will develop both sides of our nature—both sides of the Christian paradox of losing self and finding self. After all, as discussed in chapter 5, the Atonement is fundamentally a doctrine of human development.

In addition, simply through the normal process of human maturation that is encouraged by living the gospel, we look to the needs of others and assume such responsibilities as parenthood, teaching, or missionary service. As a result, we discover that these roles of belonging are not "external encumbrances" but are "the very forms through which one becomes an authentic and responsible adult." They "do not subvert but enrich the virtue of autonomy."[19]

Note one very practical illustration of these ideas, the theme of which is that we must lose ourselves in duty in order to find ourselves in liberty. Some single LDS men and women worry about the Church's heavy emphasis on marriage and family life. These worries are not without foundation. Sometimes the preoccupation with family values in Church talks and lessons seems so exclusive that it can make single people feel invisible and unappreciated, wondering if the Church is only for married people with children. Because so many devoted and contributing members of the Church do not live in such family settings, all of us must open our eyes to individualized reality, appreciating and supporting each person as a full-fledged child of God, regardless of family status.

However, beyond cultivating such sensitivity, the Church need not apologize for its emphasis on family belonging. *The Lord's emphasis on marriage and family is not merely for social reasons. That emphasis is primarily for theological reasons.* As discussed in chapter 11, our family bonds are our liberation. Marriage is one of the Lord's primary institutions for perfecting us individually, because taking upon ourselves

70

the unlimited commitments of marriage and parenthood will develop our core personality and character to levels that are otherwise almost impossible to find.

Therefore, the happiest and most productive single men and women will find substitute opportunities for service and commitment in extended family ties and in other places where they are needed. They will prefer this over becoming stuck in the quagmire of self-pity that is fostered by the world's current preoccupation with individualism. Cultivating such places of charity will help them anchor their search for liberty in an equally important search for duty. When that happens, they are applying successfully the same theological principle that asks them to submit to the yoke of family bonds.

Consider, finally, the example of someone who found the link between liberty and duty both within and beyond her immediate family. She enriched the virtue of her autonomy by losing herself in belonging to other people. Caroline Hemenway Harman lived in Utah nearly a century ago. By President Gordon B. Hinckley's description, she was an "unknown and unsung" woman "who held together, nurtured, loved, and reared to useful maturity two large families . . . in an environment of grinding adversity."[20] Caroline married George Harman in 1895 and bore seven children, one of whom died in infancy. When she was thirty-nine years old, her husband passed away suddenly. A few years later, her sister died in an influenza epidemic, and Caroline took her sister's new baby boy, Pete, into her home.

Within three weeks of her sister's death, Caroline's own daughter, Annie, passed away, and Caroline—or "Aunt Carrie," as she was called—collapsed from the strain of these events. She recovered but continued to suffer a serious case of diabetes. Not long afterward, she married her deceased sister's husband—thus becoming a mother to thirteen children. Five years later, her second husband died from the effects of a terrible chemical accident. Aunt Carrie consequently assumed responsibility by herself for all the children and for the family's large farm. In addition, for eighteen of these years, she was a ward Relief Society president. Caroline was living proof that "charity never faileth"; she looked after the welfare of nearly one thousand ward members with the same devotion she gave her family. She later married again, but not long afterward her husband suffered a stroke. She cared for all his needs until his death five years later. She then passed away at age sixty-seven.

Many things have changed since Aunt Carrie's day, some for the better, some for the worse. One of these changes is that people are now more prone to ask whether giving their hearts to God—or to other people—will bring them freedom or slavery. Those who knew Caroline Harmon describe her as one who intuitively and daily drank from the meaning of Harry Rowe Shelley's line from "The King of Love My Shepherd Is:" "I nothing lack if I am His,/And He is mine forever." Like many other men and women who have worn out their lives in quietly giving themselves to those within their circle of belonging, her example of inspiration, courage, and self-fulfillment touched a multitude of lives with an influence that continues nearly a century later.[21] As Wendell Phillips once said, "How 'prudently' most men creep into nameless graves; while now and then one or two forget themselves into immortality."[22]

Was Aunt Carrie "liberated"? Many today would say no. Imagine yielding one's life in perpetual service to husbands, children, and neighbors whose needs consumed her very life. Some might have said to her, "Aunt Carrie, get out from under all that. You're entitled to a little happiness of your own. It's time somebody waited on you for a change. Don't let them do this to you. You don't *belong* to them."

But Aunt Carrie knew better; for the King of Love was her shepherd. She loved and served him by loving and serving those to whom she fully and freely belonged. She was theirs, and they were hers—forever. In thus belonging, she who gave her life a day at a time in serving others for the Master's sake also found her life and her liberation, for she came to know the truth, and the truth made her free. She grew to be more like her Maker in that freedom, outside the shadows of domination, in the full, warm light of day.

Part II

THE ATONEMENT AND BELONGING TO GOD

Eve Heard All These Things and Was Glad: A Developmental Perspective on the Atonement

B elonging as taught by the gospel encourages rather than stifles the development of our personal identity. This developmental process occurs in our belonging to God, as it does in other forms of belonging. Thus, because of the Atonement of Jesus Christ, we may *learn* from our experience without being *condemned* by our experience. In this way, the Atonement uses the oppositions of mortality to nourish the personal capacities we must develop in order to return and eternally belong to God.

In other words, it is often when we are *lost* that we are most likely to *find* Christ and the meaning of his mission. A few years ago we made our first trip to the BYU Jerusalem Center in Israel. On our first day in Jerusalem, Bruce attended a meeting in the old part of the city. When the meeting concluded earlier than expected, he decided he had time to walk through the old city back to the BYU Center, which he could see on a distant hill. As he made his way through old Jerusalem, he thought that if he could choose only one spot to see on this solo excursion, it would be the Garden of Gethsemane. However, he had been in Israel just once several years earlier, and recalled only having seen the garden at the bottom of a deep valley. He assumed it would be too far away to reach by foot.

Soon he emerged beyond the city wall, but he could no longer see the BYU Center on Mt. Scopus. As he looked for a better vantage point, he found his pathway moving down a steep road. Then he realized that the road carried heavy traffic, but the street allowed no place for walking. He found himself clinging to a wall to avoid cars and trucks as he stumbled down the busy street. When he reached the bottom of the hill, he realized that he was lost. He had no sense of which direction to look for the Center. With some embarrassment, he looked around for someone he might ask for directions, but he saw no one on foot.

As he walked across a nearby street, a familiar feeling came over him. He rounded a corner, and his eyes rested on a small, quiet area lined with trees. Puzzled, he felt he had seen this spot before. As he moved closer, he saw a small sign: "Garden of Gethsemane." He had found the place where the Atonement occurred, but he had found it when he was lost.

Adam and Eve were the first mortals to discover the Atonement, and they found it only when they were lost. Not long after they were left to wander as outcasts in the lone and dreary world, the Lord sent angels, then came himself to teach them: "As thou hast fallen thou mayest be redeemed." (Moses 5:9.) He urged them to accept the Atonement by repenting and calling upon God in the name of the Son forevermore. He promised not only to forgive their transgression in Eden—he would also cause the sorrow and the bitterness of both Eden and mortality to become the source of great meaning and joy.

When Adam, in his lost and fallen state, realized that his experience with sin and suffering could enlighten and exalt him rather than condemn him, he exclaimed: "Blessed be the name of God, for *because of my transgression* my eyes are

78

opened, and in this life I shall have joy, and again in the flesh I shall see God." (Moses 5:10; emphasis added.) He had discovered that in being lost, he could find God in a way that would not otherwise have been possible.

Eve had the same astonishing insight: if they accepted the gospel, their sad experience would not destroy them—it would actually sanctify them! "Eve, his wife, heard all these things and was glad, saying: Were it not for our transgression we never should have had seed, and *never should have known* good and evil, and the joy of our redemption, and the eternal life which God giveth unto all the obedient." (Moses 5:11; emphasis added.) This insight is a central message of the temple endowment, taught to us through the story of Adam and Eve.

A friend once said, "If the temple is our holiest place of worship and learning, shouldn't it teach the Atonement, our most sacred and central doctrine? And to do that, shouldn't the endowment focus on the life of Christ rather than on the lives of Adam and Eve?"

The temple endowment does teach the Atonement, but it focuses on Adam and Eve to teach the story of *receiving* the Atonement. The Savior's life is the story of *giving* the Atonement. We who must receive the Atonement can identify with the lost feelings and the sorrows of Adam and Eve so fully as to say, "That is the story of my life." When we see how much their story is our story, perhaps we too will exclaim, as Adam might have said, "Blessed be the name of God! Because Christ came, mortality is not my enemy—it is precisely because of my mortality that, in this life, I shall find joy, understanding, and even the presence of God." This is because *the Atonement is fundamentally a doctrine of human development, not a doctrine that simply erases black marks*.

A woman who was preparing a Church lesson on the Atonement said that she had always believed the Atonement plays no role in our lives until we stand before the judgment bar of God. She said our lives and sins would then be weighed in the balance, measured against the degree of our repentance. If we had repented, she thought, the Atonement would remove the stain of our sins and we could be exalted. If that is how it works, she wondered, what can the Atonement possibly have to do with our daily mortality? Our response is that the Atonement blesses us not only on judgment day but also in the here and now of daily life. It is not a mere abstraction for some other place and time. Just as we get lost in mortality, God will find us in mortality.

Moreover, because of the Atonement's developmental purpose, it also sanctifies *all* of our distress, not just the distress caused by our sins.

For example, many parents ache from losing children, both physically and spiritually, and they wonder—did they fail their children, or did their children fail them? In addition, some people are harmed by the sins of others under circumstances that make them feel like transgressors themselves.[1] And we know a good and spiritual man who lost his business and his self-respect through misjudgments that were caused by a serious emotional disorder, not by his conscious choices. Yet, even when the degree of their accountability is unclear, many good people take upon themselves full and admirable responsibility for whatever happens to them. Much of this is as it should be. But not all of it, for we suffer not only from acting but also from being acted upon.

We hear often today that those who are hurting and emotionally wounded can be helped by therapy. Often they are—there is, in fact, a healer's art at work in much professional treatment. But some people assume that religion is of little help in solving serious personal problems, because they view religion as just so many clichés and abstractions, so much history, so much irrelevance. In this view of religion, the Atonement is at best a sterile set of philosophical abstractions that deal only with sin and apply only after death.

But Jesus is the Great Healer, and his Atonement is the heart of our theology. No therapist can match that healing power. When is the power of the Master Healer accessible to us? Should we be surprised to discover that the Atonement—the core doctrine of the gospel—applies to the core problems of our mortal lives—all of them?

The story of Adam and Eve teaches us that the Atonement is for all of our losses and all of our lives, each day of our lives. The Savior's gracious power not only heals and comforts—it is also a source of personal growth and development, leading to an understanding of life and a fulness of joy. The Atonement is thus developmental and practical, not static and abstract.

According to Lehi, if Adam and Eve had not transgressed, they would have remained in the garden of Eden "in a state of *innocence*," having no children and knowing neither misery nor joy. (2 Nephi 2:23; emphasis added.) The Fall was therefore an essential step in their development. It introduced the misery and sorrow of a sinful world, but the Fall was not a mistake or an accident. Rather, the Fall was consciously designed—misery and all—to bring us joy and freedom: "Adam fell that men might be; and men are, that they might have joy. And the Messiah cometh in the fulness of time, . . . that they . . . become free forever, knowing good from evil; to act for themselves." (2 Nephi 2:25–26.)

The Lord taught Adam this same understanding of life. He said Adam's children would experience the bitterness of mortality, but "they taste the bitter, that they may know to prize the good." (Moses 6:55.) Indeed, "if they never should have bitter they *could not* know the sweet." (D&C 29:39; emphasis added.) The role of the Atonement in this process is to compensate for, thereby healing us from, the effects of the bitter, once we exert our best efforts: "It is by grace that we are saved, after all we can do." (2 Nephi 25:23.)

Thus does the grace of Christ, unlocked by his atoning sacrifice, heal us from the wounds of our sins and all our other "infirmities." (See Alma 7:12.) As we repent of our conscious sins, accept the gospel, and do all else in our power to do, we enter into a holy relationship with our Savior based on the two-way covenants made possible by his Atonement. Through our covenant relationship with him, he heals us in at least four distinct ways:

1. He satisfies the eternal law of justice, paying for our sins, so long as we repent of them.

2. His influence interacts with our righteous yearnings and our repentance to change our hearts until we desire goodness continually.

3. He bridges any chasm that separates and estranges us from God, thereby healing our feelings of shame, bitterness, and worthlessness. Many causes can create this sense of alienation—unintentional mistakes or undeserved discouragement and confusion, as well as sin. Regardless of whether his sheep run away or lose their way or are stolen away, the Good Shepherd will search for them when they are lost, pick them up, and carry them home, making them "at one" with him and his Father. That is the work of the great "at-one-ment."

4. Once we have done all we can do to make restitution, the Savior will help to compensate for the harm we may have done, or the harms done to us, repairing and restoring our spiritual and psychic losses, whether caused by sin or other factors.

Among these four sources of healing, only the first two deal exclusively with the effects of conscious sin. We may become alienated from God, or we may injure other people, not only through sinful acts but also by careless mistakes or by the consequences of unavoidable adversity. From the cumulative effect of these causes, we experience the bitter tastes that can teach us to know the sweet and prize the good. The grace of Jesus Christ makes this sweetness both possible and lasting by purging, healing, and cleansing us from the stains of all mortal bitterness, so long as we in good faith do "all we can do." (2 Nephi 25:23.) This lets us *learn* from our experience without being *condemned* by that experience. Thus does the Atonement enable our growth and our understanding. No wonder "Eve heard all these things and was glad."

Beyond these ways of healing, the Lord's grace also offers a fifth, more affirmative dimension: He endows and blesses us with hope, charity, understanding, and joy as we move beyond forgiveness and healing toward the eternal life of possessing a divine nature. At that crowning stage, we will not only *desire* the good, or even just *do* good. We will, as the Lord said to Adam, "*prize* the good" (Moses 6:55)—savor it, enjoy it, comprehend it. A developmental perspective helps us see that, as desirable as it is for us to avoid evil or to repent from it, that is not the same as doing—let alone prizing—the good.

A father once scolded his son a few days before Christmas because the little boy was terrorizing the house and creating a constant mess. The father said, "If you aren't good, Santa won't bring you anything." Soon the father wondered where his boy had gone—things were too quiet. He found the little guy lying very still on his back, looking stonily at the ceiling. "What are you doing?" the father asked. "I'm being good," said the boy. He was avoiding evil by avoiding movement. That is not what it means to prize the good. We seek more than neutrality, more than avoidance. We seek to *be* good, as the character of God himself is good in its very nature. And that state of being is, like charity, ultimately a gift of Christ's Atonement, bestowed upon the humble and obedient followers of Christ, after they learn from experience all they can discover by themselves about prizing the good.

So, does the Atonement work in our lives as an event or as a process? If it is an event, life is a simple test that we either pass or fail. We compile a certain number of black marks and white marks. At life's end, we add up the marks, compute our repentance points, and check the score. Above some fixed level of repentance, the Atonement applies, our sins are paid for, and we go back to square one. With this approach, repentance is essentially another white mark— something we do to *earn* forgiveness. But something is missing here. For one thing, if the Atonement simply returns Adam and Eve to Eden, theirs is a story with no plot, no character development. Nothing *happens* to them, because the Atonement seems to erase what has happened to them. There is nothing here about what it means to have *learned* to recognize evil and to prize the good.

Moreover, this view sees our repentance as mechanically earning enough grace to offset our black marks. If that is how we think the Atonement works, we are unlikely ever to feel the full freedom and meaning of forgiveness and belonging to Christ. As long as we believe that we totally *earn* forgiveness, we will still feel guilty, because we will sense intuitively that we do not have the power to make ourselves completely whole. The Lord's forgiveness is ultimately an act of grace—it comes as his gift, not as something we have a "right" to, even though we must repent as a condition of receiving it.

Consider, however, the Atonement in our lives as a process rather than an event. The process of Atonement applies not just once but, potentially, throughout our lives. Along this path of life, Adam and Eve did not simply return to Eden; rather, they moved onward from Eden through the telestial world. Because they accepted the gospel, then learned to cast Satan's influence from their lives, they kept moving with the blessings of the priesthood into the terrestrial world, and finally into the celestial presence of God.

During this arduous journey, our first parents learned from their own experience to distinguish good from evil. By the sorrow and sweat of earthly life, they learned the taste and, ultimately, the very meaning of the sweet and the good. They did not come to this understanding merely by partaking of the forbidden fruit. Their first taste of the tree of knowledge was but the beginning of a lifelong quest for meaning—not an event but an extended process, marked by having children and discovering misery, sin, goodness, joy, and the very meaning of eternal life.

When, after all this, Adam and Eve returned to the Lord's presence, we could describe their homecoming with the lines of T. S. Eliot:

> We shall not cease from exploration
> And the end of all our exploring
> Will be to arrive where we started
> And know the place for the first time.[2]

To illustrate, consider what happened in Eve's experience. As God's literal spirit daughter, Eve probably desired to become like her parents. Perhaps the serpent in the garden played to this natural desire when he told Eve that if she would eat of the tree of knowledge, she would "be as gods, knowing good and evil." (Moses 4:11.) The Lord had forbade her to partake of this fruit. But Elder John A. Widtsoe taught that this commandment was primarily a "warning," simply disclosing to Adam and Eve that the choice to seek knowledge would bring death and great sorrow.[3] They made the brave choice, perhaps sensing that this was the pathway not just to knowledge but also to eternal life—which is to become like God.

The last line in the song "I Am a Child of God" originally read, "Teach me all that I must *know*/To live with him some day." Later it was changed to "Teach me all that I must *do*."

Perhaps it might read, "Teach me all that I must *be* to live with him some day." Satan cunningly misled Eve when he said she would become as the gods by simply knowing good and evil. Partaking of the tree of knowledge destroyed her innocence, but that was only the beginning of her quest to be as the gods. She and Adam had to leave the security of the Garden and face the full fury of mortality. They needed to repent and obey God rather than wander in Satan's misery-bound search for knowledge without obedience. Through the interaction of their obedience and God's mercy, they could then actually become like him, moving beyond just knowing "about" the good toward literally "being" good.

The interaction between our effort and God's grace is represented by the covenants of the Atonement, described in the sacrament prayer. Our part of that covenant is not that we may never make a mistake; it is, rather, that we are *willing* to take upon ourselves his name, *willing* to always remember him, and *willing* to keep his commandments. And that willingness shows where our hearts really are. On this condition, he will always be with us, to heal, to compensate, to strengthen us by the gifts of his Spirit—for those gifts are "given for the benefit of those who love me and keep all my commandments, *and [those] that seeketh so to do.*" (D&C 46:9; emphasis added.) The Lord offers the gifts of the Spirit not only to those who *do* but also to those who, willing but struggling, *seek to do* his will.

What must life have been like for Eve, whose willingness to live righteously was constantly tested and battered by the growing pains of mortality? She had no precedent, no one to call for advice who had been through her experience. She couldn't call her mother on the phone and ask, "Mom, what did you do when your children argued and fought?" She and Adam had only each other—and the Spirit of the Lord; but, over time, how they grew in that total interdependency! When they were first together, Adam was defensive about his choice to eat the forbidden fruit. Under the Lord's firm questioning, he said, "*The woman* thou gavest me, and commandest that *she* should remain with me, *she* gave me of the fruit . . . and I did eat." (Moses 4:18; emphasis added.) But after their shared experience brought them, together, into the depths of humility and the heights of marital commitment, "Adam and *his wife* mourned before the Lord, because of Cain and his brethren." (Moses 5:27; emphasis added.) Their love grew as they learned *together* the tastes of bitter and sweet, and the joy of their redemption.

Arta Romney Ballif once wrote a poem called "Lamentation,"[4] in which she imagined Eve's experience as a mother and a wife—her questions, her cries for understanding, her quest to know God. Note the symbols here—the "fruit" of both the garden and the body; the "storm," the repetition of "multiply" and "sorrow." Consider how the Atonement could help Eve with the anguish she describes here:

And God said, "BE FRUITFUL, AND MULTIPLY—"
Multiply, multiply—echoes multiply

God said, *"I WILL GREATLY MULTIPLY THY SORROW—"*
Thy sorrow, sorrow, sorrow—

I have gotten a man from the Lord
I have traded the fruit of the garden for fruit of my body
For a laughing bundle of humanity.

And now another one who looks like Adam
We shall call this one "Abel."
It is a lovely name, "Abel."

Cain, Abel, the world is yours.
God set the sun in the heavens to light your days
To warm the flocks, to kernel the grain
He illuminated your nights with stars
He made the trees and the fruit thereof yielding seed
He made every living thing, the wheat, the sheep, the cattle
For your enjoyment
And, behold, it is very good.

Adam? Adam
Where art thou?
Where are the boys?
The sky darkens with clouds.
Adam, is that you?
Where is Abel ?
He is long caring for his flocks.
The sky is black and the rain hammers.
Are the ewes lambing
In this storm?

Why your troubled face, Adam?
Are you ill?
Why so pale, so agitated?
The wind will pass
The lambs will birth
With Abel's help.

Dead?
What is dead?

Merciful God!

Hurry, bring warm water
I'll bathe his wounds
Bring clean clothes
Bring herbs.
I'll heal him.

I am trying to understand.
You said, "Abel is dead."
But I am skilled with herbs
Remember when he was seven
The fever? Remember how—

Herbs will not heal?
Dead?

And Cain? Where is Cain?
Listen to that thunder.

Cain cursed?
What has happened to him?
God said, *"A fugitive and a vagabond?"*

But God can't do that.
They are my sons, too.
I gave them birth
In the valley of pain.

Adam, try to understand
In the valley of pain
I bore them
       fugitive?
       vagabond?

This is his home
This the soil he loved
Where he toiled for golden wheat
For tasseled corn.

To the hill country?
There are rocks in the hill country
Cain can't work in the hill country
The nights are cold
Cold and lonely, and the wind gales.

Quick, we must find him
A basket of bread and his coat
I worry, thinking of him wandering
With no place to lay his head.
Cain cursed?
A wanderer, a roamer?
Who will bake his bread and mend his coat?

Abel, my son dead?
And Cain, my son, a fugitive?
Two sons
Adam, we had two sons
Both—Oh, Adam—
       multiply
       sorrow

Dear God, why?
Tell me again about the fruit
Why?
Please, tell me again
Why?

This poem movingly depicts Eve's anguish—yet it does not tell us why she and Adam lost their sons. They may not have known why. They must have wondered if those losses were their own fault. Had they failed as parents? The poem imagines that in her very uncertainty, Eve felt estranged from God, cut off, not at all "at one" with him. And it is fair to assume that Adam's and Eve's questions and fears in losing Abel and Cain were literally "multiplied" on other dark days throughout their lives. Like Eve, sometimes we do not know—perhaps cannot know—how fully we are at fault for the bitterness we taste. When we taste the bitter, we, like Eve, can only keep trying, and wondering, and asking for understanding. We might then cry out as Joseph Smith did: "O God, where art thou? And where is the pavilion that covereth thy hiding place?" (D&C 121:1.) Does the Atonement speak to such questions? We testify that it does.

Carlfred Broderick, a former stake president and well-known psychotherapist, relates the following incident. He was invited to a Young Women program in his stake. The program theme was based on the Wizard of Oz story, hoping to teach young people that if they will follow the yellow brick road of the commandments, they will find their way safely to Oz. As the program ended, a leader asked President Broderick to say a few words. He told them that even if they keep the commandments, life will not always be a yellow brick road. He said he had just come from two wrenching hours of counseling with two faithful, devoted women in their stake. Despite their faithfulness, they found life crumbling around them. So he taught the young women and their parents what he had tried to teach the two women: Obedience to God's commandments surely protects us from much harm. But ultimately, the gospel of Jesus Christ was not given us primarily to *prevent* our pain. The gospel was given us to *heal* our pain. That is the promise of the scriptures: the Atonement not only heals us—it can sanctify our trying experiences to our growth.

We know a deeply religious woman who literally could not pray for *months* after losing her seventeen-year-old son in a motorcycle accident. She said to her husband, "What can I say to the Lord?" She was asking the questions Eve asked. But her faithfulness was stronger than her anguish—so finally she, like Eve before her, found that the healing balm of the Atonement began to soothe and heal her wounded heart.

This healing, strengthening power is not a vague abstraction of distant hope. This power flows from the fully developed theology of the Atonement. Our most fundamental doctrine truly does speak to our most fundamental problems. The Lord can and will *sanctify our experience for our growth and development.* Remember the fourth and fifth verses of our hymn "How Firm a Foundation":

> When through the deep waters I call thee to go,
> The rivers of sorrow shall not thee o'erflow,
> For I will be with thee, thy troubles to bless,
> And sanctify to thee thy deepest distress.
>
> When through fiery trials thy pathway shall lie,
> My grace, all sufficient, shall be thy supply.
> The flame shall not hurt thee; I only design
> Thy dross to consume and thy gold to refine.[5]

As suggested by this song from the first LDS hymnbook, published in 1835, the doctrines of the Restoration are full of Atonement theology. But often we don't see the breadth and the strength of our own theology. Our doctrine is not just that adversity can help us learn and grow; rather, it is that Christ, because of what flows from the redemption, gives us the power to make weak things strong, to sift beauty from the ashes of our fires.

When it is our turn to ask the questions Eve asked in Sister Ballif's poem, let us "always remember him," for he will never forget us. His sacrifice for us binds his heart to ours. His words etch an indelible impression: "Zion hath said: The Lord hath forsaken me, and my Lord hath forgotten me—but he will show that he hath not. For can a woman forget her sucking child, that she should not have compassion on the son of her womb? Yea, they may forget, yet will I not forget thee, O house of Israel. Behold I have graven thee upon the palms of my hands; thy walls [symbols of our problems and needs] are continually before me." (1 Nephi 21:14–16.) Note the echoes of *amae* here in the relationship of a mother and her nursing child. More significantly, note the symbolism of the palms of his hands. The heart of his doctrine and the heart of his love find their source in his having bought us with his blood.

Not long ago, after two frustrating years of infertility, our son and his wife were excitedly expecting their first baby. Then they were devastated with the report from an ultrasound examination that the baby had a serious congenital heart defect. When he was born, their little Devin weighed over eight pounds. He had a head full of dark hair, but he was, quite literally, born with a broken heart. We watched through the window of the intensive care unit as the doctors hooked up the wires and tubes that became Devin's lifeline. Then, while his mother held him, his father, his grandfather, and his uncle placed their big, adult hands on his tiny newborn head to give him a name and a blessing.

Our Devin struggled mightily for three weeks, but then we gathered under a large and lonely tree in the Lehi city cemetery. Family and friends and a few flowers surrounded his little coffin. The wind literally "galed" as our daughters played on their violins, "I am a child of God," and "Teach me all that I must do"—and we thought "all that I must be." We watched then, and thereafter, as Devin's parents followed in the footsteps of Adam and Eve. We watched as their unanswerable anguish turned gradually into a mellow bonding with the other side of the veil. Now, even with the questions that remain, they know and feel and understand in ways that are otherwise undiscoverable. They have found "the peace . . . which passeth all understanding." (Philippians 4:7.) Thus, their lives bear witness that the Savior takes upon himself not only our sins but also our infirmities. (See Alma 7:11–12.) It is by sharing those infirmities with the Lord that we, like Eve, may come to know "good and evil, and the joy of our redemption, and the eternal life which God giveth unto all the obedient." (Moses 5:11.)

Eve's experience as a mother opens our understanding of the Atonement's developmental nature. She eventually learned that the Lord heals our separation by making us "at one" with him. He does this not by returning us magically to Eden but by leading us through a process of learning and growing day by day toward spiritual maturity. The Lord also draws on our understanding of a woman's perspective when he teaches us that he feels toward us the way a mother feels for her child: "Can a woman forget her sucking child, that she should not have compassion on the son of her womb?" Just as a mother could never forget her child, he said, "I [will] not forget thee." And just as a mother's body may be permanently marked with the signs of childbirth, he said, "I have graven thee upon the palms of my hands." (1 Nephi 21:15–16.) For both a mother and the Savior, those marks memorialize a wrenching sacrifice, the sacrifice of begetting life—for her, physical birth; for him, spiritual rebirth.

How does such a mother view her child's mistakes? Certainly not as the child does. Think of a frustrated little girl, crying and miserable because she always makes mistakes, loses her shoes, and leaves untidy debris around the house. Her mother does not view the child's mistakes as hopeless disasters. She views those mistakes as growing pains. Her mother holds her, dries her tears, and tells her not to be discouraged. She will learn. She will grow. Everything will be all right. With her mother's encouragement, she picks up all she can from the debris of her travail. And when the child is exhausted, her mother picks up after her. Mother picks up what her daughter cannot reach, what she cannot find, what she cannot see. Cleaning up everything can be so hard when you're little.

The Lord views our mistakes—our messy debris—as a mother would. To us, they can seem like overwhelming failures. To him, our mistakes are growing pains. He will hold us. He will comfort us. And then, if we do our best, he will pick up after us. Even when we try our hardest, cleaning up everything by ourselves can be so hard when we're little.

A little girl we know was once so tired that she just lay down and fell asleep on the edge of a dangerously busy road. Prompted by inspiration, her mother discovered her there, picked her up, and carried her to safety. We thought of her when hearing another woman describe her worry about Lehi's dream and the iron rod leading to the tree of life. She said, "My problem is not that I might leave the iron rod and wander off into the mists of darkness. My problem is that sometimes I just get so tired that I sit down in the middle of the path, unable to go on, though still clinging with my hand to the iron rod." She might have sung, "Sometimes I feel like a motherless child, a long way from home." But the Lord, like a mother, will pick up a tired child and take him or her by the hand toward home.

So we grow and learn, and he leads us along, saying, "Behold, ye are little children and ye cannot bear all things now; *ye must grow* in grace and in the knowledge of the truth." (D&C 50:40; emphasis added.) That is how Adam and Eve gained a full knowledge of good and evil. And that is how they found the joy of their redemption—not just in one grand gesture that balanced the scales at the end of their lives. Instead, they grew gradually, in grace and in their knowledge of the truth. This understanding of life's *develop-*

mental nature tells us that, even in looking for the meaning of Christ's Atonement in our lives, we should focus on ordinary, accumulated experience more than on such "bottom line" judgments as whether we are saints or sinners, or whether society thinks of us as visible or invisible people.

The Russian author Leo Tolstoy teaches this difference between small-scale development and heroic moments on a grand stage. The real heroes of his novels are not the generals, the aristocrats, or the dramatic figures. Rather, the characters he admires are the ordinary people who "lead undramatic lives, [but lives that] are rightly lived moment to moment and which unfold only as a background to the" stories of the visible heroes.[6]

In this vision of life's meaning, writes Tolstoy scholar Gary Morson, one of the best examples of the moral and spiritual life is "the moment-to-moment conscientiousness of a good mother."[7] A good mother—like other good people—is always working, reaching, responding to others' needs. Of course she will make mistakes, many of them. She can't always be right in her judgments or anticipate other people's responses. But, over time, her "moment-to-moment conscientiousness" moves her along, through growing pains, through sunshine and shade, tears and troubles, until she, with the constant help of the Lord, becomes a *moral virtuoso*. We develop moral virtuosity the way we develop musical virtuosity—by daily, demanding *practice*. When we practice, we learn from our mistakes, and the Lord helps us compensate for them—as we also do all we can.

Would such a mother be aware of her goodness? Probably not. One of Tolstoy's stories, *Father Sergius*, tells of "a proud man" who "trains himself to attain sainthood by grand gestures and noticeable acts of self-sacrifice." But "his quest fails, because no matter what he does to humble his pride, he is still proud of his very humility. When he at last meets a true saint, he discovers that she is unaware of her exceptionality. She is a mother who supports her daughter and the daughter's [very ill] husband, and [she] reproaches herself for not going to church. She lives a life of daily kindnesses that are entirely undramatic, undiscerned, and inimitable."[8] This reminds us of what Elder Neal A. Maxwell once said about President Spencer W. Kimball: "Part of what makes him so special is that he has no idea of how special he really is."

Tolstoy believed that women often seem to understand better than men do that the moral, spiritual life is most fully lived at the prosaic level of daily toil. He believed that the typical abstract interests of men—politics, sports, the military, and "sterile philosophizing"—are really quite unimportant compared to "moment-to-moment conscientiousness." We know a few men, as well as a few women, who feel such a need to worry about politics or other "big things"—like who will win the Super Bowl, the election, and the latest far-off civil war—that they happily leave to their spouses the "little things," like seeing that the children are fed, educated, and exalted. In distinguishing between this abstract, superficial world of "the great," and the deep, everyday world of "the prosaic," Tolstoy believed that the exquisite quality of the prosaic life well lived is best described in "women's language." For him, "almost everything important" and especially "anything that has positive moral value" occurs most naturally within the world of marriage, family, and daily labor that some people commonly regard as the realm of women.[9] That is indeed the realm of greatest moral value, not only for women but also for men. That is the Lord's own realm of choice: it is "[his] work and [his] glory—to bring to pass the immortality and eternal life" of his children. (Moses 1:39.)

If the Atonement is concerned with the *process* of our spiritual and moral development, where is the Atonement's meaning most likely to be found? Is it in long discussions of philosophical implications, or in knowing every detail of the last hours of the Savior's life? As valuable as such knowledge may be, the true knowledge of personal meaning of Christ's atoning sacrifice is to be found in the resolution of some person's secret sorrow, as in the story of Adam and Eve.

Consider this symbolic example. The first mortal to see the resurrected Jesus was Mary. Why had Mary and the other women gone to the tomb so early on that hushed Easter morning? Did they go in search of grand theological fulfillment? No—they went to care for the body and change the linen. Some would call that "women's work." And Mary found him there, in the midst of workaday tasks of compassionate drudgery. We too will most likely find him there—not in abstract experience detached from mortal cares, not solely at the end of life before the grand judgment bar, but here, now, in the tears and needs of obscure and lonely sorrow.

King Benjamin clarified this thought in his theology of the Atonement. In his final address, Benjamin spoke of God's goodness and his Atonement; then he described the conditions on which we find salvation:

> Repent of your sins and forsake them, and humble yourselves before God; and ask in sincerity of heart that he would forgive you; and . . . if ye have . . . tasted of his love, and have received a remission of your sins, which causeth such exceedingly great joy in your souls, . . . ye should . . . always retain in remembrance, the greatness of God, . . . and his goodness and long-suffering towards you, . . . and humble yourselves . . . , calling on the name of the Lord daily. (Mosiah 4:10–11.)

Benjamin then taught that the cultivation of this daily *attitude* of a meek and lowly heart following our baptism is *"for the sake of retaining a remission of your sins from day to day,* that ye may walk guiltless before God." (Mosiah 4:26;

97

emphasis added.) And "if ye do this ye shall *always rejoice, and be filled with the love of God,* and always retain a remission of your sins; and ye shall *grow* in the knowledge of . . . that which is just and true." (Mosiah 4:12; emphasis added.) This describes, in its highest sense, the moment-to-moment conscientiousness of a good mother—or father, or any child of God.

The Atonement of Jesus Christ allows us to learn from our experience without being condemned by that experience. When we repent and come unto him daily in lowliness of heart, he will take upon himself all our sorrows and infirmities. He will, himself like a conscientious mother, pick up after us, and even at times pick us up from our collapses of fatigue along the path of the iron rod. As we move through each growth stage of life, we will experience the bitter that we may know to savor the sweet and prize the good. The conversion of bitter to sweet is like a catalytic process of energy creation. It leaves behind some toxically bitter wastes. After we clean up as much of that waste as we can, the Lord himself absorbs the residue, for he alone drank the bitter cup. He continually nourishes and heals us, from all our losses and all our pain, whether caused by our acts or caused by our being acted upon. Each member of the Church is his spirit child, and he will not forget the children of his compassion, for he has graven us upon the palms of his hands. He will find us when we are lost; and when we hear his voice, we, like Eve, will be glad.

CHAPTER SIX

The Restored Doctrine of the Atonement: The "Authentic Theology"

A friend of ours is a successful physician and stake president who lives with his family in the southeastern part of the country. He and his wife enrolled several of their children in an academically strong Christian school, where their children were among the school's best and most popular students. Not long ago, because of the fears of other parents who were convinced that Mormons are not Christians, the school required these parents to withdraw their children permanently. Another friend, who is a community-oriented priesthood leader in a West Coast city, recently applied for membership in an interdenominational organization of local Christian religious leaders. He was told that a Mormon would fit more appropriately with the city's association for non-Christian religions.

A substantial part of these puzzling attitudes can be attributed to widespread and erroneous perceptions about Latter-day Saint doctrines concerning the Atonement and grace of Christ. As *Newsweek* magazine put it a few years ago in an article entitled "What Mormons Believe," "Unlike orthodox Christians, Mormons believe that men are born free of sin and earn their way to godhood by the proper exercise of free will, rather than through the grace of Jesus Christ. Thus

Jesus' suffering and death in the Mormon view were brotherly acts of compassion, but they do not atone for the sins of others. For this reason, Mormons do not include the cross in their iconography nor do they place much emphasis on Easter."[1]

We find massive irony in these profoundly mistaken impressions, for it is our thesis in this chapter that the Restoration through Joseph Smith actually made the Atonement and the grace of Jesus Christ relevant and accessible to individuals in a way that traditional Protestant and Catholic doctrines have simply been unable to do. And this good news has come at a time when the contemporary society is starving with spiritual hunger.

We introduce this thesis by referring again to McDannell and Lang's *Heaven: A History*,[2] which recounts how the Christian world has thought about heaven throughout Western history. When this historical study considers the twentieth century, it reports two major findings. The first finding is that the large majority of Americans still believe in a life after death and in a heaven where family members may reunite. This study's discovery that seven out of ten Americans believe in heaven is corroborated by other research showing that a similar fraction of the population believes in the existence of angels.[3] Most people think of heaven as a real place inhabited not only by friends and family, but also by a God so real and approachable that many people say they look forward to embracing him.[4]

When we learned of this widespread hunger to "hug God," our knowledge of gospel teachings on that sacred subject made us feel like Alma of old: "O that I were an angel, and could have the wish of mine heart" (Alma 29:1), to let these thousands of hopeful people know the glad tidings of the Restoration. In the Lord's words to Joseph and Oliver, "Be faithful and diligent in keeping the commandments of God, and I will encircle thee in the arms of my love." (D&C

6:20.) Or as Mormon put it, "that this people had not repented that they might have been clasped in the arms of Jesus." (Mormon 5:11.)

McDannell and Lang's second finding about the idea of heaven in twentieth-century America is more sobering. After first describing the surprising strength of today's personal beliefs in a real heaven, these authors observe that the mainline Christian churches offer little serious theological response to the natural intuition of their members. Rather, today's "ideas about what happens after death are only popular sentiments and are not integrated into Protestant and Catholic theological systems."[5] Modern Christian theology seems to assume that its earlier ideas about immortality are no longer socially relevant and, besides, are too speculative to be acceptable to contemporary scholarship. "For some of the most prominent Protestant and Catholic theologians of this century, heavenly life—if heaven exists at all—cannot be described by reason, revelation, or poetic imagination."[6]

But then, as noted in chapter 1, these historians describe one "major exception" to their generalization regarding today's theological vacuum among Christians about heaven—"the theology of The Church of Jesus Christ of Latter-day Saints."[7] They then summarize in respectful and knowledgeable terms a range of LDS teachings from eternal marriage and genealogy to ordinances for the dead. They conclude that "the understanding of life after death in the LDS church is the clearest [known] example of the continuation of the modern heaven into the twentieth century."[8]

It is poignant that so many people would instinctively yearn for a sense of genuine belonging in everlasting relationships of loving, intimate meaning, not only with other people but also with God. How sad and ironic, then, that today's Christian theology hardly offers a serious response to these deeply felt needs. If McDannell and Lang are correct that this "deep and profound longing in Christianity" is a key to understanding Western culture, then Western culture is a theological wasteland scorched with loneliness and alienation. Perhaps these are the days of which Amos spoke, days of "a famine in the land, not a famine of bread, nor a thirst for water, but of hearing the words of the Lord: And they shall wander from sea to sea, . . . they shall run to and fro to seek the word of the Lord, and shall not find it." (Amos 8:11.)

Despite this virtual absence of theological support, many Americans continue to dream of a heaven where families are reunited and where God himself might welcome them in a divine embrace. The Restoration offers these people not only the hope of such an embrace but also a full understanding of its meaning, which offers the promise of "peace in this world, and eternal life in the world to come." (D&C 59:23.) This is because being clasped in the arms of Jesus symbolizes the fulfillment of his Atonement in our personal lives, here as well as in heaven, becoming literally "at one" with him, belonging to him, as he will belong to us.

The Restoration's theological foundation for this fulfillment touches upon several major doctrines, including the Fall, the Atonement, salvation, the nature of man, grace, and repentance. These doctrines are summarized in *The Broken Heart*. Thus, this chapter suggests only the general idea that, just as the Restoration offers the most complete and satisfying available theology about heaven, the Restoration also fills a similar—and more substantial—theological void about the Atonement of Jesus Christ. Moreover, the Restoration teaches of Christ's mission in a way that lets his life and his death speak to our most profound human needs in everyday life, just as an understanding of heaven fulfills our hopes for the life after death. There is an answer to the unfulfilled longings that plague the modern wasteland. That answer is found in the teachings of the Restoration about our relationship with the Savior.

This bold assertion of the Restoration's revolutionary implications for Christianity's most central doctrine finds strong support in the work of a noted scholar on the Protestant Reformation, John Dillenberger. In a 1978 essay comparing Martin Luther with Joseph Smith on the question of grace and works, Dillenberger commented on Mormonism's doctrinal uniqueness: "Mormonism brought understanding to what had become an untenable problem within evangelicalism: how to reconcile the new power of humanity with the negative inherited views of humanity, without abandoning the necessity of grace." In this way, "perhaps Mormonism . . . is the authentic American theology, for the self-reliance of revivalist fundamentalist groups stood in marked contrast to their inherited conception of the misery of humanity."[9]

To explore the meaning of Professor Dillenberger's provocative observation, we must take a brief journey through the history of certain ideas in Western civilization. Any sketch of this kind runs the risk of being simplistic, but sometimes even a few headlines from history can provide needed perspective.

Since the fourth century A.D., the teachings of traditional Christianity on man's nature and the role of Christ's grace have begun with the assumption that each person born since the fall of Adam and Eve has an inherently evil nature. According to Catholic teachings, this effect of original sin can be overcome only by the grace of Christ as that grace is dispensed through the official sacraments of the Church. General Protestant theology on this subject is even more pessimistic about the degree to which humankind's inherent evil is uncontrollable. Moreover, Protestantism's primary departure from Catholic doctrine is its claim that the source of grace is not in Church sacraments but only in the unearned gift that God may choose to bestow, at his option alone, directly upon an elect few. Let us consider the historical origins of these major premises that form the basis for so much Christian reasoning.

Leading Christian scholars commonly acknowledge, as BYU's Stephen Robinson has pointed out, that by the fourth century A.D., Christianity's basic doctrines had undergone a "radical change from the theology of the New Testament Church."[10] The extent of this change is illustrated by the *Harvard Theological Review*'s recent publication of a skillful article by BYU's David Paulsen, which documents that "ordinary Christians for at least the first three centuries" after Christ believed that God had a body.[11] Brother Paulsen shows that, beginning in the fourth century, Christianity gradually abandoned its belief in God's physical body, because that idea was unacceptable to the Greek philosophy that pervaded the Roman empire. This change erected one of the first conceptual barriers against human identification with a personal God. That the *Harvard Theological Review* considers this evidence of the great apostasy to be worthy of serious treatment by a BYU scholar is, like *Heaven: A History*, an encouraging sign. As we thoughtfully remove whatever bushels conceal the Restoration's light, Latter-day Saint perspectives can and will play a legitimate part in restoring the gospel of Jesus Christ to its rightful place in today's otherwise impoverished public and private conversations about the religious life.

Another significant doctrinal change during and after the fourth century was the widespread acceptance of St. Augustine's view about man's fallen and evil nature, which has had a profound effect on Christianity's understanding of both the need for and the meaning of the Atonement and the grace of Christ. In another candid acknowledgment of the great apostasy, Princeton religious scholar Elaine Pagels's recent book, *Adam, Eve, and the Serpent*, describes in some detail how Augustine's highly original "teaching on 'original sin' became the center of [the] western Christian tradition, displacing, or at least wholly recasting, all previous views of creation and free will."[12]

Augustine's reasoning began with his despair over his perceived inability to control the way his body responded to sexual stimuli. He finally concluded that all human seed is infected with the contaminated seed of Adam, thereby transmitting to each human person Adam's fallen nature. In his view, "no human power" could remedy this inborn human failure, but only the power of Christ, who was fathered without mortal seed. As a result, only the Church and its clergy could bestow God's grace by administering "to sick and suffering humanity the life-giving medication of the sacraments."[13]

We infer from this logic that the Catholic doctrine of Real Presence (Transubstantiation), whereby sacramental bread and wine are believed to be literally transformed into the flesh and blood of Christ, is the only way, under Augustinian thinking, to achieve a gradual, physical conversion of a fallen part of the body of Adam into a redeemed member of the body of Christ.

Professor Pagels's research shows that Augustine's ideas were a radical departure from both the moral freedom taught by the Old Testament and the ideas of free will and personal responsibility that had prevailed among Christians since the time of Christ. Given Augustine's heretical "decision to abandon his predecessors' emphasis on free will,"[14] Pagels asks, why were his views embraced rather than condemned by the Christian leadership? One answer must be that Augustine's writings demonstrated great intellectual power. But Professor Pagels found a further explanation in historical and political reality.

The Roman emperor Constantine had accepted Christianity and declared it the official religion of the vast Roman empire not long before Augustine began writing. Augustine's views offered a perfect justification for the asser-

tion of both governmental and religious power over a plu-
ralistic and unruly population: because people by their fallen
nature could not govern themselves, they required the help
of a powerful state as well as a forceful Church structure.
Thus Augustine's theology of the fall made "the uneasy
alliance between the Catholic churches and [the] imperial
power [of the Roman state] . . . not only justifiable but necessary."[15] This political imperative moved Augustinian doctrine "into the center of western history," surpassing the
influence "of any other church father." From then on, it was
heresy to teach the earlier Christian view of human freedom,
which had once been "so widely regarded as the heart of the
Christian gospel."[16]

In the centuries that followed, the Church of the middle
ages erected an elaborate structure of both doctrine and
practice on the foundation of Augustine's assumptions about
man's evil nature. This structure included the monastic
orders. By the time of Martin Luther in fifteenth- and six-
teenth-century Germany, the Church's influence was waning
and the former Roman empire had fragmented into many
nationalistic states that began giving higher priority to their
own interests than to the dictates of papal authority. New
political, economic, and intellectual forces had emerged that
would make the Renaissance into one of Western history's
greatest watersheds. Nevertheless, Martin Luther was about
to reinforce Augustine's notion of natural human depravity
as the linchpin of Christian theology.

Himself an Augustinian monk, Luther struggled with his
personal weaknesses in an ordeal very similar to Augustine's.
He tried in vain to satisfy his desperate desire for grace
through the Church's sacraments. Eleven hundred years earlier, Augustine had found guidance in Paul's New Testament
letters. Luther looked to those same sources and, while he
developed his own theological vision, he also accepted
Augustine's major premise about man's evil nature.[17] He then

launched the Reformation era by concluding, as part of his critique of the Church, that God bestows undeserved grace not through Church sacraments but directly on chosen individuals. This reasoning removed any need for the Church as an intermediary.

Luther, perhaps unintentionally, thus broke the Catholic Church's control over the sources of grace, thereby permanently undermining the Church's social and political authority. In another echo of Augustine's experience, Luther's theology provided a rationale for the claims of potent new political forces throughout Europe that sought to overthrow rather than sustain centralized authoritarian structures. Luther was courageous and articulate, but as had happened with Augustine, a historic political need gave wings to his ideas that their religious merit alone might not have warranted.

This historical sketch illustrates John Dillenberger's comment about the "negative inherited views" of "the misery of humanity" that have come to characterize western Christianity. In the years following Luther, numerous doctrinal differences emerged among the various Christian denominations; however, in the post-Reformation era, Augustine's essential pessimism about humankind's depraved nature continued as a permanent inheritance in Christianity's general tradition. By 1820, these ideas had painted Christianity into an impossible corner, because neither the intellectual developments of recent centuries nor popular common sense in the U.S. seriously supported the notion of man's inherently evil nature. As Dillenberger put it, Protestantism had thus developed "an untenable problem"; namely, how to reconcile the "new power of humanity" and the "self-reliance" of Christian religious groups with the Augustinian heritage without nullifying the meaning of grace.

For example, a leading authority on Puritanism (which traces its theological lineage to Martin Luther through John Calvin) writes that within a century after the Puritans originally came to America in 1620, "the theory of the utter dependence of man on . . . God ceased to have any relevance to the facts of the Puritan experience. [Still,] the preachers continued to preach [the doctrine of man's inherited evil nature] and the laymen continued to hear it; not because either of them believed it, but because they cherished it. . . . Thus the sense of sin became a genteel tradition, cherished in the imagination long after it had been surrendered in practice. The Puritan insistence on . . . [human] depravity became the . . . justification of Yankee moral complacency."[18] In other words, one might say with a wink, we might as well be sinful—that's just human nature.

One reason people became less inclined to believe seriously in man's evil nature was that European and American history between Luther's time and Joseph Smith's time demonstrated such irresistible evidence for the wonder of humankind's abilities. Drawing on classic Greek optimism about man's rational powers, the Renaissance and the Enlightenment fueled true revolutions in the sciences, the arts, the commercial/industrial world, and the political sphere—as witnessed by the French and American revolutions. The turmoil of the French Revolution and its aftermath tempered some Europeans' enthusiasm for these ideas, but by 1830, much of Europe as well as the independent and robust United States of Joseph Smith's time were fairly bursting with confidence in the ability of men and women to subdue the earth and take charge of their lives.

However, the great danger of the new optimism regarding human nature and mankind's effort was that, taken to its logical extreme, that optimism would finally have no need for the grace of Christ. As illustrated by Goethe's *Faust,*[19] leading nineteenth-century European and American writers increasingly emphasized the self-realization made possible by the indomitable spirit of human striving. Because these writers often regarded man's discoveries and personal quests as being "without inner or outer limits,"[20] the limitless Faustian journey by itself—wherever it led, with or without grace—could serve life's limitless purpose. And that is exactly what happened as humanistic self-confidence gained the upper hand over self-deprecating theology in the nineteenth and twentieth centuries.

As a result, the Protestant Christianity that dominated nineteenth-century America was increasingly unable to reconcile its pessimistic heritage with the nation's frontier optimism. Humankind's widely recognized powers and accomplishments contradicted traditional beliefs in man's evil nature to the point that many people not only saw little practical need for God's grace, but they gradually adopted the humanistic assumption that people are good by nature. Then, given the centuries-old belief that humanity needs grace primarily to overcome its evil nature, the assumption that man is naturally good eliminated in the minds of many the need for Christ's grace altogether. Individuals still violated divine laws, but the new line of thinking concluded that poverty and other collective failures were more persuasive explanations for these failings than was any idea of inborn depravity.

The abstractions of Christian theology seemed increasingly out of touch with daily experience in the twentieth century—to such an extent that in 1964 Protestant theologian Harvey Cox pronounced Christianity quite irrelevant to modern society. In a book called *The Secular City,* Cox symbolically and literally rejected Augustine's preoccupation with the evil of this world and the goodness of God's world as described in Augustine's famous book from the fourth century, *The City of God.* Cox urged the Christian churches to give up dreaming of heavenly cities and to focus on the social problems of earthly cities. Until the churches heeded this message, said Cox, Christianity would hardly play a meaningful role in American life.[21] Despite the continuing belief in Augustine's assumptions about humankind's evil nature among a few theologically conservative Protestant groups today, most Christian churches and theologians have clearly taken Cox's advice.

For instance, one noted theologian said of Americans' current popular interest in the existence of angels, "If people want to get in touch with their angels, they should help the poor [or work] at a soup kitchen [rather] than attending a seminar."[22] And in a recent talk to students entering Yale Divinity School, Dean Phillip Turner acknowledged that Augustine's thought "now appears unsatisfactory and in certain ways rather destructive." One of Augustine's errors, he said, was to place so much emphasis on the first commandment—loving God—that he ignored the second commandment to love one's neighbor. Yet "many theologians in the modern period, partly in reaction [against this Augustinian heritage], have executed a reverse maneuver," in which they emphasize love of neighbor so much that they now exclude the love and worship of God.[23] Dean Turner urged his students to put the study of divinity—God—back into divinity school. The deficiency Turner sees echoes the lack of interest in heaven among modern theologians that we noted earlier.

As we survey the contemporary wreckage of a once-elaborate Christian theological structure, Dillenberger's observation about Mormon doctrine seems even more compelling: "*In stressing human possibilities, Mormonism brought things into line, not by abandoning the centrality of grace but by insisting that the [obvious abilities] of humanity . . . reflected the actual state of humanity as such. . . . Perhaps Mormonism . . . is the authentic American theology.*"[24]

With the error and the impracticality of Augustine's teaching now unmasked, we must next ask, What *is* this authentic American theology? *The Broken Heart* attempts to summarize the Restoration's unique theology of grace and the Atonement, suggesting the general relationship between human nature, the Atonement, and the way in which belonging to Christ can sustain us in times of personal need. We are drawn to the personal dimension in this book because we are saddened by seeing so many decent people outside (and inside) the Church who have no theological support for embracing and belonging to the authentic, personal Christ—not only in heaven but also on earth. The Restoration, like the Atonement, offers not only an abstract historical message but also an intensely personal one.

According to the Savior's original doctrines as restored through Joseph Smith, the fall of Adam and Eve made the Atonement both possible and necessary. Moreover, human nature is inherently neither good nor evil. We *become* good or evil based on interaction between the Lord's influence and the choices we make.

Because of their transgression, God expelled Adam and Eve from Eden into a world that was subject to the forces of life and death, good and evil. But the Lord soon taught Adam that "the Son of God hath atoned for original guilt"; therefore, Adam's children were not evil but were "*whole* from the foundation of the world" (Moses 6:54; emphasis added.) Thus, "every spirit of man was *innocent* in the beginning; and God having redeemed man from the fall, men became again, in their infant state, *innocent* before God." (D&C 93:38; emphasis added.)

As the descendants of Adam and Eve then become accountable for their own sins at the age of eight, they all taste sin to one degree or another as the result of their curiosity and their experiences with temptation in a free environment. Those whose cumulative experience leads them to love "Satan more than God" (Moses 5:28) will to that degree become "carnal, sensual, and devilish" (Moses 5:13; 6:49) by nature—"natural men." On the other hand, those who accept Christ's grace by their faith, repentance, baptism, and continued striving will yield to the "enticings of the Holy Spirit," put off "the natural man," and become "saint[s] through the atonement of Christ the Lord." (Mosiah 3:19.) Thus, after taking the initiative by faith to accept the grace made available by the Atonement, one may then nourish one's faith by obedience that interacts with grace until one "becomes a saint" by nature, thereby enjoying eternal or godlike life.

In LDS theology, therefore, grace is the absolutely indispensable source of three categories of blessings. First are the unconditional blessings—free and unmerited gifts requiring no individual action on our part. God's grace in this sense includes the very Creation, as well as making the plan of salvation known to us. It also includes resurrection from physical death and forgiveness for Adam's and Eve's original transgression.

Second, as an act of grace, the Savior has atoned for our personal sins subject to the condition that we repent. Personal repentance is thus a *necessary* condition of salvation, but it is not by itself *sufficient* to assure salvation. Without the Atonement, our repentance availeth nothing.

Third is the bestowal of grace after baptism along the path toward a Christlike nature. Once we have repented and have been baptized unto forgiveness of sin, we have only "entered in by the gate" to the "strait and narrow path which leads to eternal life." (2 Nephi 31:18–20.) The Lord does not expect perfection during this postbaptism stage of spiritual development, but he does require our good-faith effort to "endure to the end" (2 Nephi 31:20) of becoming perfect, "even as [our] Father which is in heaven is perfect" (Matthew 5:48). This effort includes our receiving the higher ordinances of the temple and continuing our repentance as needed to "retain a remission of [our] sins" from day to day. (Mosiah 4:12.)

According to Martin Luther, a Christian who performs

righteous acts after receiving Christ's grace is not acting from personal initiative but is only reflecting the spontaneous fruit of internal grace. For Luther, man's fallen nature made self-generated righteousness impossible. In LDS doctrine, by contrast, "men should . . . do many things of their own free will, and bring to pass much righteousness; for the power is in them, wherein they are agents unto themselves." (D&C 58:27–28.)

Yet we clearly lack the capacity to develop a fully Christlike nature by our own effort alone. Thus, the perfecting attributes, which include hope, charity, and finally the divine nature that is part of eternal life, are—as Mormon put it so eloquently—ultimately "*bestowed* upon all who are true followers of . . . Jesus Christ" (Moroni 7:48; emphasis added) by the grace that is made possible by the Atonement. In LDS theology, this interactive relationship between human and divine powers derives both from the significance the theology attaches to free will and from its optimism about the "fruit[s] of the Spirit" (Galatians 5:22) among "those who love [God] and keep all [his] commandments, *and him that seeketh so to do*" (D&C 46:9; emphasis added).

God bestows these additional, perfecting expressions of grace conditionally, as he does the grace that allows forgiveness of sin. They are given "after all we can do" (2 Nephi 25:23)—that is, as a supplement to our best efforts. We prove worthy and capable of receiving these gifts not only by obeying particular commandments, but also by demonstrating certain personal attributes and attitudes such as "meekness, and lowliness of heart" (Moroni 8:26) and developing "a broken heart and a contrite spirit" (3 Nephi 9:20).

In addition, those who enter into the covenants of the gospel of Jesus Christ also enter a precious and ongoing relationship with the Savior, by which he nourishes them with personal and spiritual sustenance. This is the relationship of belonging to—or being children of—Christ.[25] We celebrate and renew this relationship each time we partake of the sacrament. Through this covenant relationship, the Savior not only grants a continuing remission of our sins, but he will also help compensate for our inadequacies, heal the bruises caused by our unintentional errors, and strengthen us far beyond our natural capacity in times of acute need. Both we in the Church and those outside the Church need this Atonement-based relationship more than we need any other form of therapy or support.

Sometimes Latter-day Saints seem to have little idea of the strength of the Church's position on the most basic doctrines of Christianity. This remarkable strength derives not just from family values and healthy living, as important as those are; it derives from the "authentic theology" of the restored gospel, which is the last, best, and only hope of Christianity, and of all mankind. The Restoration not only resolves post-Augustinian Christianity's central doctrinal dilemmas; it also offers the most complete solution to our greatest problems, whether social or personal.

Yet the gospel's insights remain relatively hidden from a society that has been consciously and cleverly persuaded by the adversary himself that the Church of the Restoration knows least—when in fact it knows most—about making Jesus Christ our personal Savior. Satan knows exactly what he is doing. What frightens him and his allies is not that the Restoration teaches so little about the Atonement and grace of Christ, but that it teaches so much. To conceal that reality, he has been engaged in one of history's greatest cover-ups.

Increasingly now, not only the LDS lifestyle but the far more fundamental contribution of the restored Church's doctrine is coming forth from obscurity. The widespread circulation in major libraries of the new *Encyclopedia of Mormonism* is a wonderful step in that direction. And a recent survey in the United States of five thousand of its readers by the Book of the Month Club recently asked people what was the most influential book in their lives. They reported that the Bible still ranks first, and the Book of Mormon now ranks eighth.[26] Only a few years ago, the Book of Mormon would never have shown up on such a list in a national survey. But now, as the Book of Mormon's influence spreads, so will spread the good news that access to the *living grace* of the *living God* has been restored in fulness.

Today many people feel a longing for heaven, where, they want to believe, they will be welcomed not only into the arms of their families but also into the arms of God. The Restoration offers a complete fulfillment of that longing, not just as momentary emotion but as the fully developed doctrine of the gospel of Jesus Christ. He is saying to all those, within and outside the Church, who hunger and thirst to find him in these times of trauma and famine: "Be faithful and diligent in keeping the commandments of God, and I will encircle thee in the arms of my love." (D&C 6:20.)

Forgiveness and Christ Figures: The Atonement and Being Harmed by the Sins of Others

One of the most significant questions we have encountered since the publication of *The Broken Heart* is whether and how the Atonement can heal the emotional wounds inflicted by the sinful acts of other people. This question is both natural and important—natural because so many suffer from these wounds, and important because some of this suffering runs so deep as to seem beyond repair. This issue also raises a question about belonging and *amae:* What do we do when those on whom we depend violate our trust?

One woman told us that, as a child, she had been the victim of extensive sexual abuse. Years later, as she tried to cope with the wrenching trauma caused by that experience, she prayed and searched the scriptures to find healing and relief. She knew that the Atonement is the source of God's most potent healing power, but she thought the Atonement compensated only for her sins. In the dark time of her childhood, she was not a sinner but had been sinned against. How could she repent when she was the victim? Yet her pain and her self-loathing felt much like the "exquisite pain" that Alma said is suffered by those who commit serious sin. (See Alma 36:21.) That somehow made her feel like a transgressor. She also felt, as did the sinful Alma, shut out by feelings of estrangement from the presence of God. And she yearned, like Alma, for the healing and forgiving balm of Christ's love. Could she find what Alma had found in the Atonement of our Lord? Could the Atonement heal her from being hurt by the sins of another person? She longed for understanding.

The answers to these questions draw on two assumptions on which the present volume rests: first, that the Atonement's healing power in fact extends beyond healing us from our own sins; and second, that the Lord's grace is a powerful and active force not only in our relationship with him but also in our relationships with other people.

We heard Catherine Thomas tell about growing up in circumstances of emotional abuse, the child of an alcoholic father. After joining the Church, marrying, and having children of her own, she was plagued with recurrent feelings of fear, guilt, and anger that seriously impaired her relationships at home. Late one night, she reached a crisis point while waiting for an absent teenage child. She cried out in anguish to the Lord for deliverance from her "indefinable distress." The words "go home" came to her clearly but without explanation.

She acted on this impression by flying immediately to her parents' home, where she found her father just concluding a rehabilitation program that invited her participation as his adult child. The program opened a new world of understanding, identifying previously hidden connections between the emotional deprivations of her own childhood and her adult confusion. She saw that her preoccupation with her own troubles had caused her to pass some of that distress on to her own family. Through great effort over much time, she then learned to "repent of bad mental habits: fear, self-pity, self-condemnation, [and] unforgiveness." Yet, significantly, she writes, "I found I did not have this power fully in myself to reshape and heal my mind, but Christ did."[1]

117

This story finds an important echo in the pathbreaking work of BYU clinical psychologist Allen Bergin on the place of religious values in psychotherapy. Brother Bergin has identified the concept of the "transitional figure" as a key professional tool that draws on the religious concepts of sacrifice and redemption. By this means, a client suffering from psychological harm can be "taught to become a transitional person in the history of his or her family."[2]

The victims of various forms of abuse commonly stand as a link in a great family chain, holding the hands of ancestors on one side and descendants on the other. Within this chain, one may pass along to the next generation, like an electrical current, the emotional harms one has suffered. This occurs when a parent who was damaged in childhood later traumatizes his or her children, whether consciously or not, in confused attempts to be free of distress. (For example, research shows that 80 percent of those accused of sexually abusing children were once sexually abused themselves.)[3] The "transitional figure," a personal link in the pathological family's intergenerational chain, halts the process by simply *absorbing*, rather than passing along, the current of harm. "Instead of seeking retribution, one learns to absorb the pain, to be forgiving, to try to reconcile with forebears, and then become a generator of positive change in the next generation."[4]

Brother Bergin illustrates this with the story of a young woman whose therapist encouraged her to place herself in such a transitional role, temporarily setting aside years of bitter feelings toward the father who had abused her. Like Catherine Thomas, she also "went home." There, rather than confronting her father again over the pain he had caused her, she simply spent time with him, learning about his identity and experiences, including tape-recording and transcribing her interviews. Her therapist reported that this became "a gentle experience occurring in a forgiving atmosphere," and it "caused a dramatic reconciliation between the woman and her father," helping him "to face certain realities he had never faced."[5]

Those who would become transitional figures confront the question about human nature raised so powerfully in Shakespeare's *Hamlet*: which is more human—to forgive being wronged, or to avenge the wrong? As Hamlet became convinced of the identity of his father's murderer, he stated this question as: "To be or not to be?" Could he, more educated and reflective than most, muster the moral strength to offer mercy, rising above the standard impulse to seek revenge? Would he extend mercy unto forgiveness, absorbing great injustice—or would he, like most others, simply avenge it? "Whether 'tis nobler in the mind to suffer/The slings and arrows of outrageous fortune/Or to take arms against a sea of troubles/And by opposing, end them."[6] Then again, would Hamlet really "end" the chain of harm by "opposing" it? The blood-soaked stage at the end of *Hamlet* tells us that his choice to seek vengeance only extended the outrageous fortune. But true transitional figures find ways to suffer the slings and arrows—and thereby stop their flow.

Children who stop the intergenerational flow of affliction act in fulfillment of Isaiah's prophecy regarding those who fill the void left by a former generation and raise a new foundation for the next, thus repairing the breach in the intergenerational linkage: "They that shall be of thee shall build the old waste places: thou shalt raise up the foundations of many generations; and thou shalt be called, The repairer of the breach; the restorer of paths to dwell in." (Isaiah 58:12.) Christ himself was the greatest of all transitional figures in this sense, because he "repaired the breach" that afflicted all the members of his human family.

Let us generalize still further from these experiences of transitional figures. A team of BYU professors led by Dr. Anne Horton recently completed a significant study of the healing process among the victims of child sexual abuse. The researchers knew from experience—as the public is increasingly coming to know—that child abuse is among the most damaging and intractable of all human problems. No matter what healing techniques are employed, the process is so long and so difficult that it discourages both therapists and victims. Indeed, many therapists have questioned whether such victims "could *ever* fully recover. The wounds [sometimes seem] just too deep and too irreparable to heal."[7] So the Horton team identified and then studied the experiences of people who had apparently recovered from abuse, trying to understand what causes healing to occur.

The study's preliminary findings identified three important elements in recovery-from-abuse cases that go beyond normal emotional healing: (1) "final family closure," (2) "resolution of sexuality issues," and (3) "spiritual recovery, which almost always involves some form of forgiveness."[8] The survivors felt above all a need "to be believed and understood" as an essential step in overcoming their own shame and guilt, despite their absence of actual responsibility. The third finding, which revealed the need to forgive, surprised the researchers. Perhaps only a significantly religious survey group would report such data. (Because this was a BYU-sponsored study, many of the survivors who elected to respond were Latter-day Saints.) As a typical survivor wrote: "In order to truly feel healed, there must be a type of spiritual recovery, where victims are able to forgive those they feel wronged by, whether that be the perpetrator, or family members who allowed the abuse to happen, or even God, whom victims often blame for not intervening on their behalf."[9]

These remarkable findings offer significant new data for abuse victims and therapists to consider. The data also raise important theological questions: Will the power of the Atonement heal us from the effects of harm caused by others? If so, what must we do to qualify for such blessings? We cannot repent when we have not transgressed. Is there some process analogous to repentance in such cases? What can we learn from the experience of abuse victims that applies to other life experiences?

The surprising responses of the abuse survivors, like the experiences recorded by Catherine Thomas and Allen Bergin, suggest at least some answers to these questions: Of course the Atonement's healing power is available to the victims of other people's sins, because its power can heal any pain and bridge any gap that separates us from God. As explained more fully in chapter 9, the first step in this healing process is that we must come unto Christ with a broken heart and a contrite spirit, repenting of our actual sins and accepting the ordinances of baptism and the gift of the Holy Ghost. By thus entering into the covenants of the Atonement, we establish a relationship with the Savior that becomes a fountain of further blessings—a well of water springing up unto everlasting life. (See John 4:14.) Along with such gifts as hope and charity, these blessings include the healing of spiritual wounds and compensation for spiritual losses. As we continue to do "all we can do" (2 Nephi 25:23) on our own power, the Savior closes the remaining gaps. However, the victims of other people's sins must take an additional step: forgiveness. This step, like repentance for our own sins, is far easier to talk about than to live, but it is essential.

We must immediately acknowledge that in cases of severe abuse, in all the ugliness of its variant forms, forgiving often does not simply mean forgetting. "Survivors don't need to forget their memories, they need to learn to take control of them so they are no longer run by them."[10] Such cases can be extremely complex, which means that telling a victim to "just be forgiving" may seem so superficial as to compound rather than solve existing problems. Each individual case is unique, requiring any therapist or counselor to develop a personalized and specific understanding of the case.

Nevertheless, the theological principle, now verified by important field experience with abuse victims, is clear: Unless we forgive, we cannot be fully healed. If we do forgive, the Savior's atoning power descends upon us in relief. "Ye ought to forgive one another; for he that forgiveth not his brother his trespasses standeth condemned before the Lord; for there remaineth in him the greater sin. I, the Lord, will forgive whom I will forgive, but of you it is required to forgive all men." (D&C 64:9–10.)

This does not mean, of course, that an abuse victim who seeks to be forgiving would never help bring a criminal perpetrator to justice, for the Lord continued, "And him that repenteth not of his sins, and confesseth them not, ye shall bring before the church . . . And this ye shall do that God may be glorified—not because ye forgive not, having not compassion, but that ye may be justified in the eyes of the law, that ye may not offend him who is your lawgiver." (D&C 64:12–13.)

In all cases involving wrongs inflicted by others, we must search to know why failing to forgive is "the greater sin." Because the Lord has commanded us to forgive as a distinct spiritual obligation, obviously our failure to forgive by itself creates a need to repent: "And ye shall also forgive one another your trespasses; for verily I say unto you, he that forgiveth not his neighbor's trespasses when he says that he repents, the same hath brought himself under condemnation." (Mosiah 26:31.)

Yet the commandment to forgive can be very difficult to obey. Here are people, often totally innocent, who have been thrust into the depths of shame, despair, and years of psychic pain—not by their own mistakes, not even by natural adversity, but sometimes by the deliberate crimes of degraded transgressors. It seems fair to ask why the victims of abuse should be required to do *anything* to deserve the Lord's vast healing powers in such a case. Because abuse victims suffer so many of the same symptoms of guilt and estrangement from God as do willful transgressors, the irony that they should need to forgive those who have wronged them is almost overpowering.

Still, there lurks between the lines of the scriptures on forgiveness a message of transcendent meaning—not only about abuse victims but about all of us, and about all of the Atonement.

Consider the "transitional figure." What are we doing when we are willing to absorb a terrible trauma of the spirit, caused not by our own doing but by one who claimed to love us—and we absorb the trauma even to help the sinner? That picture somehow has a familiar look—we've seen all this before. Of course, because this picture depicts the sacrifice of Jesus Christ: he took upon himself undeserved and unbearable burdens, heaped upon him by people who often said, and often believed, that they loved him. And he assumed that load not for any need of his, but only to help them.

So to forgive—not just for abuse victims, but for each of us—is to be a Christ figure, a transitional point in the war between good and evil, stopping the current of evil by absorbing it in every pore, thereby protecting the innocent next generation and helping to enable the repentance and healing of those whose failures sent the jolts into our own systems.

The Lord has told us: "Among them who know their hearts are honest, and are broken, and their spirits contrite, and are willing to observe their covenants by sacrifice—yea, every sacrifice which I, the Lord, shall command—they are accepted of me. For I, the Lord, will cause them to bring forth as a very fruitful tree which is planted in a goodly land, by a pure stream, that yieldeth much precious fruit." (D&C

97:8–9.) Could it be that we, not only abuse victims but all of us, will be accepted of the Lord only as we observe our covenants by the sacrifice of participating in *his* sacrifice—extending to others the grace he extends to us, and helping to absorb the undeserved trauma that he himself absorbed?

Perhaps it is in the nature of belonging to Christ that we "follow him" by letting ourselves belong to others as he does—approximating even in small ways his sacrifice for us through our sacrifice for them. Perhaps only when we begin to approximate his sacrifice will we comprehend it enough to realize the full impact of its blessings. Perhaps when his effort combines with ours to move our hearts beyond being broken to being pure and full of charity, in some small way our lives, like his on a larger scale, may represent a fruitful tree, even like the tree of life. We may then stand like a tree by a pure stream, bearing fruit that helps others develop a taste for the fruit of the real tree of life. In small and simple ways, we may be participants in his Atonement, agents of his grace through being agents of his charity.

CHAPTER EIGHT

Belonging to the Church of Christ

The idea of giving our hearts to someone we love has meaning in the language of faith as well as in the language of romance. Recall, for instance, the old hymn formerly in the LDS hymnbook, "Come, Thou Fount of Every Blessing." One of its verses reads, "Let thy goodness, as a fetter,/Bind my wandering heart to thee./Prone to wander, Lord, I feel it,/Prone to leave the God I love;/Here's my heart, O take and seal it;/Seal it for thy courts above."[1]

Possessive pronouns also carry much meaning in both romantic and religious language, as when sweethearts whisper, "I'll be yours forever." King Benjamin described the fulfillment of our relationship with the Savior in possessive terms: "That Christ, the Lord God Omnipotent, may *seal you his*." (Mosiah 5:15; emphasis added.) As Ardeth Kapp once put it, we must not only know *who* we are but also *whose* we are.

However, belonging to Christ is more than a matter of language—and more, even, than a matter of love. Just as family members take upon themselves a family name, true Christians take upon themselves the name of Christ. They become his, and he becomes theirs, forever—for he bought them with his blood. As he undertook the holy Atonement, Jesus prayed in Gethsemane, "Holy Father, keep through thine own name *those whom thou hast given me*, that they may be one, as we are. . . . I in them, and thou in me, that they may be made perfect in one." (John 17:11, 23; emphasis added.)

As individual followers of Christ accept the oneness made possible by his "*at-one*-ment,"[2] they enter into a solemn covenant, offering him their broken hearts in exchange for Christ's offering his broken heart to them. They do this unto "the purifying and the sanctification of their hearts, which sanctification cometh because of their yielding their hearts unto God." (Helaman 3:35.) And in this act, his followers say to him, "Here's my heart, O take and seal it;/ Seal it for thy courts above."

But we now live in a day when strong forces of thought and attitude are driving wedges between those who would belong to one another, in all relationships of the heart, whether romantic or religious.

A few years ago we read the work of two contemporary thinkers about the religious dimension of this problem in a piece of graffiti on a wall in Jackson, Wyoming. As graffiti goes, these expressions were quite philosophical. They were written in two parts—the second writer had obviously edited the first writer's work. The original lines read: "The way to find purpose in life is to allow Jesus to save your worthless soul. Religion is a rock." The second writer had evidently pondered the meaning of this message and found it wanting. He first crossed out the word "worthless," a change with which we agreed. He also changed the word "rock" to "racket," and after the word "soul" he added, "and become a socialized robot." As edited, the statement read: "The way to find purpose in life is to allow Jesus to save your soul and become a socialized robot. Religion is a racket." To a society that prizes individual autonomy, the idea of salvation through Christ can sound like a robot-producing racket.

Society's declining sense of belonging thus affects our attitudes not only about personal relationships but also about our relationship with God—and with his church. This phenomenon is but one dimension of a large and complex cultural problem that has developed in American society over the past generation. Clearly influenced by anti-establishment attitudes originating in this recent movement, a few Latter-day Saints have now begun transferring U.S. culture's general skepticism about authority and institutions to their relationship with the Church.

The Western tradition of questioning the institutional authority of churches actually goes back five centuries to the time of Martin Luther, whose theological contentions challenged the authority of the Catholic church in ways so fundamental that he altered the entire course of history. As a result of Luther's doctrinal theory,[3] the entire Protestant movement was based upon ideas that emphasized a direct, unmediated relationship between each individual and God, rejecting the emphasis on institutional and community authority that had characterized both the Catholic and Jewish traditions. Given the Protestant attitudes that dominated the thinking of those who founded the American republic, skepticism about institutional authority then became a central element in defining the very nature of democracy and democratic institutions.

Indeed, one of the hallmarks of American society, both in Joseph Smith's time and now, is the idea that political authority begins within individual citizens, who may choose to create a government, a corporation, or a church. This concept undergirded Jefferson's formulation of the Declaration of Independence and is embodied in the U.S. Constitution. The Founding Fathers' ideas about democracy make institutions accountable to the people who create them. This accountability helps explain why public criticism of governmental and other institutions is such a time-honored and important American tradition. An electoral process informed by wide-open and often critical discussions of public policy is essential in keeping democratic governments under the control of the citizenry.

Against this background, the divinely initiated restoration of the Lord's church and his priesthood authority in nineteenth-century America clearly ran against the grain of historical momentum. The Church derived its ultimate authority not from the people who organized it but directly from God, who took the initiative to call Joseph Smith to re-establish the Lord's Church according to His detailed instructions. Of course, the principle of common consent has always played an important role in encouraging individual Church members to express themselves about sustaining those called to Church positions. Moreover, Church leaders at any level seek to be worthy of the members' trust. Yet the accountability of these leaders is not only to the members of their congregations but to the Lord and his authorized representatives.

At the same time, the restored gospel teaches the pre-eminent value of individual worth and independence. We are, indeed, beings who are co-eternal with God.[4] And the Restoration makes it possible that "every man might speak in the name of God the Lord." (D&C 1:20.)

By extracting these individualistic doctrinal strands from their complete gospel context—a context having much to say about belonging and humble submission—then mixing them with anti-authoritarian democratic political ideals, a few contemporary Church members are beginning to regard the Church in essentially the same way as they regard other man-made institutions. While they may see the Church as serving generally useful purposes, some seem to believe that their own views about Church policies and practices have equal validity with the views of those the Lord calls to lead the Church. Even for those who are still willing to accept direction from God himself, this point of view makes it difficult to think of yielding to the institutional authority of the Church as part of yielding one's will to God.

When this form of skepticism is directed toward the Church, it asks anew Luther's centuries-old question about the place of institutional religion: is a church a catalyst or a barrier in the individual's relationship with God?

The assumptions and concerns of those who worry about the balance between institutional and individual strength within the Church are not without foundation. Salvation *is* finally an individual matter. Moreover, the gospel does have a broader reach than the institutional elements of the Church. For example, Jacob's phrase that "the keeper of the gate is the Holy One of Israel" (2 Nephi 9:41) symbolizes the reality that each person who accepts the Atonement and the gospel of Jesus Christ enters into a unique and everlasting relationship with the Savior—and that relationship is one-to-one. Jacob describes the gate to the strait and narrow path that leads to eternal life, a gate that each of us enters by the ordinance of baptism. Because Christ "employeth no servant there" (2 Nephi 9:41), we do not maintain this relationship through an agent or intermediary, even though many others may assist us—including the missionaries or parents who teach us, the bishop who counsels us, or the priesthood holder who baptizes us.

Similarly, while marriage is for any man or woman a prerequisite to entering the highest degree of the celestial kingdom, each worthy woman and man also enters into and eternally enjoys a private, personal relationship with the Lord. No woman needs to "go through a man" to gain access to the Lord's influence in her daily life. Each woman and man prays directly in his or her own language. There is no translator between God's language and our own, for he knows every tongue and recognizes every voice.

In addition, the Church organization plays a less permanent role than the role played by the eternal family unit or
by eternal gospel principles. In the eternities, the family will
ultimately supersede the Church as the primary organizational vehicle for spiritual and all other activity. Even today,
Church leaders emphasize that parents are our most fundamental gospel teachers and that the home is our children's
most fundamental classroom. Studies of the activity of the
Church's young people have shown that personal and family
religiosity are more significant predictors of future missionary service and temple marriage than are such institutional
influences as Church programs and Church teachers—even
though the teachers' significance is second only to the significance of parents. Additionally, general Church officers
have frequently reminded local leaders to spend more of
their time "ministering" to the Saints in needed but unstruc-
tured ways than in "administering" formal Church programs.

Moreover, we should not be surprised by claims of
human flaws in the institutional Church. The fact is that,
despite their best efforts, some bishops, Relief Society and
quorum presidents, or other priesthood and auxiliary leaders
really are at times insensitive. The work of the Lord's church
is done by imperfect people. Indeed, the Lord said through
Joseph Smith that "almost all" of those who receive "a little
authority, as they suppose" will "immediately begin to exercise unrighteous dominion" over other people. (D&C
121:39.) Unfortunately, when we act "to cover our sins, or to
gratify our pride, our vain ambition, or to exercise control or
dominion or compulsion upon the souls of the children of
men, *in any degree of unrighteousness*, behold, the heavens
withdraw themselves; the Spirit of the Lord is grieved; and
when it is withdrawn, Amen to the priesthood or the authority of that man." (D&C 121:37; emphasis added.)

What this means, as Hugh Nibley has pointed out, is that
"of all those who 'hold' the priesthood almost none really

possess it." Any time someone uses priesthood-authorized power to "show off," to enjoy "prestige," or just to "give orders to another," he undermines the source of his own authority. By contrast, those who exercise divinely sanctioned authority in righteousness will be among the "humble, unpretentious and unworldly people [who are] the 'few humble followers of Christ.'"[5]

There is nothing new about human limitations and insensitivities among well-meaning but imperfect leaders. The Savior's chosen, closest associates more than once tried to discourage him from casting the net of his ministry as broadly as he did. For instance, when the blind beggar pleaded with Jesus for mercy and healing, the disciples who were with him "rebuked" the beggar, saying "that he should hold his peace." (Luke 18:39.) But Jesus ignored them and healed the man. And when people brought a number of little children forth to be healed, some of the Savior's disciples, perhaps in an attempt to protect him, "rebuked them." However, Jesus taught his disciples a lesson in compassion and tolerance: "Jesus called them unto him, and said [to his disciples] . . . forbid them not: for of such is the kingdom of heaven." (Luke 18:16.) And he proceeded to bless and heal the little ones.

Consider the story of the Samaritan woman at the well, to whom Jesus taught his sermon on the living water of the gospel. If Jesus had followed Jewish tradition, he would not have taught this woman as he did. For one thing, she was a Samaritan, for whom the Jews had a long-standing hatred; for another, she was a woman, and the women of that day were not customarily involved in religious discussions with Jewish men. Probably for such reasons, his disciples "marvelled that he talked with the woman: yet no man said, . . . Why talkest thou with her?" (John 4:27.)

Elder Richard L. Evans once observed that those who will live and work only with perfect people will soon be all alone. Because of our mortal limitations, some human failings will inevitably influence the Church's institutional character. At the same time, however, we must maintain a balanced perspective, valuing both the individual and the institutional dimensions of Church membership. If organizational elements predominate over personal elements, we may overlook the private, customized dimension of spiritual development. But if we regard the institutional dimension as trivial, or if we are put off too much by the human limitations of fellow Church members, we may miss out on opportunities for growth and service that are found only through the blessings of complete activity and membership in the Church.

One of those blessings is simply belonging among the Saints of the Most High. In an essay entitled "Belonging: A View of Membership," Elder Jeffrey R. Holland once described membership in the Church as coming "into the fold of God, and to be called *his [Christ's] people*." (See Mosiah 18:8; emphasis added.) A fully participating member of the Church is involved in a community of compassion and interconnectedness that is "more than boys' clubs or civic associations . . . more than house parties and welcome wagons. . . . This fellowship is ultimately of the Spirit and comes because Christ is our eternal head."[6]

This is the fellowship of which Alma spoke to those he baptized at the waters of Mormon, brothers and sisters in the gospel who "are willing to bear one another's burdens, that they may be light; yea, and are willing to mourn with those that mourn; yea, and comfort those that stand in need of comfort." (Mosiah 18:8–9.) As described by a third-century Christian named Cyprian in a letter to a friend, "It is really a bad world, yet in the midst of it I have found a quiet and holy people. They have discovered a joy which is a thousand times better than any pleasure of this sinful life. They are despised and persecuted, but they care not. They have overcome the world. These people, Donatus, are the Christians and I am one of them."[7]

A more particular blessing of Church membership is that the bond of belonging to Christ and his people extends our level of deeply committed interaction beyond the narrow circle of family and friends to a circle of brotherhood and sisterhood that is a cross-section of all humanity. As we give ourselves over to that broader circle in wards and stakes based on geography, led by lay leaders, and typically populated by a broad socioeconomic spectrum, we give ourselves to the true spirit of charity in its unadorned, daily reality. And in that process, we discover hidden wellsprings within ourselves, we discover gifts and truths in others we would never otherwise know, and we taste in intensely practical ways the love—the charity—the Savior has for all mankind.

From such experience, Eugene England learned that "the Church is as true as the Gospel," because the Church organization is "the best medium apart from marriage (which it much resembles in this respect), for grappling constructively with the oppositions of existence." This experience occurs very naturally through Church callings that help us "serve people we would not normally choose to serve," thus providing us with "opportunities to learn to love unconditionally." These intimate and long-term relationships with "brothers and sisters" in the bonds of Church belonging also teach us through the experiences of others how the Atonement applies—not just in theory but also in the plain though richly varied crucible of mortality.[8]

Another cluster of rich blessings, which Elder Bruce R. McConkie once called "the blessings of the priesthood,"[9] is also made available only through our membership in the Church. Significantly, nearly all of these blessings are available not just to those who hold the priesthood but to all Latter-day Saint women and men, whose Church membership lets them tap fully into the opportunities and powers that flow through the Church by virtue of the Church's *institutional* access to the Aaronic and Melchizedek priesthoods. While great blessings come to those who "hold" the priesthood, it is not just "holding the priesthood" that produces most of "the blessings of the priesthood" in our lives; rather, it is our having become members of the institution—the Church—in which the priesthood resides.

For example, two of our daughters have served as full-time missionaries. Each was called, set apart, and assigned by priesthood authority to preach the gospel as an authorized representative of the Church. Each was entitled to, and received, constant inspiration. Each was accountable for the missionary work in her assigned area. Each experienced the receipt of spiritual gifts and advised both members and investigators concerning important personal problems and needs. When our daughters marry in the temple, virtually all of the blessings of the priesthood will be within the reach of their doctrinally based, priesthood-authorized promises. As essential as is their personal relationship with the Savior, they could not realize these blessings without the callings, ordinances, and associations made possible only by the institutional Church with its foundation of priesthood authority.

Among the most significant "priesthood blessings" of Church membership is continual access to the counsel of living prophets, who teach us in contemporary terms what the Lord would have us know. As he said, "Whether by mine own voice or by the voice of my servants, it is the same." (D&C 1:38.) Modern prophets typically teach us what Elder John A. Widtsoe called "a rational theology." But we also live by faith, at times accepting the counsel of the Lord and his servants without a complete rationale. For instance, because science has now discovered the terrible health hazards of tobacco, we have recently lived through a fascinating culture change on the social acceptability of smoking. We might wonder why the Lord didn't just tell us in the 89th section of the Doctrine and Covenants about the risks of lung cancer. Instead, he gave only his conclusion and a promise—no more explanation than that tobacco "is not good for man." (D&C 89:8.)

Thus have the Lord and the prophets always worked. We have an entire theology explaining why it is better for our spiritual development when we freely choose to be believing rather than waiting until we are compelled—even by scientific evidence—to believe.[10] The believing attitude is not always easy, especially for Church members educated in the tools of rational skepticism. But our long-term experience in observing the outcomes of prophetic counsel to the Saints constantly verifies, as suggested by the tobacco example, why the Lord warned the Church: "All they who receive the oracles of God, let them beware how they hold them lest they are accounted as a light thing, and are brought under condemnation thereby, and stumble and fall when the storms descend, and the winds blow, and the rains descend, and beat upon their house." (D&C 90:5.)

One further dimension of membership in the Church is tied directly to membership in the family of Christ, which means belonging to Christ. When the Savior talks about those who "are *mine*," he is referring to the Saints of God, the members of *his* Church. The members of that body are not just those shown on the dues-paying roster of some collective association bound by common interests. Rather, they are all of the individual souls who have chosen to come forth out of the world, one here and two there, into the covenants of the Atonement with him. They are the humble followers of Christ, the members not only of *the* Church (see D&C 115:4) but "the elders and people of *my* Church of Jesus Christ of Latter-day Saints, scattered abroad in all the world." (D&C 115:3; emphasis added.)

As the Lord taught Alma, who organized the Church at the waters of Mormon and in Zarahemla, "Blessed art thou

because thou hast established a church among this people;
. . . and they shall be *my people.* Yea, blessed is this people
who are willing to bear my name; for in my name shall they
be called; *and they are mine."* (Mosiah 26:17–18; emphasis
added.) This membership in the institutional body of Christ is
but a time of preparation for the day when the Saints who
endure to the end will enter his permanent presence in the
celestial kingdom, where "all things are theirs, whether life
or death, . . . *and they are Christ's,* and Christ is God's. . . .
These shall dwell in the presence of God and his Christ forever and ever." (D&C 76:59–60, 62; emphasis added.)

The members of the Church are, then, all those whom
Christ has "spiritually begotten." (Mosiah 5:7.) They are
called the children of Christ; therefore, they call each other
brother and sister. Alma described them as "all the true
believers of Christ, who belonged to the church of God . . .
And [they] were faithful; yea, all those who were true believers in Christ took upon them, gladly, the name of Christ, or
Christians as they were called, because of their belief in
Christ who should come." (Alma 46:14–15.)

As a transition between the idea of belonging to the
Church and the idea of belonging to Christ, we should note a
basic perspective that affects both forms of religious belonging: unchecked skepticism about the very idea of belonging
can poison the wellsprings of religious faith altogether, shut-
ting off our willingness to accept the spiritual bonds of either
Church membership or membership in the family of Christ.

Nothing is more fundamental to authentic religion than
the attitude of faith, that childlike willingness to become "as
a child, submissive, meek, humble, patient, full of love, willing to submit to all things which the Lord seeth fit to inflict
upon [us], even as a child doth submit to his father." (Mosiah
3:19.) As we read in Proverbs, "Trust in the Lord with all
thine heart; and lean not unto thine own understanding."
(Proverbs 3:5.) For the sublime example, picture Abraham,

the Father of the Faithful, standing over his only son, Isaac, with a raised knife. God had asked him to *submit* his will to God's direction under circumstances so utterly contrary to reason that Abraham could only bow his head in "fear and trembling." (Philippians 2:12; see also Mormon 9:27.)

By stark contrast, today's anti-authoritarian skepticism would instantly reject all requests for the submission of one's will to any cause or any other person, because being let alone is so important to this skepticism that it rejects any sense of dependency on others. The sad stories of those who have in fact exploited the dependency of people who trusted them are not to be denied. This uncomplimentary human record calls for extreme caution in yielding ourselves to others—whether in the yielding of romantic love or religious faith. But we must be equally cautious about the adversary's clever exploitation of today's intellectual currents. In the final showdown in the war for our souls, he has unveiled an attack that undercuts and even mocks the most basic religious attitude—simple faith and trust in God.

His strategy is clear: he must attack the core *idea* of belonging, presenting it always as a subversive invasion—a kind of psychic rape—of our inner selves. Thus he portrays any form of belonging, no matter how voluntary—no matter how fruitful, how yearned for, or how sought after—as a kind of slavery. Belonging to God, belonging to the Church, belonging to those who love you—in his cunning posturing he taunts, "All this is but a pretense by those who seek to control you for their own selfish ends."

So we feel confused about what we once believed were opposites—love and slavery. In our confusion, Satan will try to persuade us that submission to God will cost us our liberty, when in reality, it is only by yielding our hearts to God that we can possibly know the unbounded freedom of sanctification. (See Helaman 3:35.) "Know the truth," said he who was and is the Truth, "and the truth will make [us] free."

(John 8:32.) *Enslaved* fools for the sake of Christ? No, for only "where the spirit of the Lord is, *there* is *liberty.*" (2 Corinthians 3:17; emphasis added.)

Satan's attack on belonging is full of irony, because the ultimate end of his strategy is not to leave us free, alone, and autonomous; rather, he wants us to belong to *him.* Consider: the invitation to yield our will to God's appears at first to restrict our freedom, yet acceptance of the invitation eventually blesses us with the full-blown liberty of eternal life. Experience in many realms teaches us that obedience to law is liberating, not confining, because lawful obedience is the key to intelligent action. Because of the law of gravity, we can walk; the rules of grammar make coherent communication possible; only by conforming scrupulously to the physical laws of sound and motion can we compose beautiful music and send rockets to the moon. The Greeks saw this principle very early: by discovering and following the laws of the universe, humanity could master the universe rather than be mastered by it.

In contrast, Satan always offers early freedom, as if freedom requires no price. Yet that seductive beginning ultimately ends with his ensnaring his victims in the full-blown bondage of eternal slavery. As both a literal and symbolic example of this enslavement, drug addiction—like other addictions—begins with the promise of a mind-expanding adventure; then it ends in a mind-destroying tragedy. No wonder we shudder to read, "Satan . . . had a great chain in his hand, and it veiled the whole face of the earth with darkness; and he looked up and laughed, and his angels rejoiced." (Moses 7:26.) This chain symbolizes the bondage that awaits Satan's followers through his ironic imitation of the fatherhood of both God and Christ: "Satan shall be their *father,* and misery shall be their doom." (Moses 7:37; emphasis added.) This conclusion is no surprise, for Satan disclosed long ago to Moses his intention to demand our eternal allegiance: "Satan cried with a loud voice, and ranted upon the earth, and commanded, saying: I am the Only Begotten, worship me." (Moses 1:19.)

According to Lucifer's classic bargain, he offers immediate short-term freedom in exchange for long-term slavery. He gives us what we desire in our momentary myopia, but then we are obliged to give him our souls. Incredibly, many are willing to pay this price to feel short-term "cheap thrills," even when he has warned them in advance of the long-term costs! It is a story as old as Cain, as memorable as Faust, or as modern as the musical play "Damn Yankees." In the latter case, Mephistopheles (Satan) promises a twentieth-century sports nut that he will temporarily be a superstar for the New York Yankees, if only he promises to deliver his soul to Mephisto when the cheering crowds have gone home. As in each version of this old story, Mephisto eventually comes to collect his eternal reward—to lead his subject into the ever-closing system of eternal damnation. Mephisto's arrival is never a surprise, because he discloses the terms of his bargain from the very beginning.

With Christ, there is an opposite sequence: we submit to the commandments, and we give ourselves to him through the two-way covenants of the Atonement; then he blesses and tutors us with ever-expanding freedom. The ultimate goal of this process is to help us develop into beings who are free in the ultimate sense—enjoying the unfettered freedom of eternal life, the result of which is a fulness of joy. If we are faithful, the promise is clear: "Ye shall sit down in the kingdom of my Father; yea, your joy shall be full, even as the Father hath given me fulness of joy; and ye shall be even as I am, and I am even as the Father; and the Father and I are one." (3 Nephi 28:10.)

Some may think the choice to reject God is no more than choosing to be left alone. But, as the classic paradigm of the Satanic bargain makes clear, the choice to reject the divine alternative—which we may view initially as being "left alone"—is ultimately the choice to belong to Satan. The question is not whether we belong to anyone at all, but whether we finally belong to Satan or to Christ. One of them will surely possess us and be the father of our souls and the shepherd of our flock. We will finally be *sealed* to one of them or the other.

Amulek taught, "That same spirit which doth possess your bodies at the time that ye go out of this life, that same spirit will have power to possess your body in that eternal world." (Alma 34:34.) We might interpret this as a reference to the nature of our own spirits; however, Amulek continued, "If ye have procrastinated the day of your repentance even until death, behold, ye have become subjected to the spirit of the devil, and *he doth seal you his;* therefore, the Spirit of the Lord hath withdrawn from you, and hath no place in you, and the devil hath all power over you; and this is the final state of the wicked." (Alma 34:35; emphasis added.) Thus, the spirit that will possess our souls in the eternal world is either Satan's or Christ's. For if we are redeemed, Christ will "seal [us] his." (Mosiah 5:15.)

Alma preached the same doctrine: "If ye are not the sheep of the good shepherd, of what fold are ye? Behold, I say unto you, that the devil is your shepherd, and ye are of his fold." (Alma 5:39.) And Jacob adds, "Prepare your souls for that glorious day when justice shall be administered unto the righteous . . . that ye may not remember your awful guilt in perfectness, and be constrained to exclaim: . . . the devil hath *obtained* me." (2 Nephi 9:46; emphasis added.) Therefore, "*reconcile yourselves* to the will of God, and not to the will of the devil and the flesh." (2 Nephi 10:24; emphasis added.) The Greek root for *reconcile* is to become one with: "To set estranged persons *at one* again." (*Oxford English Dictionary;* emphasis added.) We will reconcile ourselves to—become one with—either Satan or Christ.

The inevitability of belonging either to Satan or to Christ is graphically portrayed by the scriptural imagery of that most human expression of belonging—to be embraced, or as the scriptures say, "to be encircled about." Those who follow Christ until they are accepted into his covenants of true belonging will one day be, as was Father Lehi, "encircled about eternally in the arms of his love." (2 Nephi 1:15.) That is why Mormon lamented in his "sorrow for the destruction of [his] people": "They will sorrow that this people had not repented that they might have been clasped in the arms of Jesus." (Mormon 5:11.) Mormon's sorrow was not just that his unrepentant people would be left unattended to continue wandering as they desired; rather, Mormon knew, as Alma explained, that "this was a snare of the adversary, which he has laid to catch this people, that he might bring you into subjection unto him, that *he might encircle you about with his chains*." (Alma 12:6; emphasis added.)

We usually associate the term *possessed* with Satan. But eternal liberty and eternal life mean being possessed by— belonging to—Christ. For being "reconciled to the will of God" is not only to be at peace with Christ but also to belong to him in the sense of being "at one" with him and, therefore, like him; for the "at-one-ment" can close all the gaps that once left us estranged from him. Thus did he say to Adam, "Behold, thou art one in me, a son of God; and thus may all become my sons." (Moses 6:68.) The highest reward of mortal faithfulness, the Lord says, is "to receive a crown of righteousness, and . . . to be with me, that we may be one." (D&C 29:13.)

CHAPTER NINE

Belonging to Jesus Christ

Today's waning of belonging may inflict many losses on us—a weakening of family bonds, a loss of civic community, and a diminished feeling of genuine "member-ship" in the Church. But the greatest loss of all occurs when this alienating loneliness keeps us from Jesus Christ, for being kept from belonging to him is to be kept from letting his Atonement be ours to claim and keep.

When Jesus completed his atoning act, he uttered these words from the cross: "It is finished." (John 19:30.) When the meaning and purpose of his Atonement are first realized in our lives, we may say, "It has begun." What has begun? The process of becoming forever "at one" with him—belonging to him.

The Savior has frequently taught his people about this dimension of his Atonement by referring to familiar forms of belonging—marriage and child-parent relationships. He commonly described his relationship with ancient Israel as a marriage. So when Israel descended into patterns of sustained disobedience to Jehovah's commandments, Israel was "unfaithful," like an unfaithful spouse. The Lord thus warned through Moses that Israel should not worship other gods, for Jehovah "is a jealous God: Lest thou make a covenant with the inhabitants of the land, and they go a whoring after their gods." (Exodus 34:14–15. See also Leviticus 17:7; Deuteronomy 31:6; Judges 8:33.) Said Jehovah through Jeremiah, "Turn, O backsliding children, saith the Lord; for I am *married* unto you" (Jeremiah 3:14; emphasis added); and "My covenant they brake, although I was an *husband* unto them, saith the Lord" (Jeremiah 31:32; emphasis added). In expressing the permanence of his covenants with Israel, again the Lord used the language of marriage: "I will *betroth* thee unto me forever . . . and I will say to them . . . thou art my people; and they shall say, Thou art my God." (Hosea 2:19, 23; emphasis added.)

New Testament writers also expressed the Lord's relationship to the Church using the metaphor of marriage. The parable of the ten virgins, for instance, likens the faithful Saints to the virgins who trim their lamps with oil, that they who are ready when the bridegroom cometh may go "in with him to the marriage." (Matthew 25:10.) John the Revelator wrote of "the marriage of the Lamb" to "his wife . . . arrayed in fine linen, clean and white," which linen is "the righteousness of saints. . . . Blessed are they which are called unto the marriage supper of the Lamb. " (Revelation 19:7–9.)

Paul made the comparison between the bonds of marriage and Christ's ties to the Saints especially vivid: "The husband is the head of the wife, even as Christ is the head of the church. . . . Husbands, love your wives, even as Christ also loved the church. . . . He that loveth his wife loveth himself. For no man ever yet hated his own flesh; but nourisheth and cherisheth it, even as the Lord the church: For we are members of his body." (Ephesians 5:23, 25, 28–30.)

Those who come unto Christ also enter into a spiritual child-parent relationship with him. They take upon themselves his name—not only "Christians" in a general sense, but as King Benjamin wrote of those who accepted Christ's Atonement and his gospel, "ye shall be called *the children of*

Christ, his sons, and his daughters; for behold, this day he hath spiritually begotten you." (Mosiah 5:7; emphasis added.) In this way, the concept of being born again suggests not only a change of heart but also the profound beginning of a new life—a parent-child relationship in which the child develops and grows toward the maturity of being like the parent. For the ultimate end of belonging to Christ is that the child may become as He is: "Ye may become the sons of God; that when he shall appear we shall be *like him,* . . . that we may be purified even as he is pure." (Moroni 7:48; emphasis added.)

The unlimited parental commitment the Savior feels for those who are in this sense his children is anchored deeply in the sacrifice of his Atonement. A mother descends into the dark valley of pain and death, risking her life to bring forth the life of her child. And when the child is born, she feels the awesome limitlessness of maternal bonds that are stronger than the cords of death. This sacrifice, understandable to any parent, yet most understandable to mothers, mirrors both the Savior's sacrifice and his everlasting commitment to nourish and cherish the children of Christ for whom he offered his body and his blood. (See 1 Nephi 21:15–16.)[1]

Moving from the metaphorical to the doctrinal, the two-way relationship of our coming unto Christ arises in the covenants of the Atonement, which represent the irreducible center of the gospel of Jesus Christ: "Now this is the commandment: Repent, all ye ends of the earth, and come unto me and be baptized in my name, that ye may be sanctified by the reception of the Holy Ghost, that ye may stand spotless before me at the last day. Verily, verily, I say unto you, this is my gospel." (3 Nephi 27:20–21.) Yet the fulfillment of this commandment is but the beginning—"the gate" or "the way"—of our being justified, then taught, then sanctified by the Savior: "For the gate by which ye should enter is repentance and baptism by water; and then cometh a remission of your sins by fire and by the Holy Ghost. And then are ye in this straight and narrow path which leads to eternal life; yea, ye have entered in by the gate." (2 Nephi 31:17–18.)

As noted earlier, the keeper of this gate is "the Holy One of Israel; and he employeth no servant there." (2 Nephi 9:41.) "The way" opened up by the gate "is narrow, but it lieth in a straight course . . . and there is none other way save it be by the gate." (2 Nephi 9:41.) Once upon this course, we "must press forward with a steadfastness in Christ, . . . feasting upon the word of Christ," on the way to "eternal life." (2 Nephi 31:20.) And "this is *the way;* and there is none other way nor name given under heaven whereby man can be saved in the kingdom of God. And now, behold, *this is the doctrine of Christ.*" (2 Nephi 31:21; emphasis added.)

What is the way? He is the way. When Thomas asked, "Lord, we know not whither thou goest; and how can we know the way? Jesus saith unto him, *I am the way.*" (John 14:5–6; emphasis added.) What is the law of the true way? He is the law, for he told the Nephites that the law of Moses had an end in him. (See 3 Nephi 15:2–8.) As Paul said, the Mosaic "law was our schoolmaster to bring us unto Christ." (Galatians 3:24.)

Once the laws of the lesser priesthood—repentance and baptism—have led us to "come unto Christ," we enter the order of a new way and a new law: a personal master/apprentice relationship with the Master himself. The lesser law has a purpose and an end—to bring us to him. And when we enter *that* "way," he tells us as he did the Nephites after their baptism, "Behold, *I am the law,* and the light." (3 Nephi 15:9; emphasis added.)

But what do we do? How can we know where to look and where to turn when we have the new law and are upon the new way of belonging to Christ as his children? Where are our instructions?

Nephi responded to such questions: "My beloved brethren, I suppose that ye ponder somewhat in your hearts concerning that which ye should do after ye have entered in by the way. But, behold, why do ye ponder these things in your hearts? . . . I said unto you, feast upon the words of Christ; for behold, the words of Christ will tell you all things what ye should do. . . . Again I say unto you that if ye will enter in by the way, and receive the Holy Ghost, it will show unto you all things what ye should do. Behold, this is the doctrine of Christ." (2 Nephi 32:1, 3, 5–6.)

The Savior taught this doctrine of Christ most fully in what might be called "the doctrines of the last supper," where he combined his teachings about the sacrament, the Atonement, the Holy Ghost, charity, friendship, and eternal life into a moving and coherent whole.

First he introduced the sacrament of the last supper (see Luke 22:19–20), which enables the renewal of our baptismal covenants—a reaffirmation of the covenant relationship of "at-one-ment" with him. For us, the sacrament renews the faith, the repentance, and the baptismal covenant through which we previously accepted his atoning sacrifice, entered into the bonds of mutual belonging symbolized by accepting his name, and pledged to obey and remember him always. For him, the sacrament renews the offering of his body and his blood, thus reaffirming the cleansing, healing power of the Atonement with the assurance that his spirit—his power and influence—will literally be "with us"—"at one" with us. The sacrament ordinance is not by itself a means of securing remission of sin, which comes only through the well-known processes of repentance. But it does renew and symbolize the ongoing relationship by which Christ forgives, nourishes, and sustains us in all the turmoil of our lives.

As the Savior taught the Nephites, "He that eateth this bread eateth of my body to his soul; and he that drinketh of this wine drinketh of my blood to his soul; and his soul shall never hunger nor thirst, but shall be filled." (3 Nephi 20:8.)

Our assimilating this sense of the Atonement into our souls, symbolized by the physical assimilation of eating and drinking the sacramental bread and water, creates a spiritual umbilical cord between Christ and the children of Christ. He spoke of this life-giving nourishment in the teachings of the last supper: "I am the vine, ye are the branches: He that abideth in me, and I in him, the same bringeth forth much fruit." (John 15:5.) And the sustenance of this "true vine" (John 15:1) will bless us with "the fruit of the spirit," which includes both hope and the gift of charity, along with "joy, peace, longsuffering, gentleness, . . . faith, [and] meekness." (Galatians 5:22.)

The primary agent by which this power is manifested in our lives is the Holy Ghost, "the Comforter . . . whom the Father will send in [Jesus'] name" (John 14:26), not only to teach us, not only to comfort us in affliction, but also to be within us a well of living water that sustains us with an ever-lasting flow of hope and love for others.

Jesus taught us through Moroni about the same relation-ships, the same sequence, and the same blessings of which he taught the Twelve the evening of the last supper: "The first fruits of repentance is baptism; and baptism cometh by faith unto the fulfilling the commandments; and the fulfilling the commandments bringeth remission of sins; and the remission of sins bringeth meekness, and lowliness of heart; and because of meekness and lowliness of heart cometh the visitation of *the Holy Ghost, which Comforter filleth with hope and perfect love,* which love endureth by diligence unto prayer, until the end shall come, when all the saints shall dwell with God." (Moroni 8:25–26; emphasis added.)

In both a literal and symbolic expression of continuing "at-one-ment" between Christ and those who belong to him, the doctrines of the last supper teach us about entering into and remaining in his presence. Our sins and other sources of estrangement separate us from God. We will remain outside his presence until the Atonement reconciles us, heals us, and carries us home to him. His presence is thereafter accessible to us, if we honor our portion of the covenants of the Atonement: "He that hath my commandments, and keepeth them, he it is that loveth me: and he that loveth me shall be loved of my Father, and I will love him, and will manifest myself to him." (John 14:21.) This is also the promise of the sacramental prayer. If we "always remember him and keep his commandments which he has given" us, we will "always have his Spirit to be with" us—our spirit with his spirit, belonging to one another in continual "at-one-ment." (D&C 20:77.)

Our unity with the divine presence thus brings us peace and comfort, at first through the Holy Ghost. But that is not all; for not only the Holy Ghost may abide with us, but the good Master too: "I will not leave you comfortless: *I will come to you.*" (John 14:18; emphasis added.)

The term *comfortless* in this passage of the New Testament is translated from the Greek term for *orphans*, suggesting that the Savior might have said, "I will not leave you orphaned." This usage would underscore the parent-child relationships between Christ and his followers, and it echoes the sense of *amae* and parent-like bonding we have seen elsewhere in describing the Savior's bonds with us.[2]

Regarding the Lord's statement "I will come to you," Joseph Smith taught:

> After a person has faith in Christ, repents of his sins, and is baptized . . . and receives the Holy Ghost . . . , which is the first Comforter, then let him continue to humble himself before God, hungering and thirsting after righteousness, and living by every word of God, and the Lord will soon say to him, Son, thou shalt be exalted. When the Lord has thoroughly proved him, and finds that the man is deter-

mined to serve Him at all hazards, then the man will find his calling and his election made sure, then it will be his privilege to receive the other Comforter [as promised in John 14:12–17]. . . . Now what is this [second] Comforter. It is no more nor less than the Lord Jesus Christ Himself.[3]

Jesus taught the doctrines of the last supper as his final sermon in mortality, explaining to his apostles the meaning of what he was about to do in Gethsemane. These teachings are, then, the mature doctrines of the Atonement. The tender and sacred relationship between himself and his followers that he described in this "last lecture" was possible only because he ransomed and "bought" them from the grasp of divine justice with his infinite sacrifice. Therefore did he pray in Gethsemane in the very hour of his agony,

And now, O Father, . . . I have manifested thy name unto the men which thou gavest me out of the world: thine they were, and thou gavest them me; . . . I pray for them: I pray not for the world, but for them which thou hast given me; for they are thine. And all mine are thine, and thine are mine. . . . Holy Father, keep through thine own name those whom thou hast given me, that they may be one, as we are. . . . I in them, and thou in me, that they may be made perfect in one. (John 17:5–6, 9–11, 23.)

Thus he describes *those whom he has redeemed* in the language of belonging and possession. As Paul wrote, "Ye are bought with a price." (1 Corinthians 7:23.) Similarly, the Lord said of the Saints in Missouri: "Yet I will *own* them, and they shall be *mine* in that day when I shall come to make up my jewels." (D&C 101:3; emphasis added.)

Among the Lord's most intimate and personal reassurances to us are his words in modern revelation to the children of Christ, teaching us that belonging to him in this doctrinally based sense is the ultimate source of safety and

149

peace—the spiritual fulfillment of our *amae:* "Fear not, little children, for *ye are mine,* and I have overcome the world, and you are of them that my Father hath given me; and none of them that my Father hath given me shall be los.." (D&C 50:41–42; emphasis added.)

The doctrine of belonging to Christ clearly derives from his Atonement: "Look unto me in every thought; doubt not, fear not. Behold, the wounds which pierced my side, and also the prints of the nails in my hands and feet." (D&C 6:37.)

Does it matter that these supernal promises to us find their source in his Atonement? At an earlier time in our lives, we were generally aware that the Lord blesses and helps us in times of need, but we did not see the connection between those blessings and the Atonement. We saw things much as did another Church member who once wrote in a personal letter that "although the Savior can heal many of our pains, this has nothing to do with the atonement." He believed that "through the Spirit of Christ and the Holy Ghost we can be comforted from the stresses of this world, but the Atonement is only for the sins of mankind." What, then, does the Atonement-based theology of belonging—"the doctrine of Christ" (2 Nephi 31:21) as well as the teachings of the last supper—tell us about the relationship between being "his people" and being healed by his Atonement?

The Broken Heart states that "the Atonement is not just for sinners,"[4] meaning that the Savior's Atonement can be the healing power not only for our sins but also for carelessness, inadequacy, and any other form of mortal bitterness that separates us from God. For example, some Church members feel weighed down with discouragement about the circumstances of their personal lives, even when they are making sustained and admirable efforts. Frequently, these feelings of self-disappointment come not from wrongdoing but from stresses and troubles for which they may not be fully to blame. The Atonement applies to these experiences because it applies to all of life. The Savior can wipe away *all* of our tears.

Alma had this broad reach of the Atonement in mind when he wrote that Christ would "go forth, suffering pains and afflictions and temptations of every kind; and this that the word might be fulfilled which saith *he will take upon him the pains and the sicknesses* of his people. And *he will . . . take upon him their infirmities,* that his bowels may be filled with mercy, according to the flesh, that he may know according to the flesh how to succor his people according to their infirmities." (Alma 7:11–12; emphasis added.) These words echo Isaiah's earlier prophecy that Christ would be "a man of sorrows, and acquainted with grief: . . . *Surely he has borne our griefs, and carried our sorrows.*" (Isaiah 53:3–4; emphasis added.)

Part I of *The Broken Heart* describes life as a school, a place for us to learn and grow. We, like Adam and Eve, experience "growing pains" through the sorrow and stress of a lone and dreary world. These experiences may include sin, but they also include mistakes, disappointments, and the undeserved pain of adversity—all of the pains, infirmities, and griefs the Savior will carry for us as he heals and cleanses us from the contaminations of the mortal experience. As Jesus himself described that mission, quoting from Isaiah: "The Spirit of the Lord God is upon me; because the Lord hath anointed me to preach good tidings unto the meek; . . . to bind up the brokenhearted, to proclaim liberty to the captives, . . . to appoint unto them that mourn in Zion . . . *beauty for ashes.*" (Isaiah 61:1, 3; emphasis added.) He not only heals and cleanses—he also beautifies, consecrating our afflictions for our gain.

The Atonement's healing power thus cleanses our spirits, upon condition of repentance, when our souls are soiled with sin. It can also compensate, after we in good faith do all we can, for many of the adverse consequences of our sins, as well as for the harmful effects of our ignorance, our neglect, and our inadequacies. Beyond that, the Atonement infuses into our lives other blessings of the Savior's grace, endowing us with affirmative gifts that fill our souls with hope, charity, and, ultimately, all of the perfecting attributes of a divine nature, which is what it means to have eternal (godlike) life.

The concept of belonging to Christ is the doctrinal context that explains how all of these blessings flow from the Atonement. When we "come unto Christ" through repentance and baptism, we enter into a covenant *relationship* with him. Our faith and our repentance qualify us to enter that relationship, just as the Savior's Atonement qualifies him to enter it. As the Master taught his disciples in the doctrines of the last supper, *this relationship* becomes the medium by which the unlimited range of the Atonement's blessings begins its everlasting flow.

As important as this relationship is, it does not supersede our relationship with the Father, nor is it to be pursued with exclusive, excessive zeal. Elder Bruce R. McConkie once counseled Church members to "have a proper relationship to each member of the Godhead," since each performs "separate functions." We pray to God, who is the Father of our spirits and is "the God we worship." We also seek the constant companionship of the Holy Ghost, who "bears record of the Father and the Son" and "dispenses spiritual gifts." Yet "salvation comes by" Christ the Redeemer, whose name we take and whose commandments we keep. Our relationship with him, as with all members of the Godhead, is one of "worshipful adoration rather than being excessively personal and intimate."[5]

Since we have a relationship with Elohim as the father of our spirits and with Christ as the father of our spiritual birth, we may wonder how those two relationships differ from one another. For one thing, Christ is our advocate with the Father, suggesting that when the Father is our judge, Christ pleads our case before him.[6] In addition, in modern revelation the Lord has suggested that our relationship with Christ may somehow parallel his relationship with the Father. He teaches us that we "may understand and know how to worship, and know what you worship, that you may come unto the Father in my name, and in due time receive of his fulness. For if you keep my commandments you shall receive of his fulness, and be glorified in me as I am in the Father." (D&C 93:19–20.) Clearly, as we come to Christ, he helps us come to the Father.

As we come to the Savior in this spirit, we are initially forgiven of our sins, with the Atonement satisfying the law of justice.[7] Then we receive the sanctifying power of the Holy Ghost, which cleanses us from the effects of our sins. Since no unclean thing may dwell in God's presence, this cleansing is essential to our regaining his presence, both now and eternally. Still largely through the medium of the Holy Ghost, our covenant-based and Atonement-based relationship with Christ goes on to bless us with the affirmative endowments of hope[8] and charity,[9] gifts that are extended and bestowed as Christ, the father of our reborn spirits, guides and nourishes each of us toward a Christlike nature. In addition, the same power that compensates for and heals us from the effects of our conscious sins also compensates for and heals us from the same kinds of effects—the pain, the bitterness, the sorrow—caused by our unintentional mistakes and the natural adversities we suffer.[10]

Those who have not embraced the covenants of the doctrine of Christ are not entitled to this continuous and permanent healing influence in their lives, even though at times their prayers may be answered and special blessings given to them. This is the primary difference between having the gift of the Holy Ghost and being touched temporarily by its influence for some particular purpose. That holy gift is a result of the Atonement: "The Father giveth the Holy Ghost unto the children of men, because of me," the Savior said. (3 Nephi 28:11.) This gift is available to all who forsake their sins and embrace the gospel, thereby entering the gate that enables not only forgiveness but also all the blessings of belonging to Christ.

Our repentance and our continued obedience are thus necessary prerequisites to our receiving the sustaining, healing, and compensating power that flows from belonging to Christ—not because we can "repent" of our undeserved pains and infirmities, but because we must repent of our sins to be entitled to the *relationship* whose healing and nurturing influence will wipe away all our other tears. That such incomprehensible blessings are unlocked through the two-way covenants of the Atonement unveils an entire body of well-developed, powerful doctrine that gives meaning, life, and theological foundations to our search for peace and personal growth. Because we are *his* and he is *ours*, the Lord will continually "at-one for" our separation and estrangement from him, whether that separation has been caused by our sins, our mistakes, the sins of others, or any other cause.

These are the blessings of belonging to Christ, ultimately made possible by the power of his Atonement: "O Israel, Fear not: for I have redeemed thee, I have called thee by thy name; *thou art mine.* When thou passest through the waters, I will be with thee; and through the rivers, they shall not overflow thee: when thou walkest through the fire, thou shalt not be burned; neither shall the flame kindle upon thee. For I am the Lord thy God, the Holy One of Israel, thy Saviour." (Isaiah 43:1–3; emphasis added.)

These sublime promises describe the Savior not as our judge but as our *advocate.* So has he described himself: "Lift up your hearts and be glad, for I am in your midst, and am your *advocate* with the Father." (D&C 29:5; emphasis added.)

His advocacy—his *defense* of us before the judgment bar of the Father—derives directly from his atoning act for us: "In mine own name, by the virtue of the blood which I have spilt, have I pleaded before the Father for them." (D&C 38:4.) In that role, as our champion, he "is pleading [our] cause before [the Father], saying: Father, behold the sufferings and death of him who did no sin, in whom thou wast well pleased; . . . spare these my brethren that believe on my name, that they may come unto me and have everlasting life." (D&C 45:3–5.)

We must always seek to be on the Lord's side; but what good news it is to know that *he is on our side.*

His powerful advocacy in our behalf is not limited to pleading our case before the Father, for "your advocate . . . knoweth the weakness of man and how to succor them who are tempted." (D&C 62:1.) It is the advocate's role to present our case in its most favorable light, refuting the challenges of the adversary who opposes us and who presents our case in its worst possible light. Even in our thoughts about ourselves, we must resist the adversary's attempts to convince us of our worthlessness by interpreting our life circumstances in a negative light; rather, let us listen to him who knows our weaknesses fully yet believes in us more than we may believe in ourselves. What glorious news, not only that the greatest advocate of all is willing to represent those who are guilty, but also that he will take *our* case! "I am the first and the last; . . . I am your advocate with the Father. . . . Therefore, lift up your heads and rejoice. . . . Let the hearts of all my people rejoice." (D&C 110:4–6.)

These perspectives may help to explain the depth and the everlasting nature of belonging to Christ as his eternal "friends." He said, "Greater love hath no man than this, that a man lay down his life for his friends." (John 15:13.) His friends are those for whom he made the atoning sacrifice, not only by laying down his life but also by paying for their sins and bearing the burden of their infirmities: "Ye are they whom my Father hath given me; ye are my friends." (D&C 84:63.)

Part of Christ's sacrifice benefits his enemies as well as his friends; but only his friends obey him enough to receive the fulness of his blessings. "Ye are my friends, if ye do whatsoever I command you," he says. (John 15:14.) His friends are thus those who keep the covenants they made at baptism and then renew those covenants continually through the relationship of belonging to Christ. Moreover, they keep not only his general commandments but all of the covenants that arise from coming to Christ. This includes adherence to his ongoing inspiration and guidance—"the words of Christ," which "tell you all things what ye should do" after entering in by the gate. (2 Nephi 32:3.)

As this tutorial continues, he is a faithful master to his friends, not as in a master-servant relationship, but as in a master-apprentice relationship: "Henceforth I call you not servants; for the servant knoweth not what his lord doeth: but I have called you friends; for all things that I have heard of my Father I have made known unto you." (John 15:15.)

In modern revelation, the Savior has again spoken of his "friends" in the doctrinal context of promising the inheritance of eternal life, the ultimate blessing of the Atonement: "I will call you friends, for you are my friends, and ye shall have an inheritance with me." (D&C 93:45.) Those who belong to him—his children, his friends—are, to use Joseph Smith's phrase, "joint heirs with Christ," heirs of the promises of celestial or God-like life. The Prophet used this language in expounding one of the underlying themes of our total sense of belonging to Christ—the theme of sacrifice. For just as Christ laid down his life for his friends—just as he sacrificed all, withholding nothing—so we must sacrifice everything, not even withholding our lives.[11] Since the moment of the Atonement, the law of sacrifice no longer asks for the animal sacrifices required under the law of Moses as that law looked forward to Christ; rather, the law of sacrifice now asks each of us to sacrifice our own hearts in the sacrifice of a broken heart and a contrite spirit. (See 3 Nephi 9:18–20.)

When we accept the modern law of sacrifice through the two-way covenants of the Atonement, our willingness to give the Lord everything we have mirrors his willingness to give us everything he has—our broken heart for his broken heart.[12] The combination of his sacrifice with ours in the miraculous chemistry of this mutual belonging then gives us the *power* "to contend against all the opposition, tribulations, and afflictions which [we] will have to encounter in order to be heirs of God, and joint-heirs with Christ Jesus."[13]

This mutual sacrifice is totally without limits, for that is the nature of true belonging: "I nothing lack if I am his, and he is mine, forever."[14] Or as Paul wrote, "Neither death, nor life, nor angels, nor principalities, nor powers, nor things present, nor things to come, nor height, nor depth, nor any other creature, shall be able to separate us from the love of God, which is in Christ Jesus our Lord." (Romans 8:38–39.)

Relationships of belonging, both in the language of romance and in the language of faith, derive from unlimited, unqualified commitments—as distinguished from relationships that are, by definition, limited to the terms of a "contractual" understanding.[15] In most human interaction, our commitments are of limited scope and duration. Thus if we ask, "How long must I do this?" or "How much of this must I take?" there is some identifiable point at which we may say, "That is enough." But when we belong to Christ and he belongs to us, as when parents and children truly belong to one another, both will stay as long as it takes, and both will give all there is. For the children of Christ, Jesus is a parent, not a baby-sitter.

He taught the unqualified nature of his commitment to us, and ours to him, in the parable of the Good Shepherd. Note here the difference between a *limited* contractual commitment and an *unlimited* commitment of belonging: "He that is *an hireling*, and not the shepherd, *whose own the sheep are not*, seeth the wolf coming, and leaveth the sheep, and fleeth. . . . The hireling fleeth, because he is an hireling, and careth not for the sheep. I am the good shepherd, and know *my sheep*, . . . and *I lay down my life for the sheep.*" (John 10:12–15; emphasis added.) When he is mine, and I am his, his commitment is utterly boundless.

And so must be our commitment to him. Because our belonging is mutual, we must be willing to lay down our character and reputation, our houses and lands, our brothers, our sisters, and even our lives, "counting all things but filth and dross for the excellency of the knowledge of Jesus Christ. . . . [For] a religion that does not require the sacrifice of *all things* never has power sufficient to produce the faith necessary unto life and salvation."[16]

One of the fruits of such complete belonging through the covenants of the Atonement is the gift of charity.[17] That is, as our assimilation of the Atonement matures, the Lord bestows upon us the very love he feels for all the rest of mankind. Hence our belonging with and to Christ both precedes and enables our belonging to, serving, and giving ourselves to other people. It is only then that we become his true undershepherds ourselves, when we look upon his other sheep not as "an hireling" would, but as the Good Shepherd himself would.

This link between our belonging to him and our belonging to others is expressed in the Savior's last words to Peter near the end of his mortal ministry: "Simon, son of Jonas, lovest thou me?" If so, said the Lord, "feed my sheep." (John 21:16–17.) Peter knew he must care for the Lord's sheep not as the hireling would care for them—that is, until the gathering wolves put the hireling's convenience or safety at risk. Rather, Peter—and we—must feed them as the Good

Shepherd would feed them, not withholding even our lives. In this sense, our belonging to Christ begets our belonging to spouses, children, and others; and when this occurs we will love one another, as Christ has loved us. Then, "by this shall all men know that ye are my disciples," when, nourished by the true vine, our lives reflect the fruit of pure charity, as we "have love one to another." (John 13:34–35.)

Ten Insights from King Benjamin about the Atonement

As a summary of the relationship between the Atonement of Jesus Christ and the concept of belonging to Christ, consider King Benjamin's answers to ten common questions about the Atonement.

1. *What is the source of our knowledge about the Atonement?* Our understanding of the nature and meaning of the Atonement is not the result of human imagination. More than one hundred years before the birth of Jesus, Benjamin told his people that the angel of the Lord awoke him from his sleep one night to teach him the "glad tidings" of Christ's coming. Most of Benjamin's address, one of the greatest known sermons about the Savior's life and atoning mission, was given him by an angel—with express instructions for the king to "declare [this message] unto [his] people, that they may also be filled with joy." (Mosiah 3:4; unless otherwise specified, scriptural citations in this chapter refer to the book of Mosiah.)

This pure source of direct instruction reaffirmed an ancient pattern of revelation, for Adam also received his understanding of Christ's mission directly from an angel. This messenger came to teach Adam and Eve that the sacrifices the Lord commanded them to offer were in "similitude of the sacrifice of the Only Begotten." (Moses 5:7.)

2. Does the Atonement compensate for more than deliberate sins? Yes. At its most fundamental level, the Atonement compensates for the transgression of Adam and Eve. Then, upon condition of our repentance, it also compensates for our personal sins.[1] The angel told Benjamin that Christ's Atonement also redeems the sins of those who died not knowing God's will concerning them, as well as the sins of those "who have ignorantly sinned." (3:11.) Benjamin contrasted the state of those who sin in ignorance with "him who knoweth that he rebelleth against God," noting that there is no atonement for *deliberate* sins "except it be through repentance." (3:12.)

This comparison suggests that the extent of our required repentance is directly proportional to the willfulness of our sins. As the Lord said elsewhere, "Of him unto whom much is given much is required; and he who sins against the greater light shall receive the greater condemnation." (D&C 82:3.) This also implies that we must repent of our conscious sins before the Atonement can provide the further blessing of healing and compensating for our careless mistakes and misjudgments that are not caused by deliberate sin.

3. How did the Atonement help those who heard the gospel before the time of Christ? God sent certain prophets, such as Benjamin, who gave their people an opportunity to hear the gospel of Jesus Christ and to be baptized for the remission of their sins. Those who believed "that Christ should come" received "remission of their sins, and rejoice[d] with exceedingly great joy, even *as though he had already come among them*." (3:13; emphasis added.)

This assurance repeated the ancient pattern. Adam and Eve had also found that as they repented and called upon God according to the angel's instructions, "the Holy Ghost fell upon Adam," teaching him that "as thou hast fallen thou mayest be redeemed. . . . And *in that day* Adam . . . was *filled*," declaring, "Because of my transgression my eyes are

161

opened, and *in this life I shall have joy"* because of Christ's redemption. (Moses 5:9–10; emphasis added.) Thus, the Atonement has always played an active role in people's mortal lives—it is not just a promise of future blessings.

4. *What is the relationship between the Atonement and the nature of man?* Since the 4th century A.D., the Christian tradition has held that human nature is inherently evil because of Adam's fall.[2] Clearly rejecting this idea, the Restoration teaches that because the Atonement universally "redeemed man from the fall" of Adam, "men became again, in their infant state, *innocent* before God." (D&C 93:38; emphasis added.) Thus all children are born in an innocent state. But when children reach the age of accountability, "that wicked one cometh and taketh away light and truth through disobedience." (D&C 93:39.) As a result, many of Adam's children "loved Satan more than God. And men began from that time forth to be carnal, sensual, and devilish." (Moses 5:13.)

King Benjamin taught that by choosing to follow Satan, each of these "natural men" became to some degree an "enemy to God" and would remain so "forever" unless each "yields to the enticings of the Holy Spirit, and putteth off the natural man and becometh a saint through the atonement of Christ the Lord, and becometh as a child, submissive, meek." (3:19.)

To the extent that we have become "natural" in this sense—that is, have become carnal, sensual, and devilish—we must repent before the Atonement can bring us complete forgiveness and remove the stains of evil. However, the Atonement also blesses us with the power to move beyond forgiveness, helping us develop our nature toward being a "Saint"—presumably having a God-like or perfect nature. We are then "like God," namely, good by nature.

5. *How, then, does the Atonement bring us more than the forgiveness of our sins?* As suggested by Mosiah 3:19, when

we repent and accept the covenants of the gospel of Christ, his influence begins to interact with our good-faith desires and our obedience, *developing* our character and attributes toward a true saintly nature. Benjamin taught his people that after receiving the initial remission of their sins, which brought them such joy (4:11), they should continue to believe in God (4:9) and to remember his greatness and their relative unworthiness (4:11). If they did so, he promised, they would lose their previous desire for evil, and their lives would reflect the goodness and fruits of divine character. (See 4–5.)

In addition, as noted more fully in item 9 below, the *relationship* the Savior's Atonement creates between the Lord and his followers forms the basis for an unending flow of related blessings, including the gift of the Holy Ghost, the comfort of the Lord's presence, and the power of his influence.

6. *How must we live, after baptism, to receive this blessing of becoming as a Saint—must we be "perfect"?* According to King Benjamin, we must be meek, like a little child (3:19), have great humility (4:11), pray daily (4:11), and be "steadfast and immovable, always abounding in good works" (5:15). This pattern is less a matter of error-free obedience to multiple commandments than it is a basic *attitude* that helps us cope patiently with our failings: "Humble yourselves even in the depths of humility, calling on the name of the Lord daily, and standing steadfastly in the faith of that which is to come, which was spoken by the mouth of the angel." (4:11.)

7. *If we live as Benjamin directed, what will be the effect of the Lord's influence in our lives?* Even while on the path of righteousness, we, like Adam and Eve, must wade through much affliction and sorrow, facing continual and surprising patterns of opposition. At the same time—often literally at the same time—we may enjoy glorious, life-changing blessings. If we strive with fulness of heart to emulate the atti-

tudes Benjamin described, we will experience recurringly (even in the midst of affliction) a comforting sense of joy and hope—we "shall always rejoice, and be filled with the love of God, and always retain a remission of [our] sins." (4:12.) In addition, we will sense that we are undergoing honest personal development, outgrowing our weaknesses, and increasing our understanding of God: "*ye shall grow* in the knowledge" of God and the "knowledge of that which is just and true." (4:12; emphasis added.) For most of us, these blessings feel more like a gradual process of development than a once-in-a-lifetime event.

As part of this Atonement-based growth pattern, Benjamin taught that we will develop tender feelings of kindness, not having "a mind to injure one another, but to live peaceably." (4:13.) As parents, we will feel an increased measure of love and new abilities to teach our children "to love one another, and to serve one another." (See 4:15.) Our feelings of charity for other people will then extend beyond our own families, until we are moved with compassion for people having all forms of personal need, and we "will succor those that stand in need of [our] succor." (4:16.) As we thus extend to others the love and grace the Lord has given us, we are gradually purified of our worldly desires until we feel "a mighty change in us, or in our hearts, that we have no more disposition to do evil, but to do good continually." (5:2.) This is the process of becoming "a saint through the atonement of Christ the Lord." (3:19.)

8. *So is the Atonement for judgment day, or is it for this life?* The Atonement is surely weighed in the balance when we face the day of judgment, but it is also clearly a doctrine for every day.[3] Indeed, once we have received the initial remission of our sins through baptism, Benjamin told us what we must do to "*retain* a remission of [our] sins" each day of our lives. In addition to his other counsel, he instructed us to "watch yourselves, and your thoughts, . . .

and observe the commandments of God, and continue in the faith . . . even unto the end of your lives." (4:30.)

Benjamin was also realistic, urging us not to try to solve every complex personal problem in one grand gesture. Life is lived and growth occurs incrementally, a step at a time: "See that all these things are done in wisdom and order; for it is not requisite that a man should run faster than he has strength. . . . All things must be done in order." (4:27.) It is by the modest life of practical wisdom, not the life of frantic fanaticism, that we will retain "a remission of [our] sins from day to day, that [we] may walk guiltless before God." (4:26.)

9. *What is our relationship with Christ as we take these blessings of the Atonement into our lives?* As Benjamin's people accepted his teachings, they entered into two-way covenants with Jesus Christ—the covenants of the Atonement, also simply called the gospel. They covenanted to become the sons and daughters of Christ, taking upon themselves his name and pledging to live his teachings throughout their lives. (See 5:5–7.) In turn, Jesus promised them forgiveness, the power to become Saints, and the assurance that they will "be found at the right hand of God." (5:9.) They—and we—renew and celebrate these mutual promises as we partake weekly of the sacrament of the Lord's supper. The sacramental prayer describes a relationship of endless depth and breadth; for as we are truly willing to take upon us his name, to remember him, and to keep his commandments, we are not only forgiven—we "may *always* have his Spirit to be with" us. (D&C 20:77; emphasis added.)

Some people reason that such powerful, positive forces as membership in the Church, the gift of the Holy Ghost, and the Spirit of Christ operate independently of the Atonement—because they think the Atonement serves the limited function of simply paying for our sins. But membership in the Church is but one fruit of the larger blessing of accepting the first principles and ordinances of the gospel, which all flow from and center on the Atonement. The members of the Church are not just fellow members of a common institution—we are, more exactly, the very people from all across the earth who have covenanted with the Savior to accept his Atonement. In this sense, the Saints are the "true followers of . . . Christ." (Moroni 7:48.) We call each other "brother and sister" because we are all children of Christ, the father of our spiritual rebirth.

Our repentance from our sins qualifies us to enter this covenant *relationship* with Christ, just as his Atonement qualifies him to enter it with us. The hope, the comfort, and the charity we then receive through the medium of the Holy Ghost are all part of the abundant blessing of belonging to Christ by being bought with his sacrifice. This relationship unlocks the doors not only to forgiveness but also to all the promises of the Holy One of Israel, including his bearing the burdens of our pains and infirmities that are not the result of our sins. And even though we cannot typically "repent" of these infirmities, we must repent of our actual sins to be entitled to his healing power, which can wipe away all our tears.[4]

Elder Dallin H. Oaks discussed the broad significance of our personal, Atonement-based relationship with Jesus Christ in 1993, when he explored the reasons why President Ezra Taft Benson has emphasized our need to study the Book of Mormon as "his central message as President of the Church." Elder Oaks discussed President Benson's warning that "the whole church" is under condemnation for "treating lightly" and forgetting "the new covenant, even the Book of Mormon and the former commandments which I have given them." (D&C 84:57.)

Elder Oaks described this "new covenant" in general terms as the restored gospel of Christ as taught in the Book of Mormon. He described it in specific terms as "our covenant relationship with Jesus Christ. . . . The 'new covenant' . . . is that central promise of the gospel, rooted in the atonement and resurrection of Jesus Christ, which gives us the assurance of . . . eternal life if we will repent of our sins and make and keep the gospel covenant with our Savior." He illustrated the Church membership's neglect of this covenant by indicating our collective "deficiency" in teaching "those doctrinal subjects most closely related to the Atonement of the Savior."⁵

10. *What is the end of the process King Benjamin described?* If we are "steadfast and immovable" in our covenants, "always abounding in good works," the day will come when "Christ, the Lord God Omnipotent, *may seal [us] his*, that [we] may be brought to heaven, [and] have everlasting salvation and eternal life." (5:15; emphasis added.) Then those of the belonging heart belong to Christ, as he belongs to them.

Part III

BELONGING TO FAMILY

CHAPTER ELEVEN

Family Belonging: These Bonds Are Our Liberation

Many people in today's society have become unsure whether the bonds of kinship and marriage are valuable ties that bind, or are sheer bondage. Increasingly, society is having a hard time knowing whether the idea of "belonging" to another person is a manifestation of love or a manifestation of slavery. In the midst of this confusion, more people are emphasizing "the right to be let alone."[1]

One student of this trend is University of California professor Robert Bellah, who describes the present state of the waning of belonging in American family life: "In the United States the family is now regarded less as something one *belongs* to than as something at the service of the individual. Obligations to husband or wife, even to parents or children, are determined more by what suits one's own desires than the needs of the other."

Bellah believes this attitude is an extension of the "pursuit of self-interest" that Americans long ago accepted in the economic marketplace. Until recently, our society believed that the self-interested motives of the market were contrary to the common good when people applied them to their family lives or even to the public service of political activity.

But now, even "politics in the United States is increasingly regarded less as a means of democratic participation than a source of" maximizing one's personal self-interest.[2]

This chapter introduces part III by considering the waning of belonging within the sphere of marriage and family life. We first note the recent tendency of the family-related professions—primarily law—to encourage the withering of family life by backing away from their traditional expectation that people should regard family ties as a source of legal, moral, and social obligation. We will then see that some writers in the professions, along with other Americans, are beginning to feel that something is wrong with these reduced expectations. Indeed, it is becoming increasingly clear—clearest of all to ordinary people in strong and nurturing families—that our ties through kinship and marriage are actually the source of our most significant liberation.

American family law has a problem. In only one generation, we have experienced what Harvard law professor Mary Ann Glendon calls a "transformation" in the nation's family laws that is "the most fundamental shift [in the state's legal posture toward the family] since the Protestant Reformation."[3]

For example, we have taken the idea of individual freedom to terminate a marriage further than the law of any other Western nation, including Sweden. The American divorce reform movement began in California in the mid-1960s. Prior to that time, courts granted divorces only upon a showing that one spouse was at "fault" in abandoning or abusing the other. The "no fault" reforms of the 1960s introduced the concept of irretrievable breakdown, which originally meant that while a divorcing partner no longer had to prove the other partner's fault, a court would grant a divorce only if the judge found that the marriage could not be salvaged. However, courts in most states now simply grant a divorce if so requested by the parties—in many states if only one party so requests. And in granting divorces and in over-

172

seeing post-divorce financial arrangements, the American approach now exhibits a level of "carelessness" about "the economic casualties of divorce [that is] unique among Western countries."[4]

In addition, the law speaks far less now in moral terms about family relationships, having transferred "many moral decisions from the law to the people the law once regulated."[5] As a result, our society seems to have replaced its once idealistic attitudes toward marriage commitments, spousal support obligations, and sexual behavior outside marriage with a "hands off" approach in which the law seems to make few moral judgments.

We have also experienced a children's rights movement that psychologically—and sometimes legally—"liberates" parents and children from one another. Some adults welcome this movement, because they agree with federal judge Patricia Wald's charge that "the child's subjugated status [is] rooted in the same benevolent despotism that kings, husbands, and slave masters claimed as their moral right."[6]

However, it is one thing for the law to assure a personal right to be "let alone" from intrusive governmental surveillance. It is quite another when an intense but vague commitment to personal autonomy and privacy is thought to guarantee each person the right to be let alone from the obligations of marriage and parenthood.

For example, the deepest psychological and emotional needs of children require continuity and stability in their relationships with parents—relationships that can be the key factor in children's eventual development of mature, personal freedom. Ironically, the most ardent advocates of children's liberation gloss over the reality that prematurely cutting children's family ties has the effect of abandoning them.

The current tendency toward this form of abandonment evoked this response from *Time* magazine's Lance Morrow: "A motif of *absence*—moral, emotional and physical—plays

173

through the lives of many children now. It may be an absence of authority and limits, or of emotional commitment. . . . [Whatever it is,] [t]here appears to be a new form of [adult] neglect: absence."[7]

Moreover, when parents feel liberated from their children through a kind of informal, psychic divorce process, they are probably more likely to neglect, abandon, or abuse them. Hence the irony of the assumption some make that, given the vulnerability of those who live in intimate dependency, ongoing intimacy itself is the problem. Yet we seem ever more suspicious of the serious, long-range commitments on which marriage and family ties are based.

The new skepticism about relationships of belonging also profoundly affects our thinking about the very idea of marriage. For example, Albert Ellis, a psychiatrist who describes himself as representing mainstream attitudes in his profession, worries about the "emotional stability" of people who commit themselves to "unequivocal and eternal fidelity or loyalty to any interpersonal commitments, especially marriage."[8]

This reluctance to "get tied down" stems partly from the understandable fear that broken commitments and broken hearts will lead to pain and disappointment. But the same relationships and loyalties that seem to tie us down are the very sources of strength most likely to lift us up. Becoming fundamentally skeptical about such ties may reduce the risk of pain or guilt caused by disappointed expectations, but that skepticism also severely reduces the possibility of finding the highest human fulfillment.

Some legal scholars are beginning to describe the costs of our skepticism. Harvard's Martha Minow, for instance, finds that the recent individualistic family law reforms have produced "a body of family law that protects only the autonomous self," thereby failing "to nurture the relationships between individuals that constitute families."[9] Further,

Michigan's Carl Schneider observes that Americans' growing acceptance of the impossible notion of "nonbinding commitments" has begun to strip our attitudes toward family life of a sense of "prolonged responsibility."[10] The law now seems to undermine more than encourage the personal commitments that enable meaningful family life.

In their book *Habits of the Heart,* Robert Bellah and his colleagues draw on their recent nationwide empirical studies to describe how Americans have shifted their view of marriage from that of a relatively permanent social institution to a temporary source of personal fulfillment. As a result, when marriage commitments intrude on people's preferences and convenience, they tend to walk away. Yet, ironically and significantly, Bellah's group also found that despite Americans' preoccupation with self-interest, most of the people they interviewed still cling, perhaps in a hopelessly dreamy sense, to the nostalgic notion of marriage and family life based upon loving and *permanent* commitments as "the dominant American ideal."[11]

However, with its new realism, our legal system is now much less judgmental about what people should expect of one another. This creates an impression that the law has lost its normative expectation that family members should feel a sense of personal responsibility to uphold their commitments. Thus, we naturally perceive the law as no longer restraining our almost unwilling self-indulgence. The law's very absence of demands now seems to confirm our spreading fear that long-term, loving relationships are no longer possible.

We find a stirring echo of this thought in a recent anthology of American poetry dealing with the subject of father-son relationships. This collection purports to include the best American poems ever written on the theme of fathers and sons. Interestingly, nine-tenths of the selected poems were written after 1950. Stanley Kunitz, author of several poems in the anthology, believes that this disproportionate interest in father-son poetry in recent years may have occurred because family relationships were less likely to stir the poetic imagination in earlier times, when family ties were simply taken for granted. But the spirit of the recent era, Kunitz writes, is "a summons to testify about a failed intimacy, a failed life, perhaps to redeem it through a new effort of understanding."[12]

He continues: "With the disintegration of the nuclear family, the symbol of the father as a dominant, or domineering, presence is fading away. Whole sections of our nation are living in fatherless homes. Often the father is more than absent; he is lost, as he has been lost to himself for most of his adult life. The son goes in search of the father, to be reconciled in a healing embrace."[13] This is a theme with which Stanley Kunitz identifies, having earlier written as a young man after his own father's death:

> . . . down sandy road
> Whiter than bone-dust, through the sweet
> Curdle of fields, where the plums
> Dropped with their load of ripeness, one by one.
> Mile after mile I followed, with skimming feet,
> After the secret master of my blood,
> Him, steeped in the odor of ponds, whose indomitable love
> Kept me in chains.
> . . . .
> At the water's edge, where the smothering ferns lifted
> Their arms, "Father!" I cried, "Return! you know
> The way. I'll wipe the mudstains from your clothes;
> No trace, I promise, will remain. Instruct
> Your son, whirling between two wars,
> In the Gemara of your gentleness,
> For I would be a child to those who mourn
> And a brother to the foundlings of the field
> And friend of innocence and all bright eyes.
> O teach me how to work and keep me kind."[14]

Here is the paradox of loving bondage, the spirit of belonging—liberating while yet confining: "After the secret master of my blood," whose arms were like "smothering ferns," and whose "indomitable love kept me in chains." Perhaps our attitude toward morally demanding cultural and legal expectations is like our feeling about father figures— we dislike authority that temporarily represses in order to teach. When the authoritarian father, a symbol of our legal and social norms, gives in to our pleas to be left alone, we may feel a sudden yet only momentary sense of freedom.

When that sense of being set free is prolonged for a time, it can become a sense of abandonment. In this way, the cry for failed intimacy represented by the new father-son poetry sounds like an anguished reaching out for help: "O [father,] teach me how to work and keep me kind."

Such poetry, like Bellah's findings, documents Americans' recent tendency to cling to the idea of long-term belonging, even when that idea appears at odds with such normatively formal sources as law and psychotherapy. The learned disciplines are now less likely than they once were to reinforce much serious hope for the ideal of enduring relationships of commitment. As a result, many Americans now sadly but uncritically assume that an unbridgeable gap exists between their private, personal hopes and what they hear society's experts telling them to expect in family life.

Carl Schneider has noted just such a general attitudinal shift in his comparison between two concepts of morality— "aspirational morality" and "the ethic of the mean." In an earlier era, American society generally shared what Max Weber called a "heroic ethic"—an aspirational morality that "imposes on men demands of principle to which they are generally *not* able to do justice except at the high points of their lives, but which serve as sign posts pointing the way for man's endless *striving*."[15] Now, however, we have come to accept "the ethic of the mean, which is content to accept

177

man's everyday nature as setting a maximum for the demands which can be made."

The abandonment of aspirational morality is not without some benefits. For example, reducing what we expect of an intimate relationship also reduces the gap between everyday reality and the ever elusive ideal, thereby reducing both our sense of hypocrisy and our feelings of frustration and guilt when abused intimacy leads to psychological pain. Further, the new skepticism about relationships of dependency has exposed certain patterns of abuse and domination that cried out for closer public and legal scrutiny. And surely we can welcome society's increasing sensitivity to the personal needs of those who have felt the social disapproval of not fitting excessively idealistic and rigid cultural patterns.

But we must resist the naive belief that individuals can be liberated from the apparent bondage of family ties and nonetheless be assured, somehow, of the personal support systems that are found only in long-term commitments. To do this, we must be willing to take the risk that not everyone will consistently live up to such commitments. To insist on protection against all risk in our no-fault society may diminish our highest human possibilities even while it protects us against some of our fears.

Anne Morrow Lindbergh looked back on the sorrows of her life with these words: "I do not believe that sheer suffering teaches. If suffering alone taught, all the world would be wise, since everyone suffers. To suffering must be added mourning, understanding, patience, love, openness, and the willingness to remain vulnerable."[16] To nurture the value of belonging, we must be willing in some degree to remain vulnerable.

At the very least, we should not allow our attitudes toward the concept of belonging to confuse the extreme differences between love and slavery. As described more fully in chapter 16, Pitirim Sorokin's distinctions among "familistic," "contractual," and "compulsory" relationships are very helpful in illuminating those differences.[17] First, Sorokin points out that "familistic" relationships (bonds of love) involve an intermingled and organic unity in which shared commitments of mutual attachment transcend self-interest. This wholehearted and unqualified attitude springs from *unlimited* personal commitments, not only to another person but also to the good of a larger order, such as a family.

Second, "contractual" relationships, by deliberate design, are *always limited* in both scope and intensity. These limited relationships typically lack unselfish motivation, being based primarily on the respective self-interests of the contracting parties.

Third, "compulsory" relationships (bonds of slavery) are both coercive and antagonistic, like a master-slave relationship, in which the self-interest of the dominant party controls everything.

Much of today's professional and academic literature, presumably reflecting an emerging public attitude, has become skeptical about whether true "familistic" relationships exist at all. As a result, many opinion leaders imply that marriage partners and family members today have only two choices: (1) a contractual approach, based on polite self-interest and consciously limited commitments, and (2) a compulsory approach, in which one party dominates the other perpetually.

However, many Americans still want to believe in a third option—long-term, loving, familistic commitments. As Bellah's research shows, the innate human intuition to belong in familistic ways still exists. And in fact this hope is not unattainable; it is often fulfilled, at the most commonplace yet fundamental levels of human experience. When this happens, spouses and children who aspire to relationships of belonging can learn and grow in surprising ways.

They even discover that such familistic bonds are actually the source of much personal liberation.

For example, as Michael Novak has written:

> People say of marriage that it is boring, when what they mean is that it terrifies them: too many and too deep are its searing revelations. . . . They say of children that they are brats . . . , when what they mean is that the importance of parents with respect to the future of their children is now known with greater clarity . . . than ever before.
>
> No tame project, marriage. The raising of children . . . brings each of us breathtaking vistas of our own inadequacy. . . . [So,] we want desperately to blame [family life,] the institution which places our inadequacy in the brilliant glare of interrogation.
>
> The quantity of sheer . . . selfishness in . . . my breast is a never-failing source of wonder. I do not want to be disturbed, challenged, troubled. Huge regions of myself belong only to me. . . . Seeing myself through the unblinking eyes of an intimate, intelligent other, an honest spouse, is humiliating beyond anticipation. Maintaining a familial steadiness whatever the state of my own emotions is a standard by which I stand daily condemned.
>
> [Yet] my dignity as a human being depends perhaps more on what sort of husband and parent I am, than on any professional work I am called to do. My bonds to them hold me back from many sorts of opportunities. *And yet, these bonds are, I know, my liberation. They force me to be a different sort of human being, in a way in which I want and need to be forced.*[18]

A mother and father we know once discovered how such liberation can occur. One of their children came home from school one Monday afternoon and announced that if he didn't finish a certain overdue project by the next morning, the rest of his year in fourth grade was doomed. It was clear that he simply must succeed. His class was completing a unit on Native Americans, and he was assigned to build a diorama on a cookie sheet, showing the habitat of a certain tribe. But as he began stomping around the kitchen in frustration after dinner, he was clearly neither willing nor ready to begin his project.

The mother suggested that the father lead the other children in a family home evening activity while she and the fourth-grader worked in the kitchen. The father periodically heard outbursts and threats from the little diorama builder, who kept insisting that he wouldn't do another thing. At one point these vocal protests provoked the father to race into the kitchen with a threat of his own, but the mother gently waved him off. As eight o'clock became nine and later, the father started tucking the other children into bed.

Then into the bedroom came the fourth-grader, followed by his weary mother. He was grinning proudly, carrying his diorama like a birthday cake. He had obviously made every stitch of it himself. He gathered his brothers around and pointed out the bark, wigwam, trees, and little animals. His mother stood in the background smiling gently.

The boy placed his diorama on a counter and started for his bed. Suddenly he stopped and looked back at his mother, grinning a toothy fourth-grade grin beneath his freckled cheeks and tousled hair. He wasn't a demonstrative boy; but in that moment he just ran across the room, threw his arms around his mother's waist, and looked up at her with an authentic, boyish look of gratitude. As she rubbed his hair and held him close, they exchanged unspoken thoughts of much meaning—perhaps something about belonging to one another. Then he scampered off to bed.

As the mother and father left the bedroom, he asked, "How did you do it?" She said she had just made up her mind that nothing the boy could do would make her raise her voice or lose her patience. She had simply decided in advance that no matter what he said or did, she would keep helping him, even if it took all night. Then she made this significant observation: *"I didn't know I had it in me."*

And she never would have known what capacity was inside her, had she not decided that leaving him, either literally or figuratively, was simply not an alternative. It would have been perfectly reasonable for her to throw up her hands after an hour of honest effort and send him to bed. But her familistic commitment was unlimited; she couldn't do that. So she discovered within herself a reservoir of patience and endurance she otherwise would never have found. "Belonging" is for thick and thin, and this was one of the thin times.

In this sense, our bonds are our liberation. Until being "forced" by such voluntary commitments, we may never tap into the reservoirs of strength and compassion we carry within ourselves. That loss irreparably damages society, just as it weakens our own intimate relationships and our personal character. As our collective sense of belonging wanes, we are less motivated to dig deeply enough to draw upon our subsurface human powers. Thus, convinced that our growing sense of individual isolation is the emotional version of some global greenhouse effect beyond our control, our culture could die of psychic thirst—even, ironically, as we ignorantly sit atop undiscovered personal reservoirs that hold the living water of human compassion.

Our bonds liberate us in another, related sense. When our undisciplined quest to be let alone reaches some of the extremes we see today, that quest ironically undermines the mediating institutions—of which the family is an important example—that best foster the development of each person's capacity for responsible, autonomous action. In turn, that personal capacity both creates and enables political and social stability in a free and open society.[19] In this way, families bound together by belonging-based commitments prepare not only children, but also adults, to sustain a democratic society that literally depends upon each person's enlightened willingness to obey the unenforceable. The experience that best informs that willingness is a pattern of marriage and kinship nourished by wellsprings of unlimited personal commitments that constantly reveal powers we didn't know we held inside ourselves. Maintaining a family tradition is, therefore, a prerequisite to our maintaining a meaningful individual tradition. For this reason, the waning of belonging ultimately contributes, ironically, to the waning of personal freedom.

The idea that our bonds are our liberation also suggests at an introductory level what the gospel teaches in fully flowered form: marriage and family life are among the Lord's primary institutions for perfecting the individual. The demanding intimacy of familistic commitments tests us and teaches us in ways that are impossible in short-term, casual relationships. It isn't that difficult to be polite and fair toward church, business, and social acquaintances. But it requires real compassion to be patient and unselfish with those who, over many years, share the same possessions, the same checkbook, and the same name.

Our tolerance and the limits on our commitments are constantly tested by our family ties. Such testing is more a sign of normalcy than a sign of a troubled family. The real issue is how we respond to the stress—how we manage the commitment to nourish and cherish our spouses (see Ephesians 5:28–29) and the commitment never to leave, literally or figuratively, temporarily or permanently.

Actually, much more is at stake in family differences than appears on the surface, because when our commitments wane, so do the processes of discovery and personal growth. Not realizing these implications, some who are embarrassed, irritated, or just inconvenienced by their differences will simply walk away, believing they have a "right," somehow, to be free of all the interference. Many of these will in time marry someone else, only to find another set of bothersome conflicts. Once again, they may leave the person they view as the new source of their frustrations, somehow believing they are entitled to live without the intrusion of adjusting to and dealing with points of view different from their own. They may, then, never experience what it is to understand a complex situation from another person's perspective or to subordinate their own needs to those of others. As a result, they deprive themselves of discovering the meaning and the personal growth that are the blessings of belonging.

A father once said to his wife after a frustrating family day, "The Lord placed Adam and Eve on the earth as full-grown people. Why didn't he do that with our children? That would have saved everybody a lot of trouble." The mother replied wisely, "I think he gave us those children to make Christians out of us."

If we can't learn to be compassionate in the bonds of family life, we are probably not compassionate—Christlike— in any important sense. But if we let ourselves become what our bonds demand of us, we will develop the capacity to be compassionate not only with family companions but also with everyone else. That will be our spiritual liberation.

When the Savior comes, those he invites to live with him will be men and women who have learned, through experience and with his help, to live as he does. The marriages in which they are partners will then be celestial—not only in duration but also in quality. The Lord himself cannot endow us with celestial attributes unless we respond to the opportunities he provides to develop those attributes in the crucible of daily, demanding experience.

At the conclusion of Charles Dickens's novel *Little Dorrit,* a new marriage is depicted as the beginning of a *descent* out of which the only important kind of *ascent* is possible:

> Then they went up the steps of the neighbouring
> Saint George's Church, and went up to the altar,

where Daniel Doyce was waiting in his paternal character. And they were married, with the sun shining on them through the painted figure of Our Savior on the window. And they went . . . to sign the Marriage Register. . . . They all gave place when the signing was done, and Little Dorrit and her husband walked out of the church alone. They paused for a moment on the steps of the portico, looking at the fresh perspective of the street in the autumn morning sun's bright rays, and then *went down*.

Went down into a modest life of usefulness and happiness. Went down to give a mother's care . . . to Fanny's neglected children no less than to their own, and to leave that lady going into Society for ever and a day. Went down to [be] a tender nurse and friend to [those in need]. . . . They went quietly down into the roaring streets, inseparable and blessed; and as they passed along in sunshine and in shade, the noisy and the eager, and the arrogant and forward and the vain, fretted, and chafed, and made their usual uproar.

Little Dorrit gave up the life option of "that lady going into Society," preferring instead the familistic life of real belonging. She therefore "went down" into the "bonds" of a "modest life of usefulness and happiness." And here she would find her liberation.

Those who view the quiet contemplation of the church house as the essence of the religious life might not understand how there could be great religious meaning in going "quietly down into the roaring streets, inseparable and blessed" into the "usual uproar" of everyday family life. But if there is no religious meaning in the ordinary uproar of family life, there is not much religious meaning to life at all. That is where liberty, unselfishness, and heroism are most likely to be discovered as the intensely practical virtues they are. That is also where the practical, essential virtues are transmitted— if they are to be transmitted at all—to the next generation.

Of course, to "go down" from our pedestals of pride is also to slip beneath the level of the visible; for the Lord's work done within the walls of our own homes will not be in full view of an outside audience. For that reason, the insights we gain, the delights we discover, and the attitudes we shape inside our homes are unlikely to be known, much less applauded, by outside observers. The principles of love and commitment, and the silent satisfactions that flow from them, are private matters of the heart, known only to those who practice them. Yet there are no more meaningful discoveries in all of life. For as we go down, we ultimately may go up, to a celestial life that extends those same silent satisfactions "for ever and a day."

CHAPTER TWELVE

Planting Promises in the Hearts of the Children

Our teenage son recently traveled a long way from home. Distance made communication so difficult that we could send him only a brief written message with this p.s.: "Read Alma 37:35–37." In this passage Alma says, "O, remember, my son, and learn wisdom in thy youth. . . . Cry unto God for all thy support; yea, . . . let the affections of thy heart be placed upon the Lord forever . . . and he will direct thee for good."

In his equally brief reply, our boy concluded, "Read D&C 2." There we found Moroni's early words to Joseph Smith, promising that prior to the Lord's coming, Elijah will "plant in the hearts of the children the promises made to the fathers, and the hearts of the children will turn to their fathers. If it were not so, the whole earth would be utterly wasted at [the Lord's] coming." (D&C 2:2–3.)

I was moved by his response.* I wondered if he realized what deep nerves of meaning he was touching. At one level, he reflected his acceptance of the fifth commandment, to "honour thy father and thy mother, that thy days may be long upon the land which the Lord thy God giveth thee."

---

*Because this chapter draws on Bruce's relationship with his father, he writes here in first person singular.

(Exodus 20:12.) Yet Moroni's adaptation of Malachi's prophecy (see Malachi 4:5–6) extends the spirit and promise of the fifth commandment far beyond simply showing respect for parents, as important as that is. Moroni promised that the Spirit of Elijah (which is the priesthood power by which families may be sealed together) would actually *plant in the hearts of the children* a desire to realize the same promises the Lord gave to Abraham—and, for many Latter-day Saint children, the promises made to their parents in the temple. And that blessing, if realized, will save not only them but also the "whole earth" from being "wasted."

How miraculous, literally, that a thirst, even a yearning, for these marvelous blessings might actually take root in our children's own hearts. I suspect that most all parents in Zion pray every night, as we do, that this inborn hunger will be planted in the hearts of their children, supplementing all we can do to help them be receptive to it.

To explain why I was so stirred by this boy's response, I must share another story about our older son, who was born shortly after my father's death. We gave this son my father's name as his middle name. In our son's early years, he felt awkward enough about this old-fashioned name that he didn't use it. But when he took up debate in high school and learned that his grandfather had been a debater for BYU in the 1920s, he began feeling a tie to his namesake. My father had kept a journal during much of his adult life, and one day I showed my boy an entry describing his grandfather's big debate for BYU against Princeton. I left that journal volume with him, hoping he would want to read it.

Our son was a good boy, but he wasn't easy to raise. We listened, we stayed close to him, and we prayed for patience. We prayed that the seeds of faith would take root in his heart, but we knew we couldn't force that process. I thought during those days about my own older brother, who had died in an accident just as he was emerging from his own turbulent adolescence. My parents had prayed and grieved for him. One night my son left me a simple note: "I never want to do anything that would hurt you and Mom the way your brother's problems hurt your parents." I wondered how he could have known of something so personal from a generation ago. Then I remembered the journal, but I chose not to ask him any more.

A few weeks later, our son worked his way through a particularly trying experience and came to us late at night to tell us what had happened. He said, "Dad, I never knew Grandpa Hafen, but I felt he was there, helping me." I held him close that night, and I told him more about his grandfather.

Not long afterward, he was deciding how he should respond to a mission call. We were in southern Utah for a family reunion. On Sunday afternoon, with no explanation, he drove alone to the isolated little canyon where his grandfather had loved to ride his horse—the place, in fact, where he had passed away. He had read of this canyon in the journal and seen it from a distance, but he had never been in it. After hiking into the canyon, he knelt in a secluded spot and asked the Lord's help to sort through his questions about his faith, his mission, and his life. Later, at his missionary farewell, he alluded to the sacredness of that day and described the deep assurance and sense of direction he carried from his grandfather's canyon. Now, some years later, with children of his own, his life brightly reflects that assurance and direction, and I know the satisfaction my father must feel about his grandson.

I have no doubt that the Lord through Elijah planted in the heart of our child, just as he planted in my own heart, God's promises to my father. There really is a bond and a sense of belonging between the generations on both sides of the veil. This bond gives us a sense of identity and purpose.

It makes our ties with the eternal world very real, sharpening our life's focus and lifting our expectations.

In other words, as we honor our fathers and mothers by turning our hearts to them, their promises and their hearts turn to us. As that happens, in the Lord's words, our "days may be prolonged," that "it may go well with [us], in the land which the Lord [our] God giveth [us]." (Deuteronomy 5:16.) This happens because the fifth commandment "is the first commandment with [a] promise." (Ephesians 6:2.) And what is the promise? Not only that our "days may be *long*" (Exodus 21:12; emphasis added), but also that our days and lives may be blessed with personal security, happiness, and meaning. Not only that "it may go well with [us]" individually, but also that our entire culture will sustain itself with the blessings of peace and liberty. Somehow, our children's learning and accepting the accumulated wisdom of their mothers and fathers is the key to social as well as individual survival.

Yet today, to an unprecedented degree, the fabric of society is literally coming apart at the seams—those permanent seams of human interconnectedness we call kinship and marriage. In a society that seems ever more angry and unhappy, many children, parents, and spouses are turning their hearts not toward one another but toward their own self-focused needs. "They seek not the Lord, but every man walketh after the image of his own god, whose image is in the likeness of the world." (D&C 1:16.) Ours is the age of the waning of belonging.

Perhaps we are witnessing the other side of the promise associated with the fifth commandment—namely, that the earth could be "utterly wasted" at the Lord's coming. For "the earth will be smitten with a curse *unless there is a welding link . . . between the fathers and the children.*" (D&C 128:18; emphasis added.) This curse, like the blessing, was part of Malachi's conditional prophecy. Other prophecies also fore-

saw the curse of an earth that is wasted by the loss of familial bonds: "In the last days . . . men shall be lovers of their
own selves, . . . disobedient to parents, unthankful, unholy,
without natural affection." (2 Timothy 3:1–3.) "And because
iniquity shall abound, the love of many shall wax cold."
(Matthew 24:12.)

Statistics reflect some results of this problem—rising rates
of adolescent crime, out-of-wedlock births, divorce, and
family violence. Despite its relative strength, the Church population is not immune from these broad-scale trends. We
could discuss the relevant statistics, within and outside the
Church, but the *attitudes* that produce these statistics are in
some ways more revealing than the statistics themselves.
American culture seems to be changing from a society that
"strengthens the bonds between people to one that is, at
best, indifferent to them; a sense of an inevitable fraying of
the net of connections between people at many critical intersections, of which the marital knot is only one." These
"points of disintegration" have at least one common cause:
"the overriding value placed on the idea of individual emancipation and fulfillment, in the light of which, more and
more, the old bonds are seen not as enriching but as confining. We are coming to look upon life as a lone adventure,"
but it is becoming "a journey that has been rendered point-
less by becoming limitless."[1]

In addition to such individual aimlessness, this trend
gives us amnesia in our collective "group memory," the
essential knowledge each succeeding generation must possess to ensure social continuity. The fraying of human connections is choking off the transmission from one generation
to the next of the knowledge and understanding required for
meaningful survival of the culture: "Our society requires, as a
minimum for its survival, that its members share a common
set of beliefs, abide by a common set of rules, and . . . recognize their mutual dependence."[2] It was especially in this

sense that the Lord drew an explicit connection between honoring parents and living long in the land.

The fifth commandment's focus on child-parent relations calls attention to a particularly disturbing modern attitude—a new adult disinterest and neglect toward children. For instance, Marie Winn's book *Children without Childhood* describes "a profound alteration in society's attitude toward children," tracing the connections among a general erosion of institutional authority, a new sense of instability in marriage, the sexual revolution, and the emerging but unjustified tendency to treat children as if they have the capacity for unrestricted adult experience.[3] Several of these problems may appear following divorces in which a lonely, single parent by default shares every adult secret with his or her immature children in a cry for emotional support.

Another researcher found that modern TV's appeal to mass audiences erases the traditional dividing line between adults and children.[4] The commercials make us all think we should wear the same kinds of shoes and clothing styles—at age eight or eighty, everybody wants to look like Barbie and Ken. This emphasis on sameness undermines children's normal maturation process. If their parents and grandparents look just like they do and talk just as they do, how will children see that they are supposed to grow into something different as they mature?

Scholars in public education also find that current attempts by teachers to define morality may now be seen as "a form of indoctrination." People now "declare—even insist—that children are adults capable of choosing their own morality as long as they do not commit crimes."[5] Ironically, however, recent research shows that criminal behavior results primarily from a lack of self-control and an inability to delay gratification to pursue long-term goals. And "the ability and willingness to delay immediate gratification for some larger purpose" is "*a consequence of training.*"[6] Thus, most children left to themselves will simply not develop self-control.

These attitudes have also produced a "children's rights" movement that compares children to oppressed minority groups who need to be "liberated" from domination by other people. In some ways this trend has helped raise society's awareness about the seriousness of child abuse, and it has made such agencies as juvenile courts and schools feel more accountable for what they do. But rather than planting the promises made to the fathers in the hearts of the children, this movement has too often sought to liberate children from any sense of dependence upon, or even connections to, parents and other adults. For instance, one parent recently announced that she was giving her child his own first name *and his own surname* in order to set the child completely "free" to be his own person. Like some other elements of the children's rights movement, this example shows a willingness to abandon children to their "rights." However, the fact is that children's highest right is to be loved and nurtured by—to belong to—parents who honor them. Only in this way do we teach children to honor their parents—and to honor the interests of the community at large. Only this reciprocal honoring will deliver the promise of the fifth commandment.

This theme is also found in emerging attitudes about grandparents. Researchers who recently interviewed many children discovered that "the bond between grandparents and grandchildren is second in emotional power and influence only to the relationship between children and parents."[7] Yet this cross-generational tie of true kinship is seldom discussed today in studies on family life, children, or the needs of the elderly. One study found that "the isolation of grandparents from grandchildren is a recent event" that "devalues the emotional needs and attachments of children in the name of 'individual autonomy' . . . designed by and for a society of 'adults only.'"[8] Parents who neglect the development of associations between children and their grandparents violate the fifth commandment twice—both up and down the generational ladder.

Ironically, adults face conflicts of interest in thinking about the rights of children. When we "liberate" our children, we also liberate ourselves from the responsibilities parents and other adults have always assumed for the long-term nurturing of children. Child-rearing can make excruciating demands on the time, energy, and financial resources of parents and communities. To escape those demands by giving "rights" to our children is a beguiling invitation. The notion that we should "respect our children's freedom" enough to "leave them alone" can too easily justify adults whose personal convenience is also best served by leaving children alone.

By giving priority to that personal convenience, school teachers and leaders may find it not worth the patience and frustration required to provide children with meaningful discipline. Marriage partners may think it unimportant to cooperate with each other, even when that may be crucial for their children. Fathers with child-support obligations or other parents with heavy job demands or intense leisure time commitments are delighted to "set their children free."

The preference of many adults for a casual sexual environment also encourages adolescent sex, which creates another conflict between adult interests and children's needs. For example, a team of distinguished researchers concluded a large study of adolescent pregnancy with the observation that, "for ourselves, we prefer to cope with the consequences of early sex as an aspect of an emancipated society, rather than pay the social costs its elimination would exact."[9] Unfortunately, however, while that emancipated society may set a few self-centered adults free for the moment, it is already damaging today's children so seriously that it threatens to "utterly waste" our culture and its future.

The preamble to the U.S. Constitution expresses the

vision of "secur[ing] the blessings of Liberty" not only "to ourselves" but also to "our Posterity." This statement captures
the connection between the sacrifices adults make today in
defining their own rights and duties and the blessings they
secure for later generations tomorrow. The fifth commandment also stresses the parent-child relationship as the key not
only to personal happiness but also to long-term social survival. With striking clarity, the inspired Constitution tracks
this same connection between intergenerational compassion
and cultural continuity. The founders of our nation could see
that the way they defined their own freedoms and duties
would clearly control whether, for their posterity, "it may go
well with thee in the land which the Lord thy God giveth
thee." (Deuteronomy 5:16.)

Yet today, society seems confused about what parents
and children owe each other. Does kinship denote a relationship of a different order from any other relationship—or
is kinship of lesser significance because we typically do not
"choose" even our close relatives? Is the "nonbinding commitment" (notice the impossible contradiction in those two
terms) of cohabitation really that different from marriage,
when there is so much divorce? As a result of such questions,
many are uncertain now about what a family really is. Some
people seriously doubt whether our centuries-old system of
kinship and marriage—reflected in the fifth commandment—
still exists. Some argue that a legal "family" should be any
two or more persons who share resources and commitments.
One legal scholar even asserts that any "intimate association"
should enjoy the same preferred position that the
Constitution gives to marriage and kinship.

Actually, the U.S. legal system remains quite clear about
what a family is. The laws dealing with income tax, evidence, inheritance, and personal injury law, for example,
give distinct protection to relationships based on kinship,
heterosexual marriage, and adoption. A few courts have

nonetheless recognized certain *contractual* claims and some employment benefits for unmarried partners. State agencies have also become very reluctant to enforce the laws now on the books that prohibit sex outside marriage. In addition, a limited right of constitutional "privacy" has given unmarried people rights to abortion and contraception. Still, the U.S. Supreme Court has resisted attempts to grant a full right of sexual privacy to unmarried persons. Despite some increased flexibility, our legal system remains fairly certain about what a family is for the most fundamental legal purposes.

Some critics would alter this general stance—not *in spite of* the family's historic status, but perhaps *because of* that very status. In this day of passionate claims to individual rights, the existence of a legal preference makes everyone want to qualify for it. This is so even though defining a preferred category to include virtually everything renders meaningless the much-prized category itself. For example, the Hawaii Supreme Court recently became the first American appellate court to recognize that homosexual couples may have a legal right to marry.[10] As such counter-cultural pressures build, we will hear growing criticism of the traditional idea that a system based on near-permanent relationships of kinship and heterosexual marriage is crucial to society's best interests. Somehow we must remember that a society that tolerates anything will ultimately lose everything.

In the meantime, I wish to suggest four ideas that reflect society's interest in preserving family structures based on traditional ideas about kinship, marriage, and the minority status of children. This social interest, reflected in the spirit of the fifth commandment, must not be trumped by the "individual interest" that is breathlessly asserted these days—especially because preserving family stability is the best way to ensure meaningful individual liberty in the long run.

The first element is simply the needs of children. Empirical studies establish beyond question every child's need for unbroken continuity in relationships with adults. Stable relationships and environments are crucial for a child's normal psychological development. This need is so great that disruptions of child-parent relationships by the state, even to address inadequate parental care, frequently do more harm than good. This factor alone may justify the legal incentives and preferences traditionally given to permanent kinship units based on marriage.

Second, family life is the source of public virtue—what Elder Neal A. Maxwell calls the "willingness to obey the unenforceable." The tradition of individual liberty is at the heart of American culture. Yet the fulfillment of individualism's promise depends, paradoxically, upon the maintenance of a corollary family tradition that requires what may seem to be the opposite of personal liberty: submission to authority, acceptance of responsibility, and the discharge of duty. When families make and keep the mutual commitments of the fifth commandment, both children and parents experience the need for and the value of authority, responsibility, and duty in their most pristine forms.

In the words of historian Christopher Lasch: "The best argument for the indispensability of the family is that children grow up best under conditions of intense emotional involvement [with their parents]. . . . Without struggling with the ambivalent emotions aroused by the union of love and discipline in his parents, the child never masters his rage or his fear of authority. It is for this reason that children need parents, not professional nurses or counselors." A child who moves through this essential experience of personal development learns to "honor . . . father and mother" in ways that allow the child to deal productively with the entire concept of authority. The end result is that the child is able to "internalize moral standards in the form of a conscience."[11]

Our culture has an enormous stake in this process of moral learning, because we simply can't force people to live the rules of a free society. Without an inward moral light in each person, our ability to live together is doomed. And the cultivation of that light is a *learned* behavior. A voluntary sense of family duty is therefore essential to moderate democracy's tendency toward self-centeredness. Unless this tendency is checked, individualistic democracy causes people to think that they stand alone, believing that "their whole destiny is in their own hands."[12]

Third, the formal family is essential in preserving the private transmission of values in a democratic society. Our system is committed to the ideas of pluralism and diversity among all citizens, and the availability of many acceptable alternatives provides opportunity for individual choice and control. To accomplish this goal, our system presupposes a system of family units, not just of isolated individuals, partly as a way of preventing the government from asserting too much control over what values are taught to children. Indeed, the state nursery is one of the typical hallmarks of a totalitarian society.

In democratic societies, marriage itself creates an independent "family entity" that protects the autonomy of the family from outside interference. As stated by the English writer David H. Lawrence:

> The marriage bond . . . is the fundamental connecting link in society. Break it, and you will have to go back to the overwhelming dominance of the State. [In the pre-Christian era], the family was the man, as representing the State. There are States where the family is the woman. There are [totalitarian] States where the family hardly exists. Perhaps [Christianity's] greatest contribution to [our] social life is—marriage as we know it. Christianity established the little autonomy of the family within the greater rule of the State [yet] not to be violated by the State. Marriage has given man the best of his freedom, his little kingdom of his own within the big kingdom of

the State, [a] foothold of independence. Man and
wife, a king and queen with one or two subjects,
and a few square yards of territory of their own: this
is marriage. It is a true freedom.[13]

Fourth, marriage and the age-based rules that control
legal rights for children preserve legal and social stability.
Marriage and kinship involve commitments toward permanence that place them in a different category from all other
human relationships. People who believe these relationships
will continue indefinitely will *invest* in the relationship with a
reasonable belief that the promise of future benefits and
blessings justifies the sacrifice required by their personal
investment. Those who enter into "nonbinding commitments" will not make such investments; hence, they will
never discover the long-term satisfactions that flow only from
sacrificing for other people.

And if our system tried to protect child-parent or adult-
adult relationships based on personal characteristics rather
than on such fixed categories as marriage, kinship, and age
brackets, government agents would need to evaluate so
many psychological, economic, and other subjective elements that the required invasions of privacy and increases in
governmental power over personal lives would become
intolerable. In many areas of the country we are already
approaching this condition, as bewildered multitudes of
divorced families wait upon an army of family court judges
to supervise every decision from support obligations to vaca-
tion permissions. Until now, marriage, kinship, and the legal
status of children have remained fixed stars in our legal system. To the extent that they begin to drift, both as legal and
as social concepts, our society will drift from a system that
encourages stable expectations to one that discourages them.
Both individually and socially, our days will not then be
"long upon the land," meaning stable continuity of life.

The Lord instructed his Saints in D&C 98:16–17 to

"renounce war and proclaim peace, and *seek diligently* to turn the hearts of the children to their fathers, and the hearts of the fathers to the children." (Emphasis added.) As we come to understand the fifth commandment and the spirit of the work of Elijah, we will see the relationship between peace and the turning of parents' and children's hearts toward one another. The peace we proclaim and find in this way will bring peace to our minds, our homes, and our society.

How can we then "seek diligently" to call down the promises and the power of Elijah from the heavens? We will forge the Lord's peace by forging individual links, one at a time, in the great human chain of which the Prophet wrote: "a welding link . . . between the fathers and the children." (D&C 128:18.) Without that "welding together," the whole earth will be cursed and wasted. But with the welding link comes happiness and peace, the blessings of true belonging. Still, the diligent forging of human links often requires great personal sacrifice.

For example, we can see the direct connection between laboring for our children and becoming welded or bonded to them in a mother's experience as described by Camille Williams:

> When I was pregnant with my first child, I asked my mother about labor.
>
> [She] hardly looked up from her work to say, "it's not that bad." . . . She did indicate that the labor was actually harder on my father. I thought she was joking, but he [later] confirmed her account of his dismay at her experience. . . .
>
> After four labors and one emergency C-section, [I now know that those labor pains are not without purpose]. What is it I think that I have bought by my maternal pains? . . .
>
> I am forever altered by the carrying and the laboring for my children. Slow learner that I am, it took

the birth of my first child to see each person as someone else's child, someone else's pain and joy. This
radical restructuring of my world left me unable to
bear some of the misery we inflict on each other. . . .

In that relatively short time when body and soul
are straining to bring forth the daughter or the son,
some of us grasp for the first time that each irreplaceable life requires faith, patience, and more pain
than any of us would choose. Labor gives life, and
the long wait between conception and birth instills
gratitude for each delicate finger and toe, and appreciation for the beauty of the human body and all its
functions, right down to the last sleepy burp and
snore of the infant snuggled at the shoulder.

A relationship that began with the biological connection between parent and child may, through
labor and with astonishing speed, become a fierce,
inarticulate urge to protect the vulnerable newborn
whose face is seen only after long months of worry,
long hours of effort. Maybe it is the *work* of motherly
or fatherly nurture that brings about *a change of
heart linking us with those who have gone before us,
with those who will live after us.* As our children
grow, we are invited to become patient and less selfish through the presence of dependent innocents or
the pique of aggravating adolescents. As we and our
parents age, we are, in recognition of our own infirmities, enticed to be more forgiving, more repentant,
more compassionate. Perhaps it is this witness of
familial love that gives us hope beyond the present:
we were not made to turn to forgotten dust.

We are each of us bought through someone else's
pain and taught by our own suffering that every
day's breath is an infinite gift. We are none of us
simply biological creatures. Like sparrows and lilies,
we are known and accounted for; clothed by more
than mortal flesh, the end of our creation is joy.[14]

The reference here to sparrows and lilies alludes to the
Savior's comparison between God's attention to his nonhu-

man creations and his attention to his literal children. He clothed the lilies to be more splendid than Solomon's glory (Luke 12:27), and no sparrow falls without his notice (Matthew 10:29). Yet "how much more" will he clothe his children than the lilies (Luke 12:28), and "ye are of more value than many sparrows" (Matthew 10:31). The source of this incomprehensible degree of Christ's love for his children is that he, like a mother who knows labor pains, offered the labor of his Atonement for them. Our perspective on the sacrificial offerings we make for our children thus teaches us something of what it must mean that we are "known and accounted for" in the perspective of God.

This kind of diligent seeking to turn parents' and children's hearts toward one another may also be seen in contexts beyond the family. One obvious context is the turning of our hearts toward all those for whom we may perform temple ordinances—*our* dead as well as *the* dead. (See D&C 127:5.) That was the context in which the Lord taught us through Joseph Smith the need for the great welding link in section 128.

In addition, proselyting missionaries may forge their own links and feel their own "labor pains" as they seek to bring about the spiritual birth of new children of Christ. A sister missionary we know walked down a street in a French city with her companion. The sisters passed by a young family, a husband and wife with two small children. The missionaries were impressed that these people had a special character—as if, according to one of the missionaries, they had haloes above their heads. This feeling moved the two missionaries to turn around and walk back to speak to them. To their great surprise and dismay, given the strong spiritual impression they had felt, the mother rebuffed them. Only hours later did they regain their composure.

Two days later, the missionaries were reviewing their records of past investigators. They felt prompted to visit a man baptized several years earlier whom they had never seen at church. When they arrived at the man's home, the woman who greeted them at the door was the mother they had seen on the street. All three were astonished to see each other again.

The missionaries soon learned that this woman's husband had once been baptized but, because of her opposition, had drifted from activity. Over the next few weeks, the missionaries "labored" in great patience to teach the woman, her husband, and their young children the message of the Restoration. Before long, their prayers and the family's prayers were answered, and the woman was baptized. Soon afterward, her younger brother also joined the Church.

As one of these sister missionaries was then transferred, she wrote a letter home as her train sped toward a new French city:

> I feel like I'm letting my children go off to school for the first time, knowing that I won't be right by their side to help them. I literally loved [the people we taught in that city] with all my heart, mind, and strength. It's when you work for things that you learn to love them, and I worked [there] in a way that I had never been able to work in my life. Of course I have worked for things before, but a mission gives me a sense of *nurturing* that is unlike anything I have ever known. I feel like [these] people have a part of me that was the best part I knew how to give them. There is nothing in the world like seeing people grow before your very eyes, and knowing that as they continue to grow upward, there will be a little mark of growth just in the place where you influenced their lives.[15]

In these lines, we hear a clear echo from Camille Williams's experience: "Maybe it is the *work* of motherly or fatherly nurture that brings about a change of heart linking us with"[16] others in the great welding link of which the

Prophet wrote. In such changes of the heart, we experience the charity that teaches us how to nurture others, satisfying their emotional and spiritual hunger—their *amae*—and, in the process, welding us to them, and them to us, in the spirit of true belonging, the spirit of Elijah.

I began this chapter with a story illustrating how the promises made to the fathers are planted in the hearts of the children, thereby bringing those hearts together in the mutual magnetism of love—across the generations and across the veil of death. The result was a young man's clearer realization of who he was and how he should live, that his days would be long and that it might go well with him in the land the Lord has given him. This discovery blessed him, and it blessed his relationship with the larger society.

Lest it appear that such bonds arise only within traditional categories of marriage and kinship, this chapter concludes with another story illustrating how Elijah's spirit can in exceptional cases cross the boundaries of blood ties with the same spirit of honor as exists between parents and their natural children.

A woman I know was adopted as a baby into a Latter-day Saint home. When I asked her how long she had known she was an adopted child, she told me that when she was four, her father presented a family home evening lesson on the plan of salvation. In the course of that discussion, he explained to the children that sometimes parents who desperately desire children are unable physically to bear them. In such cases, the parents fast and plead with the Lord to send them special children whose biological parents are unable to care for them. Her father took her in his arms and explained that was how Heavenly Father had sent her to them. From that day forward, she sensed that it was even more special to be adopted than to be a natural child. The promises of eternal life made to this woman's adoptive parents were planted in her heart, and the result was her life-long peace of mind and sense of belonging.

In a world in which too many parents and children are drifting apart from each other, may we "proclaim peace, and seek diligently to turn the hearts of the children to their fathers, and the hearts of the fathers to the children." (D&C 98:16.) As we do so, we will see fulfilled the Lord's promise that "nothing, save it shall be iniquity among them, shall harm or disturb their prosperity upon the face of this land forever." (2 Nephi 1:31.)

CHAPTER THIRTEEN

Sustaining—and Being Sustained by— the Priesthood

In this day of confusion and uncertainty about gender issues, some people wonder how Latter-day women feel about their relationships of "belonging" to the Church and to families in which the pattern of the priesthood prevails. Some also wonder what this pattern means to single women. I can respond best to these questions by describing how the priesthood sustains me, in addition to describing how I can sustain the priesthood.*

How thankful I am for the restoration of the gospel! Because of the Restoration, the priesthood—the power and authority of God—is once more on the earth. That power sustains me in most every need and mood of my life. It also offers me the ordinances, the blessings, and the teachings of truth that give meaning to all I care about now and to all I hope for in the future.

When I think of all the ways this power of the priesthood sustains me, I wonder how my sustaining of that same power can possibly matter very much. Then I realize that my continuing support of the priesthood is intended primarily to qualify me for all our Father wants to give me.

---

*Because Marie prepared this essay from her personal point of view, she writes here in first person singular.

I have always had tender feelings for the "priesthood men" who have symbolized the Lord's love for me. I remember the kind and elderly patriarch under whose hands I was given the blessing that gives a certain focus and meaning to my life. I think of my gentle father, whose reverence for the responsibilities and blessings of the priesthood made it easy for me to envision God as both the source of law and the source of love.

I think of the blessings given me by my husband as I have faced pregnancy, childbirth, surgery, and stressful uncertainty. My children and I have thought of the priesthood he holds as *our* priesthood—as it is expressed through his hands and his voice—and we try together to be worthy of its influence in our home. I pray that our four sons will know that the priesthood they hold makes them servants, not masters.

These poignant feelings were stirred again recently when I read the words of a friend who described a dark night in her life when the power of the priesthood both rescued and reassured her. Donna is a faithful single woman whose body has been racked with the pain and stress of serious illness most of her adult life.

Looking back, Donna remembers the pleasant days of her childhood when she played quietly under the quilting frame in the little Relief Society hall in her home town, listening to the warm conversations of her mother and the other sisters about children and canning and charity. Donna assumed those would one day be the central subjects of her experience. But it was not to be, at least not as it had been for her mother and the other sisters. Through no choice of Donna's, there has been no marriage and hence no children of her own. But hers has still been a lifetime of charity as she has become a professional counselor to especially needy children.

Once, after lying in the hospital for several days, she

began to fear that she might not ever again leave her bed. She called an elder she knew, and he came the next day with a companion after fasting and prayer. She recalled: "I had not slept all night, and as the sun was coming up, I realized as I never had before that I wanted to live, that I couldn't give up life, that I wanted to have many more experiences. I wanted to spend more time with those I loved. I wanted to return to places that had meaning for me. I cherished life, held it to my heart, and desperately wanted to go on living under any circumstance.

"As the humble men came, and their tears dropped on my shoulders as they blessed me, I felt that God in his heaven was aware of our little circle."

Since that experience, Donna has continued to struggle with her health, but she has also continued serving and giving. She sustains the priesthood by the way she lives and the way she feels. She knows that even though a priesthood bearer does not live in her home, the priesthood is a key sustaining power of her life.

In the midst of such feelings, I find it difficult to put into words what it means to sustain the priesthood. I do know that doing so is central to the mission of the Relief Society and the Young Women, and that it is central in the lives of all members of the Church. I also know that the concept has several important shades of meaning.

We may see the most typical example of women who "sustain the priesthood" in organizational arrangements in which women work closely with men who serve as priesthood leaders, such as in a marriage and family, or in ward organizations. For example, a married woman sustains her husband who is a worthy priesthood holder by working in close partnership with him, doing all she can to support his righteous desires, and hearkening to his righteous counsel. If that same woman is also a ward Relief Society president, she sustains the priesthood in her ward by following the guidance of her bishop, correlating Relief Society activities with the work of the priesthood quorums and other organizations. A woman who offers these forms of support is not merely helping a man who happens to hold the priesthood; rather, she is also, but most fundamentally, sustaining the *authority* of the priesthood.

But what about my unmarried friend Donna? What does "sustaining the priesthood" mean to a single woman or a woman married to a man who does not hold or does not honor the priesthood?

My friend Carolyn is an older single woman who lives alone. She is a visiting teacher and was recently a counselor in her ward Primary presidency. All of her adult life she has longed for the blessing of having the priesthood in her home. One night Carolyn prayed with an earnest desire to understand how she might partake of at least some of the blessings of the priesthood, knowing that her dream of a temple marriage might not be realized in this life. As she prayed, the thought came to her that the Lord to whom she felt so close was himself the author and source of the priesthood. It was *his* power and influence that she sought. Because she had been baptized and confirmed by those having proper authority, she was entitled, as promised in the sacrament prayer, to "always have his Spirit to be with [her]" (D&C 20:77), subject only to her faithfulness.

With this assurance filling her heart, Carolyn promised the Lord that she would never allow anything to take place in her home or in her life that would make his Spirit unwelcome. From that day, "sustaining the priesthood" to Carolyn has included being worthy of her personal covenants with him whose power the priesthood is.

Carolyn still looks forward to the blessings of an eternal marriage to one who honors his priesthood, if not in this life then at a later time. In the meantime, the influence of the priesthood is still hers.

Carolyn's situation is shared by other women I know. Lola's husband had Alzheimer's disease and functioned for years at the level of an infant. Caring for him was her life's work. As his condition worsened and her frustrations increased, she cried to the Lord for understanding. I heard her testify that the Holy Ghost gradually began to teach her how to care for him, leading her almost as she was leading her husband—one small step at a time. Lola sustained the priesthood in her home by literally sustaining her husband, hour by hour, until his death not long ago. As she did so, she was blessed with a miraculous kind of serenity and courage.

Gaye was divorced and had three children, the oldest a thirteen-year-old boy. Because he held the priesthood, Gaye wondered if her son should be the presiding authority in her home. But of course he was not. She was the head of that Church unit—her family—and she had every right to pray for and receive spiritual guidance for her children. When they needed formal blessings and ordinances, she would call upon their grandfather or perhaps her home teachers. But she remained the organizational and spiritual leader of her family unit.

Laura was called as ward Young Women's president. She was unsure whether she and her counselors and secretary could function as a presidency unless a priesthood holder came to their meetings. Because she wanted so much to sustain the priesthood, she felt unable to make decisions affecting her teachers and her girls. When, in great frustration, she sought counsel from her bishop, he taught her that she had been called and set apart by proper priesthood authority. Of course she should take counsel regularly from her priesthood leaders, but she was to take the initiative with her organization, to do "many things of [her] own free will, and bring to pass much righteousness." (D&C 58:27.) *She* was the priesthood-appointed leader of that ward's Young Women organization. Part of sustaining the priesthood for Laura was to accept her calling from the priesthood wholeheartedly, to learn the program, to seek divine inspiration, and to love and encourage each girl in her ward.

Why are we sometimes unsure about the meaning of a phrase as basic as "sustaining the priesthood"? Perhaps it is because we use the term *priesthood* in more than one way.

First, we sometimes casually refer to an entire group of men as "the priesthood," as if the words *men* and *priesthood* mean the same things—which they clearly do not. For instance, if a few men attend a ward Relief Society meeting, perhaps to participate in the program, the sister conducting the meeting might say, "We welcome the priesthood here today." This may be an appropriate recognition of these men, but it does not mean that they stand in a position of authority to the ward Relief Society or its members. "Sustaining the priesthood" does not mean that a woman or anyone else in the Church is obliged to defer to the direction of men who are not their priesthood-appointed leaders.

Some people incorrectly believe that Mormon theology teaches that only men can receive divine revelation or hold positions of authority in the Church. I know of a young woman who nearly married a young man she did not love just because he told her that God had answered her prayers about their marriage through him. Then she realized that God would answer her own prayers about her marriage decisions. Moreover, a woman can be a priesthood-appointed leader, as in the case of a ward Relief Society or Young Women president. In those assignments, women hold important positions of authority, and they regularly receive the Lord's inspiration in fulfilling their duties.

Second, the most specific sense of "sustaining the priesthood" describes the relationship of support and loyalty we Church members feel toward our appointed priesthood leaders, especially those in the main line of ecclesiastical authority, such as the bishop, stake president, or president of the Church.

The Relief Society's sustaining of this central priesthood line is especially important, because doing so shows how fully that organization's activities are correlated with and subject to the direction of local and general Church leaders. A ward Relief Society president looks to her bishop as her priesthood-appointed leader, while she views her stake Relief Society president as a training adviser. A male Sunday School president who holds the priesthood has the same reporting relationship with his bishop and his stake Sunday School president as she has with her leaders. When the members of this woman's Relief Society unit loyally support her leadership, they are sustaining the priesthood by upholding the authority by which she was called.

This same support and loyalty applies to a married woman who sustains her husband as the priesthood leader of their family. The family is regarded as an official—even an eternal—organizational unit of the Lord's kingdom.

All other Church activities and organizations for men and women, from Sunday School to missionary work, follow this same pattern. All members and leaders at every level and in each organization are subject to the presiding direction of the ecclesiastical line, which runs from the president of the Church to the ward bishop. In that respect, men and women are treated the same. For instance, a father living in an organized ward who holds the priesthood may not baptize his own child without authorization from his bishop.

There is a third sense in which we use the term *priesthood:* as the power and authority of God, the source of all our spiritual and temporal blessings. Through the restoration of the gospel, the Church is built upon this same power. Because of the priesthood keys given to Joseph Smith and his divinely appointed successors, every worthy member of the Church has access to the blessings of the priesthood.

Under the hands of authorized priesthood representatives, each Church member may receive such glorious blessings as baptism for the remission of sins, the gift of the Holy Ghost, healings, patriarchal blessings, marriage, and the holy endowment of the temple. Through the ordinances of the priesthood, the very "power of godliness is manifest" to us. (D&C 84:20.) Because of this divine power, we may be healed, inspired, forgiven, and sanctified.

When we sustain the priesthood as it is defined in this sense, we are doing more than respecting the Lord's servants who administer the ordinances, important as that is. We are also honoring our sacred priesthood covenants and reflecting deep gratitude for our priesthood blessings.

Elder Bruce R. McConkie spoke in the October 1977 general conference about "the ten blessings of the priesthood." Women, both single and married, can enjoy almost all of these blessings by virtue of their Church membership, which is built upon the foundation of priesthood authority. Among the blessings Elder McConkie discussed are these stirring possibilities:

First, being members of the Church and receiving the fulness of the everlasting gospel.

Second, receiving the gift of the Holy Ghost and the other gifts of the Spirit.

Third, becoming sanctified by the Spirit, thereby becoming fit to dwell with God.

Fourth, representing Jesus Christ in administering salvation to mankind.

Fifth, becoming children of God in the family of the Lord Jesus Christ.

Sixth, having the opportunity of eternal marriage, without which there is no exaltation in the highest degree of the celestial kingdom.

Seventh, having the power to govern all spiritual and temporal things.

Eighth, having power to gain eternal life, the greatest of all the gifts of God.

Ninth, having power to make one's calling and election sure while yet in mortality.

Tenth, having the power and privilege, if pure in heart, to see the face of God while yet in mortality.[1]

These blessings of the priesthood are, for the most part, of the personal, spiritual kind. They enable personal growth and provide opportunities to serve others. Many of them derive from priesthood actions and ordinances, such as baptism, the gift of the Holy Ghost, being authorized and set apart in Church positions, and the ordinances of the temple. In other words, these are blessings that flow to the *receiving* end, rather than from the initial authorizing end, of priesthood activity. Thus these blessings are accessible to women as well as to men.

These blessings also include the right to behold visions and receive revelation, for the Lord "imparteth his word by angels unto men, yea, not only men but women also." (Alma 32:23.) Also included are spiritual gifts such as faith, the testimony of Christ, wisdom, tongues, prophecy, and personal revelations. As Elder Dallin H. Oaks has explained, "These gifts come by the power of the Holy Ghost and . . . are available to every member of the Church, male and female."[2]

Among the greatest of the priesthood blessings is the temple ordinance of eternal marriage. Unless we enter into this priesthood ordinance in this life or in the hereafter, we cannot receive exaltation. In some sense, exaltation is the ultimate priesthood blessing, because it finally includes all other blessings. But this privilege, though the crowning blessing of the priesthood, is not available to a worthy holder of the priesthood unless he is sealed in eternal marriage to a woman who is as worthy as he is. How significant it is for our understanding of the interdependence and equality of men and women in the eyes of God to know that neither can achieve exaltation alone! And when both finally receive exaltation, they will live and stand together forever, with all the blessings and powers of the priesthood. Thus, both of the partners in an eternal marriage "sustain the priesthood" that sealed them in the temple by striving always to be faithful to each other, and to the Lord.

All my experience teaches me that as I seek to sustain the priesthood, whether through loyalty to my husband, to my appointed leaders, or to my Savior, the priesthood sustains me, for the priesthood is the power of Him who will not forsake me.

Just as my friend Donna learned of the priesthood's sustaining power during her dark hours, the Prophet Joseph Smith also learned something about the priesthood in the terrible adversity of Liberty Jail: "Therefore, hold on thy way, and *the priesthood shall remain with thee. . . .* Thy days are known, and thy years shall not be numbered less; therefore, fear not what man can do, for God shall be with you forever and ever." (D&C 122:9; emphasis added.) Hearing this, Joseph must have felt much as Donna did when the priesthood came to her rescue.

Whether we are married or single, male or female, leaders or followers, if we sustain the priesthood by "holding on our way" as followers of Him whose power the priesthood is, "the priesthood will remain" with us. I am thankful to be living at a time when, through the Restoration, all of that is possible.

CHAPTER FOURTEEN

Women, Feminism, and Gender

I n recent years, both American society and the LDS community have experienced confusion and frustration about gender-related issues. At various times, these issues have appeared under such headings as feminism, sexism, or the women's rights movement. As challenging as these topics are for the larger society, they can be even more sensitive—even wrenching at times—for Latter-day Saints, because they can touch on deep theological nerves regarding the role of prophets, the dignity of women, and the nature of marriage. Our response to such matters can also undermine our sense of belonging, both to one another and to God. Indeed, the divisive feelings arising from today's "gender wars" are among the greatest threats to the fulfillment of our longing to belong.

Consider some examples at opposite ends of the Latter-day Saint thought spectrum. At one extreme are a few Church members who have publicly challenged the First Presidency's positions on such topics as abortion, the Equal Rights Amendment, or praying to Mother in Heaven. At the other extreme are a few Church members who are so distressed about modern threats to the traditional role of women that they have leaned over backward in overreaction. Some of these people sincerely wonder whether women should take education seriously, whether female officers of a Church auxiliary organization may make decisions when a priesthood leader is not present, or whether a divorced or widowed mother is authorized to preside in her home.

Let us first sketch a brief historical background and then consider three different ways of looking at these sometimes complicated issues. The origins of the American women's movement reach back to the late eighteenth and early nineteenth century. Since the colonists first came to America, fathers, mothers, and children had worked together in a rural and agricultural environment that typically made the *work*place the same as the *home* place. As the Industrial Revolution drew more families from their farms to the cities, more fathers began leaving home to work in factories. The increasing absence of working fathers encouraged the belief that mothers were needed at home, not only for child care but also to manage small farms and other household labor.

At the same time, the changing social and economic climate revealed women's needs for individual identity and legal protection. This growing awareness led to changes in the nation's family laws that were designed to protect the interests of women and children. Some of the first women's rights organizations also launched campaigns to assure greater equity for women in education, the labor force, and the legal system. In addition, the dislocations of urbanization drew women into social movements supporting such causes as child labor laws, public education, and temperance societies.

The Relief Society, organized by Joseph Smith in Nauvoo in 1842, eventually became one of the country's largest and most active women's organizations. Its leaders supported, with the endorsement of the Church leadership, what would become the single biggest women's issue of the day—the right of women to vote in public elections. Utah women were the first to exercise that right, in 1870. It took the nation fifty years—until 1920—to follow that example with a constitutional amendment that assured women's suffrage.

An Equal Rights Amendment to the U.S. Constitution guaranteeing general gender equality was first introduced in Congress in 1923; but with the matter of voting rights settled, the subject attracted little serious public interest. Susan B. Anthony and Eleanor Roosevelt opposed the ERA in those days, because even though they favored greater political and economic equality for women, they feared that a constitutional amendment would deprive women of needed protection. This attitude prevailed for several decades, despite the significant new levels of women's employment required to sustain the economy and the war effort during World War II. As recently as 1962, a majority of U.S. women in a Gallup poll believed that they were not victims of sex discrimination.[1]

But with the 1960s came a major change, symbolized by the publication in 1963 of *The Feminine Mystique*, by Betty Friedan. Describing a "problem that has no name," Friedan argued that the emphasis on domestic life since World War II left married women frustrated and unfulfilled.[2] This idea rode other strong reformist waves of the turbulent '60s into a period of far-reaching social change, eventually using many of the successful strategies of public protest first seen in the civil rights movement.

The women's movement of the 1960s and '70s altered the nation's consciousness. As thousands of women left their homes for new employment and greater education, more women entered such previous male bastions as corporate management, medicine, the law, and the political arena. State and federal laws regulating family life entered a period of reform that transformed not only our statutes and judicial doctrines but also our very thinking about marriage, divorce, and the status of children. Laws in other fields, ranging from employment law to constitutional law, extended to women increasing equality all across the economic and political spectrum.

This women's movement also introduced an attitudinal dimension not previously seen in American history. As described by social philosopher Robert Nisbet:

> Earlier women's rights movements were . . . efforts to achieve for women a larger share of economic, educational, and cultural benefits—*but within the family structure;* or at least without seeking to alter that structure seriously. What gives present manifestoes, political actions, and movements toward legal reform their revolutionary character is the degree to which the substance of the family is changed. For with sure revolutionary instinct, the women's liberation movement—at least in its radical expressions—goes right to the heart of the matter, which is the historical nature of the *role* of each of the sexes.[3]

Amid this change in the cultural seas, the waves of the women's movement sometimes (but not always intentionally) overlapped and then merged with other waves of change. For example, during the 1970s, the nation's economic base was changing in ways that reduced the average American family's standard of living for the first time in history. Rising inflation, declines in manufacturing, and economic demand for new workers in the low-paying service/information sector attracted many women into the workplace as they looked for ways to augment their families' levels of support.[4]

Political protests also emerged, challenging virtually every American institution and social convention. Widespread public reaction against the war in Vietnam and against the Nixon administration's handling of the Watergate affair unleashed the potent concept of investigative reporting. The media's new aggressiveness had the desirable effect of encouraging greater public accountability and candor among the nation's leading institutions; however, the visibly contentious spirit of "advocacy journalism" also bred a growing cynicism that began to erode public confidence in such fragile sentiments as patriotism and public trust. As a result, the very concepts of authority and institutional power seemed suspect in every context, from churches and schools to families, corporations, and the government. Worries about a worldwide population explosion also gave what seemed like logical support to those who already felt that legal protection for contraception and abortion was necessary to free women from what some called "biological bondage."

In addition, the public mind began showing a new willingness to question moral norms and social taboos that had prevailed as long as anyone could remember. This challenge to traditional values was reflected in new forms of drug abuse, pornographic movies, and a sexual revolution that attacked society's right to limit sexual experience and childbearing to marriage.

Then, just as Betty Friedan's book in 1963 marked the beginning of the modern women's movement, the failure of the Equal Rights Amendment in 1982 marked another key transition point. Despite having rejected similar efforts consistently since 1923, Congress in 1972 had overwhelmingly adopted a proposed amendment to the U.S. Constitution providing that "equality of rights under the law shall not be denied or abridged . . . on account of sex." Within a year, legislatures in thirty of the required thirty-eight states had ratified the amendment. But by 1982, time ran out and the proposed amendment expired. It was reintroduced in 1983 but has since lain essentially dormant.

Given the momentum at the beginning of the ERA campaign, it was surprising that the project bogged down as it did. Persuasive arguments had been mounted against the ERA, such as the First Presidency's concern about undermining family life[5] and the legal point that matters of domestic relations had historically been under state, not federal, control. However, the most logical explanation for the ERA's failure is that by the late '70s, the legal reform movement had already accomplished so much of its agenda for women's equality that the need for the amendment seemed primarily symbolic. When the case for symbolic victory was pitted against the question whether the ERA might unintentionally harm women's potential need for special protection, the drive for ratification simply ran out of steam.

Another major factor that contributed to the ERA's defeat was that the passion for equal treatment of men and women that had fueled the women's movement during the 1960s and '70s experienced gradual changes in rationale. Some of this change arose from the discovery that certain reforms in the name of women's equality and independence had actually hurt women more than they had helped them. New no-fault divorce laws, for example, often produced results that left women economically worse off and less assured of receiving child custody than before. Despite such disappointments, a national poll in 1986 found that 71 percent of American women reported that the women's movement had improved their lives and raised the national consciousness about the dignity and worth of women.[6]

At the philosophical level, growing numbers of women of varying perspectives in the 1980s began saying that inherent and significant differences between men and women called not for a system that treated men and women the same but for a system that recognized and preserved their differences. With this premise, the ERA could actually look like a mistake. These new voices expressed two very different—sometimes opposing—variations on this theme: the first was a renewed discovery of the value of motherhood and family life; the second a new understanding of feminism.

First, regarding motherhood and family life, some

observers now believe the ERA was defeated not by men but by certain women—those who realized by the late 1970s that the equality reforms they had welcomed had actually reduced the financial security of the women for whom motherhood took high priority. This made them fear what the ERA would do to the world of children and service, where many women had found their greatest opportunities for fulfillment. Hence some women who had supported the ERA began changing their minds, including changing their view of the relative importance of working compared to being with the family.

For example, Orania Papazoglou discovered what she believes other women discovered—that after years of "feminist gains in the workplace, the legislature, and the culture," by the early 1990s, ironically, the "self-respect of American women is at an all-time low." She believes this is because the women's movement of the '60s and '70s turned out to be "a revolt not against men, but against mothers, with devastating consequences."

> Heroic women who had dedicated their lives to the welfare and education of children—as mothers, teachers, nurses, social workers—were being systematically marginalized and devalued, made to feel stupid and second rate because they had taken seriously the Judeo-Christian precept that it was better to do for others than for oneself. [In addition to being a] revolt against mothers, [this attitude has made children worse off than they were a few years ago, when more parents] thought they were worth the sacrifices we had to make. . . . [Thus,] the plight of today's children can be blamed on . . . one thing alone: we no longer care what happens to them.

Papazoglou believes this outcome could have been avoided by a "feminism that would embrace *both* its career women and its career mothers." This more balanced approach would have avoided the "devaluation of motherhood," which devalues "everything else women do." She continues, "You cannot declare the primary work of most women throughout most of history to be beneath serious consideration without sending women the covert message that it is really women who are beneath serious consideration."[7] Betty Friedan expressed similar concerns in *The Second Stage*,[8] her 1981 reflections on the status of the women's movement.

A second, contrasting argument for recognizing the differences between men and women has emerged primarily in the work of feminist academic scholars. Much of the new feminist scholarship proceeds from a premise first articulated by psychologist Carol Gilligan, whose book *In a Different Voice*[9] suggests that men and women innately view the world through fundamentally different frameworks, or paradigms. Because of these differences, women may feel uncomfortable in organizational or social settings that unconsciously reflect what males value. Rather than requiring women to accept the male paradigm, as the unisex equality model of the ERA seemed to do, the new feminism urges society to begin using female frames of reference. In assessing a woman's legal claims, for example, rather than asking whether a "reasonable man" or even a "reasonable person" would interpret certain male comments as sexual harassment, we should ask how a "reasonable woman" would interpret them.

There is now a broad spectrum of feminist thought in the academic disciplines, ranging all the way from simply reaffirming basic needs for fairness and equity in gender matters to a militant, radical strain that seeks to overthrow virtually all current institutions and traditions. This radical stance proceeds from the belief some people hold that American culture is constructed to a hopeless degree on the basis of male assumptions designed to perpetuate men's domination over women. We will return to this issue shortly.

Against this historical background, we now wish to place Church teachings about gender into a comparative context. Let us consider three different perspectives drawn from the current spectrum of views about women and gender: (1) women are inherently inferior to men and should play roles reflecting that status; (2) there should be no prescription of women's roles; and (3) there are and should be role differences that are consistent with full equality.

Regarding the first perspective, a good deal of writing on women's issues since the 1960s assumes that American society has traditionally believed that women were inferior to men and should not participate in matters outside the home. Those holding this view assert that Western society has regarded women as mentally and physically inferior to men ever since the time of Plato and Aristotle. They say the early Christian thinkers believed that Eve showed typically evil female character when she deserted divine law in the Garden of Eden. They add that the English and American legal systems not long ago regarded a wife as the property of her husband. They then draw analogies between slavery and a wife's role as a perpetual servant. From this vantage point, they say, it is no wonder that pre-1960 American society often stereotyped its women as sexy temptresses, nagging bores, or useless stage props who stand helplessly watching while men solve all existing problems.

Many people have accepted some of these ideas throughout Western history, either because they believed them or because they claimed to believe them as a justification for exploiting women. Early in this century, James E. Talmage recognized the existence of this view and criticized it:

> The female sex is not infrequently referred to as the weaker of the two. As gauged by physical standards this classification may be essentially correct. And be it said to the discredit and shame of the stronger sex, man through the centuries gone has

been prone to use his superior strength to the
oppression of woman. She has suffered the greatest
humiliation during periods of spiritual darkness
when the Gospel of Christ was forgotten. . . .
Woman shall yet come to her own, exercising her
rights and her privileges as a sanctified investiture
which none shall dare profane.[10]

These words of concern and sympathy echo the Lord's
words to the prophet Jacob: "I, the Lord, have seen the sorrow, and heard the mourning of the daughters of my people
in the land of Jerusalem, yea, and in all the lands of my
people, because of the wickedness and abominations of their
husbands. . . . For they shall not lead away captive the
daughters of my people because of their tenderness, save I
shall visit them with a sore curse, even unto destruction."
(Jacob 2:31, 33.)

Nevertheless, at least some of the feminist writing in the
'60s and '70s that claimed to document cultural beliefs in
female inferiority may have been written with some exag-
geration to help justify the case for reform. For example,
Betty Friedan's call in the early 1960s for women to "get out
of the house and get an honest job" has been criticized for
the extreme way it "held the American woman in contempt.
No male supremacist in the country could have outdone her.
. . . According to Friedan, the entire occupation of American
wife and mother consisted of 'tasks for feeble-minded girls
and eight-year-olds.'"[11]

Actually, some important historical evidence suggests that
American men have long since regarded American women
with profound respect. For example, Tocqueville found in
1830 that

In the United States, men . . . constantly display
an entire confidence in the understanding of a wife,
and a profound respect for her freedom: they have
decided that her mind is just as fitted as that of a

225

man to discover the plain truth, and her heart as firm
to embrace it. . . . I do not hesitate to avow that,
although the women of the United States are con-
fined within the narrow circle of domestic life, and
their situation is, in some respects, one of extreme
dependence, I have nowhere seen women occupy-
ing a loftier position; and if I were asked . . . to what
the singular prosperity and growing strength of [the
American] people ought mainly to be attributed, I
should reply, to the superiority of their women.[12]

In addition, during the founding era of American society,
most people shared the assumptions of "republicanism"—
essentially a belief in "representative" forms of social, economic, and political action. Our political system was not
originally designed as a mass "town meeting style" democracy; rather, we originally relied on such examples of representative government as the use of "electors" in the national
electoral college and the use of state legislatures to elect sen-
ators to the national government. The complex process by
which our institutions have been gradually "democratized"
since about 1830 is beyond the scope of our present discussion. But the widely shared eighteenth- and nineteenth- (and
early twentieth-) century view of the American family as an
"entity"—something like a corporation—headed by a "representative" father had both its roots and its rationale in the
concepts of representative government and republicanism.

The older—even ancient—notion of status further ampli-
fies this understanding.[13] Thus, in the political and economic
marketplace, it was the father's role in "the little republic" of
a family to represent not just his own needs and views but
those of his family as an entity having its own collective
interests. While too many fathers may have exploited the
degree of discretion this understanding gave them, at least
this concept helps explain why our early legal and social
assumptions seemed to merge the identities of husband and
wife.

In this organizational environment, the traditional dependence of American women in a "narrow circle of domestic life" was not merely the result of a belief in women's inferiority; rather, it was partly the result of a conscious social commitment to the significance of home and family as the wellspring of cultural quality and continuity. The father represented the family in the political and economic world, often earning what many employers regarded as a "family wage" rather than purely personal income. These ideas consciously tried to protect the domestic arena from the ravages of political and economic warfare, not because women and children mattered so little, but because they mattered so much—and society wanted children raised in environments best suited to their personal growth. As George Gilder explains in *Men and Marriage,* the mothering instinct of women is the crucial force in developing long-term patterns of social stability; and one hallmark of civilized society is when men learn from their women to identify with their children.[14]

Gilder suggests that without this taming of the male wanderlust, many men, like the males of the animal species, might still be off on hunting parties, neither knowing nor caring for their offspring. Fortunately, some men have always had a natural affection for their children, but in the typical division of male and female labor since the earliest origins of our culture, women have usually been the primary developers of the moral, aesthetic, religious, and social concerns that enable and nurture our ultimate human aspirations. The "dependence" of women in this pattern has been primarily a need for physical protection, economic sustenance, and cooperation in the sharing of domestic duties—support tasks performed by men to enable and protect the primary cultural tasks performed by women.

This same domestic commitment to the rearing and education of children has eternally claimed the highest priority of God himself. As he has said, it is his "work and [his] glory to bring to pass the immortality and eternal life of man." (See Moses 1:39.) Of all the things he could have chosen to do, our Father in Heaven rivets his attention first of all on us, his children. That is why men or women who find no joy in helping their children learn and grow are not likely to be very happy in the celestial kingdom. That is also why Elder Neal A. Maxwell said of today's faithful Latter-day Saint mothers, "You rock a sobbing child without wondering if today's world is passing you by, because you know you hold tomorrow tightly in your arms."[15]

The second view of women—that there should be no prescription of women's roles—is, in significant part, a reaction against the innate inferiority view. This view rejects the very idea of women's "roles," and it does so on two different grounds—"unisex equality," which was a dominant theme of the women's movement in the 1970s, and some versions of feminism, a theme of the 1980s and '90s.

Those committed to unisex equality have argued not only that women are the equal of men but also that there are no innate distinctions between males and females significant enough to justify any difference in role, whether in domestic, political, or economic spheres. The unisex philosophy rejects any social convention that assumes there is such a thing as a "female role."

Therefore, laws against abortion are said to chain women's bodies to the slavery of a childbearing role. Proponents of this view assert that traditional attitudes about marriage make wives subservient to husbands, while the social ethic of motherhood is simply another way to keep women from pursuing career goals. They also condemn laws against homosexuality and the concept of illegitimate children on the grounds that these ideas are designed to force women into marriages with men as the condition of allowing them to have children.

Unisex feminists also condemn institutional religions,

especially those having strong patriarchal traditions, because of religion's strong influence in defining roles for men and women. In the words of Elizabeth Cady Stanton, a prominent nineteenth-century feminist, "the religious superstitions of women perpetuate their bondage more than all other adverse influences."[16] This hostility toward religion is directed at both the Old and New Testaments, which reflect implicit assumptions about the role of women in family life as well as in church organizations.

The more recent philosophy of radical feminism also condemns ideas about roles for women, but for reasons that go well beyond a belief in absolute equality. We should distinguish here between two very different forms of feminism that are frequently confused today. At one end of the broad spectrum of modern feminist thought is "equity feminism," which represents the very general goal of fairness and equal dignity for both genders. This attitude "advocates the equality of women and men and seeks to remove inequities and to redress injustices against women."[17] The Church and most Americans have shared this goal for many years, supporting gender equality and equal opportunity in a wide range of employment and educational settings.[18]

At the other end of the spectrum of feminist thought is the "radical feminist critique." Between equity feminism and the radical critique along this spectrum is a large variety of feminist ideas and approaches, many of which are now emerging in the academic disciplines. Many forms of moderate scholarly feminism emphasize the unique dimensions of women's experiences and perspectives. They also seek to broaden society's governing paradigms to include such female values as nurturing, cooperation, and personal relationships. These aspirations have great merit. Only by including women's perceptions with those of men can our social institutions reflect and foster meaningful interdependence throughout society.

This spirit of inclusion has direct applications in Church leadership councils. For example, Elder M. Russell Ballard has counseled priesthood leaders to be "seeking the vital input of the sisters in your council meetings," not just regarding women's auxiliary programs but also on missionary service, "temple attendance and a host of other matters."[19] In addition, greater awareness of women's unique experiences can help men see how their own failures to model the attributes of godliness can undermine the ability of women to develop a correct perception of God.[20]

However, as we move to the radical critique at the extreme end of the feminist spectrum, we find the hypothesis that all Western institutions were designed by men to perpetuate male power over women and that the male paradigm of meaning not only pervades but controls these institutions. Some radical feminist writers thus argue that Western institutions and ideas on every subject from marriage and family life to literature and the legal system are so contaminated with male bias that we must discard all prevailing assumptions and revolutionize the culture.[21]

For instance, the radical critique regards "the family as an institution of repression for women."[22] Some radical feminists thus claim, despite growing evidence of massive marital instability in the United States, that the two-parent family based on "lifelong commitments" may simply be impossible because, they complain, "a stable marriage system depends upon systemic forms of inequality" between men and women.[23]

Such challenges can prod us to discover limitations in ourselves and in our institutions that we might otherwise miss. But, as we have recently learned about Marxism, we must examine any single-issue explanation of human history with a healthy skepticism. The radical feminist critique's primary problem is its potential to undermine religious faith when it devalues hierarchical institutions to the point of rejecting scripture, priesthood authority, and prophets. The biggest risk of the radical critique, then, is not that it favors women, but that it can disfavor divine revelation.

For example, an uncritical application of the radical critique might describe the practice of polygamy in Joseph Smith's day as men falsely claiming divine revelation to justify the domination of women. And the same mind-set that rejects a male-dominated legislature's attempt to regulate abortion could also reject the teaching of an all-male First Presidency and Quorum of the Twelve that elective abortion is a grievous sin. Similar assumptions have led some women to pray only to their Mother in Heaven, because they believe that only a being who has a female frame of mind can fully understand a woman—as if the all-knowing God were not really all-knowing.

At the extreme, this reasoning can lead women to reject the counsel of a male bishop or to believe that marriage is by definition repressive. It can regard many forms of heterosexual intimacy as rape, since it may regard male initiative as an expression of male dominance. In its saddest form, this reasoning might ultimately lead someone to reject the Savior and his Atonement, simply because he is male.

It is not difficult to imagine that too many men over too many years have exploited and abused the very women who most deserved their trust. Any such abuse is too much. In a similar way, too many women have been "subordinate rather than privileged participants in the institutions and ideologies of male supremacy."[24] As we saw earlier in the words of Jacob, the Lord has condemned male abuses of women in the most forceful terms possible. He has also said that when any priesthood holder exercises "control or dominion or compulsion upon the souls of the children of men, in any degree of unrighteousness . . . Amen to the priesthood or the authority of that man." (D&C 121:37.)

But when one's acceptance of extreme feminist ideology

transforms legitimate questions about cases of actual abuse into a cynicism so general that it challenges all priesthood authority and then the Lord himself, one risks saying amen to his or her own religious faith. At that point, radical feminism becomes a new religion—the source of ultimate trust. When the commitment to exclusive female autonomy makes people "intent on defining themselves and their purpose for existing," they have "made [themselves] the authority over church and God."[25]

Consider now the third general viewpoint about women and gender. This is the perspective we believe the scriptures and the prophets have long taught: that women are unquestionably the spiritual and intellectual equal of men, having talents and opportunities that extend well beyond the home; yet, there are some God-given, doctrinally based differences between the sexes that we should recognize, appreciate and rely on.

For example, citing the eternal nature of each person's gender, Elder Boyd K. Packer taught in the October 1993 general conference that "different roles of man and woman are set forth in exalted celestial declarations."[26] And, noting that "we live in a day when there are many political, legal, and social pressures for changes that confuse gender and homogenize the differences between men and women," Elder Dallin H. Oaks stated in the same general conference that "maleness and femaleness" are "essential to the great plan of happiness."[27]

With this perspective, we learn that Mother Eve's initial partaking of the forbidden fruit was not a reckless mistake that left her and "her daughters . . . somehow flawed;"[28] rather, according to Elder John A. Widtsoe, what she and Adam did was an act of "sacrifice and courage," making Adam and Eve the "greatest and noblest of the human race."[29] Even though the serpent beguiled Eve, she and Adam would have had no children had they remained in the

Garden. (See 2 Nephi 2:23.) Thus, Elder Widtsoe wrote that God's commandment against eating the fruit was primarily a *warning* of the hazards and the sorrow that would accompany the choice to bear children in the lone and dreary world of mortality.[30] From the very beginning, the "mother of all living" showed the heroic maternal faith that is willing to walk down into the valley of the dark shadows, not only to bring forth a child but also to bring forth understanding and joy to his or her parents.

This view of women emulates the Savior's own attitudes. During his earthly ministry, even at a time when Jewish traditions precluded the active participation of women in discussing religious doctrine with him, Mary and Martha were among Jesus' closest friends and followers. And even though women were not accepted as competent witnesses under Jewish law, Mary Magdalene was "the first mortal to see a resurrected person."[31] And it was Mary and other women who went to the apostles to first tell them that his body was gone from the tomb.

As Elder Bruce R. McConkie once stated, "In all matters that pertain to godliness and holiness and which are brought to pass as a result of personal righteousness—in all these things men and women stand in a position of absolute equality before the Lord. He is no respecter of persons nor of sexes, and he . . . delights to honor [all] those who serve him in righteousness unto the end—both male and female."[32]

Closer to our own day, the Church's record shows great support for the idea of gender equity. The women of pioneer times were among the great figures of Church history. Utah's women were the first in the nation to exercise the right to vote. Utah produced the nation's first woman state senator, the first woman mayor, and the first editors of a women's magazine in the western United States.

President Joseph F. Smith described his perspective about women this way:

> Man and woman are begotten of the same father, are born of the same mother, possess the same life, . . . exist by the same means, both bear the divine image and possess the same divine nature. . . . Then why shall one enjoy civil rights and the other be denied them? Why shall one be admitted to all the avenues of mental and physical progress and prosperity and the other be prohibited . . . ? Shall a man be paid higher wages than is paid to a woman for doing no better than she does the very same work? Shall the avenues for employment be multiplied to men and diminished to women by the mere dictum or selfishness of men?[33]

And in stating the Church's position on the Equal Rights Amendment in 1978, the First Presidency said, "Latter-day Saint women . . . know how deeply the Church encourages them to exercise their free agency. . . . [They] are strongly encouraged to develop their individual talents, to broaden their learning and to expand their contributions to activities such as religious, governmental, cultural, educational, and community pursuits."[34] At the same time, because a mother is "the primary nurturer of the children,"[35] Church teachings have consistently taken the position that "mothers *who have young children in the home* should devote their primary energies to the companionship and training of their children and the care of their families." So these mothers "should not seek employment outside the home unless there is no other way that the family's basic needs can be provided."[36]

This perspective on women also clarifies desirable male attitudes as well. "Consider the implication of [the phrase], 'A woman leads with her heart, a man with his head.' This essentially says that a woman can't think and a man can't feel."[37] Unisex attitudes that accept this cliché sometimes cause women to reflect "macho" male tendencies—even though our society has sometimes stereotyped men as unfeeling beasts having characteristics undesirable in either sex.

The world has long tried to convince men that it is not manly to be refined, kind, or spiritually sensitive. This suggests that the hands of a "real" man would be out of place holding the hand of a child, soothing the fevered brow of a sick wife, or being placed on someone's head to give a needed blessing. But when we think of the hands of Joseph Smith or Brigham Young, Moses, Peter, or the Savior himself, we see strong, masculine hands in the posture of blessing, serving, and loving in gentleness and tenderness. When we think of the hands of an Elder (as well as Doctor) Russell Nelson, we feel a deep gratitude for hands so finely trained that they can perform surgery on the heart of a prophet of God and also be worthy to be placed on that same prophet's head in a blessing of the priesthood. We pray that our own sons will have such trained, strong, worthy, and gentle hands.

And just as it is good for a man to have tender feelings, it is good for a woman to have a thoughtful, probing, and educated intellect. Masculinity has no monopoly of the mind, and femininity has no monopoly of the heart. There are many desirable characteristics that have nothing to do with gender. As Elder Boyd K. Packer noted, "All virtues listed in the scriptures—love, joy, peace, faith, godliness, charity—are shared by both men and women."[38] Consider these descriptive, gender-neutral terms: teacher, child of God, loving parent, trained professional, student of the scriptures, faithful follower of Christ, devoted companion, loyal employee, trusted friend. Consider also the word *parent*. Women can aspire to no greater role in life than that of wife and mother; and men can aspire to no greater role than that of husband and father. Some modern critics underestimate the value of parenthood for either gender, because they overemphasize the materialistic and self-centered assumptions of careerism and competitive getting ahead—for both genders.

Unfortunately, one of the side effects of the women's movement's preoccupation with careers has been a growing public attitude that unless *society* places some tangible economic value on such domestic tasks as child rearing, the labor is of questionable worth. This makes both women and men believe they should measure the meaning of their lives according to career achievement. This discourages career-oriented men from developing nurturing instincts, denying them and their children the sweet joy of meaningful child-parent communication. It also denies home-oriented women the reassurance of feeling that their husbands recognize and value their critically important work as mothers and home-makers—valuing it enough to help carry the load.

The recent quest for gender equality in American society has sent especially confusing messages to women by devaluing not only motherhood but also "the primary work of most women throughout most of history."[39] This circumstance creates a compelling need for Latter-day Saints to reaffirm in all their relationships and conversations the gospel model of gender, which teaches both men and women to take their domestic roles more seriously than they take any other role.

In addition, the gospel model in the present climate cries out for men and women to take each other more seriously in every other phase of life. Fathers, husbands, and local priesthood leaders will note the recent pleading of the Church's leaders for men to increase their sensitivity on gender issues, avoiding any form of unrighteous dominion.[40] Priesthood leaders will include women leaders in Church council discussions.[41] They will affirm the value of being wives and mothers, and they will show as much concern about Beehive girls and Relief Society lessons as they do about deacons and high priests' meetings. LDS men attending college will respect the educational goals of their LDS women classmates, rather than implying, as some do, that women attend college for social rather than educational reasons. Young women will seek both marriage and education rather than feeling they must choose between the two. Each man and each woman will open ears and hearts to understand, respond to, and cooperate with the "different voice" of the other—rather than assuming that the other's experience is invalid when it does not match his or her own.

The generic term *feminism* seeks many of these goals, because it is essentially concerned with full human acceptance and equal human treatment. Yet so many voices and views claim allegiance to feminism today that the word itself is no longer very meaningful. For example, when we confuse equity feminism with radical feminism, not even seeing the broad spectrum between those two points, those who fear the destructive potential of radical feminism may unwittingly undermine the Church's commitment to equal treatment, dignity, and fairness for women. Thus, one of today's hazards is that, in reactions against the narrow and militant version of feminism that can choke off the roots of religious faith, some of us may unwittingly deafen our ears to "the cries of the fair daughters of this people" (Jacob 2:32), thereby enlarging "the wounds of those who are already wounded" (Jacob 2:9).

Finally, Hugh Nibley has explained that historically, both patriarchy and matriarchy have been fundamentally destructive when they are driven by the lust for power over other people: "According to the oldest mythologies, all the troubles of the race are but a perennial feud between the Matriarchy and the Patriarchy; between men and women seeking power and gain at each other's expense." This feud reflects the determination "to rule in hell rather than be ruled in heaven."[42] The adversary has long—and especially recently—exploited this will toward power, forcing men and women apart, drying up "the milk of human kindness" in both genders, pitting them against one another to destroy our divinely given aspiration toward love and belonging. Any version of feminism or patriarchy that drives such wedges between male and female comes from him who seeks our eternal misery. In either time or eternity, "neither is the man without the woman, neither the woman without the man, in the Lord." (1 Corinthians 11:11.)

CHAPTER FIFTEEN

From Status to Contract: Belonging and the Ancient Order

The very idea of permanently "belonging" to a family or a group was much more natural and instinctive for people in the ancient world than it is for people in the modern world. One of Western history's largest themes is the gradual evolution of our cultural assumptions from an emphasis on the group to an emphasis on the individual. An important reason for this evolution was that, over time, too many people oppressed and abused others, exploiting the commitments of trust and dependence that characterized the original groups. Without ignoring these abuses, we can help recover the meaning of belonging today by looking briefly into history for some understanding of humankind's original ideas about personal relationships and social roles. To that end, this chapter explores one historian's "status to contract" thesis.

The idea of belonging in family groups has such deep historical roots that, according to English legal historian Sir Henry Maine, the people of ancient times regarded society as an aggregation of families rather than a collection of individuals. The social and legal unit of ancient society was the family, while the unit of modern society is the individual. In a celebrated generalization, Maine wrote that, since primitive times, "the movement of the progressive societies has . . . been distinguished by the gradual dissolution of family dependency and the growth of individual obligation in its place." As the law reflected this development, Maine found that the interpersonal link that came to replace the intuitive sense of traditional family duties was the idea of making and keeping a voluntary contract. Hence, Maine wrote, "we may say that the movement of the progressive societies has hitherto been a movement from Status to Contract."[1]

As one result of this centuries-long trend, contemporary society now operates according to far more flexible assumptions than was true anciently about the *roles* individuals play in families, groups, or communities. This is partly because the modern mind assumes roles are to be voluntarily chosen, negotiated, and changed whenever one desires. The ancient idea of fixed, permanent roles seems foreign and even threatening to us. Thus today, the very concept of role has lost much—perhaps most—of its former meaning. Maine's insight gives us historical perspective on the individualistic forces that have shaped this change in our cultural thinking. His distinction between status and contract also helps us see that some sense of role still persists—even if not always clearly—in our thinking about "belonging" to a marriage, a family, or the Church. This is because these relationships still reflect the last remaining vestiges of the ancient concept of status.

Let us illustrate and develop the meaning of *status* in the way Maine used the term; then we can consider his historical thesis with more understanding. He spoke not of social status or economic status. Rather, his idea suggests permanent membership in groups such as kinship-based families, tribes, or sovereign nations.

One example of such status is citizenship. Because of my *status* as a "citizen"—a permanent "member" of the United States—I enjoy a wide range of benefits, and I am subject to many obligations, even though I have never agreed in any voluntary sense to assume any particular list of either blessings or burdens of citizenship. Citizenship does not exist in matters of degree. I am either a citizen or I am not. I do have the choice of totally renouncing my citizenship, but I am not allowed to pick and choose which elements of citizenship I will accept. Citizenship is not a matter of agreeing to particular clauses in a contract. So if Congress passes a new law that applies to all citizens, I am obliged to obey that law, regardless of whether I agree with it.

Being a citizen assures me of many benefits. For instance, I may pursue the occupation of my choice, even with government support for my education. By contrast, noncitizens may work in the United States only under very limited and temporary conditions. As a citizen I am allowed to vote, hold public office, and enjoy the protection of the U.S. government when I am in other nations. In a more general sense, my citizenship lets me feel an intangible but profound sense of freedom that flows from knowing I am an American, protected and sustained by the freest, strongest nation on earth. I am protected not only by the Bill of Rights—I have also been promised what the Preamble to the U.S. Constitution calls "the blessings of liberty" embodied in a constitution inspired by the Lord himself.

Citizens of other free and democratic nations obviously enjoy similar privileges, but only to the extent that the status of citizenship has the same general meaning there as it has in America. Citizens of democratic societies really are the "owners" of their societies, and their governments are ultimately accountable to those having ownership status. Such is by no means the case in totalitarian states, dictatorships, or true monarchies, where the rulers are often the "owners," even when they claim to represent the interests of their people.

Our friend, Ara Call, once had an experience that taught

241

him vividly about the meaning of both his American citizenship and his citizenship in the Lord's kingdom. Brother Call was born in Mexico but later moved to the United States, where he acquired U.S. citizenship through federal naturalization laws. His foreign birth made him a citizen of both the United States and Mexico. In the early 1960s, President David O. McKay called Brother and Sister Call to preside over a mission for the Church in Mexico. Soon after the Calls had accepted this assignment, President McKay and his counselors invited them into a special meeting and informed them that Mexico's constitution did not allow the Church to own property there in its own name. So the Church needed to record the legal title to its Mexican chapels and other properties in the personal name of a Mexican citizen in whom the First Presidency had absolute confidence. Expressing such confidence in Brother Call, the Brethren asked if they could place the Church property titles in his name.

As Ara was about to express his acceptance, the Brethren informed him of one chilling condition: the laws of Mexico required that, to be legally qualified to hold title to the Church's properties, he could not be a dual citizen; rather, he must renounce his U.S. citizenship. President J. Reuben Clark observed, "Oh, this is too much to ask of anyone." But they saw no other alternative.

This request tested to the limits Ara Call's "utmost zeal"[2] for the Church. But in great humility and soberness, he voluntarily gave up his treasured U.S. citizenship "status" because he had consecrated himself without limits to his higher "status" as a citizen of God's kingdom. In deep gratitude, President McKay placed his hand on Brother Call's shoulder and promised him that what he was doing would not impose a permanent hardship on him and his family.

Years later, pursuant to a special appeal filed after his mission, Ara was able finally to reclaim his U.S. citizenship. But the American government had given him absolutely no assurance of that outcome when he first relinquished that citizenship.[3]

Citizenship carries great blessings, but it can also impose far-reaching obligations. For example, sovereign nations may test the "utmost zeal" of their citizens' patriotism by drafting them for military service. Many thousands of Americans have laid their lives upon this altar of citizenship, giving what Abraham Lincoln called "the last full measure of devotion."

When we compare national citizenship with the status of citizenship in the church and kingdom of God, we realize the parallel implications of both *unlimited* blessings and *unlimited* commitments. Just as our nation is committed to defend its citizens to the death, if need be, its citizens are committed to defend the nation to that same ultimate degree. In the Lord's kingdom, just as the Savior has given his life for those who accept the full status of being children of Christ, Joseph Smith taught that this status may ask of them a similarly unqualified commitment—any sacrifice; if necessary, even their lives.[4] The source of this duty is not a contract of limited covenants that is enforceable at law. Rather, the *unlimited,* unqualified duties of citizenship originate in the higher law of permanent belonging that defines the very nature of status. So it is with family status.

For example, when Jesus was dying on the cross, he felt great compassion for Mary, his mother. He wanted John, his beloved apostle, to care for Mary following his crucifixion. His requests of both John and Mary vividly illustrate the meaning of family status: rather than asking John to care for Mary with a list of particular requests, he made a request for unqualified, lifelong support in the simplest expression of family status: "Woman," he said to Mary, "behold thy son!" And to John, "Behold thy mother!" Because of the ancient concept of status, both John and Mary knew what was expected of them: the status of motherhood and sonship inherently confers the concept of unlimited duty on any who carry such titles. Thus, "from that hour," John "took her unto his own home." (John 19:26–27.)

Or, in the more modern terms of Father Flanagan's Boystown motto, "He ain't heavy—he's my brother." Put another way, it doesn't matter how heavy he is, because my commitment to my brother is based on a permanent, unalterable relationship of mutual belonging, not on my having agreed to carry him as long as he isn't heavier than I can conveniently manage. Since ancient times, the kinship relationship between brothers and sisters, or parents and children, has known no limits; so the load of carrying a kinsman can, by the nature of the relationship, never become too heavy. This deeply embedded cultural assumption explains Robert Frost's declaration that home is where, when you have to go there, they have to take you in.[5]

Since our earliest history, *kinship* has conveyed—and in most societies still conveys—something about the bonds and blessings of status. In describing the foundations of kinship in nonindustrial tribal societies, the late BYU anthropologist Merlin Myers recounted the story of a Navajo friend who said that "when he was a young boy, his grandmother took him to her and said, 'My eyes have become your eyes, and my hands have become your hands.' What she meant by this was that since she had gotten old and was no longer capable of seeing and doing with [her own] eyes and hands what she had been wont to do, all would be well because the eyes and hands she had given him would now work for her. Think of the peace and security that must crown the heart of an old person in such an arrangement."[6]

Why would the grandmother assume that this boy would be willing to help her see with his eyes and feel with his hands? As with Mary and the Apostle John, her assumption—and probably the child's—originated in the implicit meaning of status in true kinship: "She isn't blind—she's my grandmother."

The concept of status is also reflected in our use of the noun *order* to describe solemn and permanent relationships that confer blessings and duties so unlimited as to transcend ordinary relationships. For instance, ever since the medieval era, history has recorded the stories of those who entered monastic orders with lifetime commitments of poverty, chastity, and obedience. And the knights of King Arthur's time entered into orders of knighthood that imposed heavy obligations and benefits upon those who pledged their skill, their devotion, and even their lives for the ultimate good of the order.

These orders may well be imitative remnants of the ancient order of the holy priesthood. Before the time of Melchizedek, the higher priesthood was known as *"the Holy Priesthood, after the Order of the Son of God."* (D&C 107:3.) Book of Mormon prophets, such as Jacob and Alma, described their status-based belonging to the priesthood as their having been "ordained after the manner of his [God's] holy order." (2 Nephi 6:2; see also Alma 4:20; Psalm 110:4; Hebrews 5:6; Ether 12:10; D&C 76:5.) Alma taught that "the Lord God ordained priests, after his holy order, which was after the order of his Son, to teach these things [the gospel] unto the people. And those priests were ordained after the order of his Son, in a manner that thereby the people might know in what manner to look forward to his Son for redemption." (Alma 13:1–2.) Elsewhere the Lord distinguished the greater or Melchizedek Priesthood from the lower or Aaronic Priesthood by stating that the greater priesthood "is after the holiest order of God." (D&C 84:18.)

The United Order of the nineteenth-century Church is another instance in which membership in or entry to a sacred order carried a status-based sense of obligation to the common good that far transcended the always-limited and self-oriented contractualism of commercial agreements. The Lord in 1834 commanded that this order "be organized and established, to be a united order, and an everlasting order for the benefit of my church . . . with promise *immutable and unchangeable*" (D&C 104:1–2; emphasis added), subject only to the faithfulness of the members of the order. Those who entered the United Order, whether in the limited form practiced in Kirtland or the full communal form practiced later in places like Orderville, Utah, all accepted the basic principles of consecration and stewardship. Brigham Young once explained that under these principles, which are also significant in the modern Church, the Saints offered "everything [they] possessed upon the altar for the use and benefit of the Kingdom of God."[7] That unqualified commitment flowed from one's permanent, status-based covenants in the order of God's kingdom.

We may also—even now—describe marriage as "the order of matrimony." This language and its echo of a true and ancient meaning may also be an imitative remnant of a sacred, eternal, and priesthood-based concept of marriage as status: "In order to obtain the highest [degree of the celestial glory], a man must enter into *this order of the priesthood [meaning the new and everlasting covenant of marriage]; and if he does not, he cannot obtain it.*" (D&C 131:2; brackets in the original, emphasis added.) Under this anciently ordered concept, marriage, like citizenship, is very different from an agreement to perform specific tasks in exchange for specific benefits. By accepting the status of being a husband or wife, marital partners under the order of the priesthood assume responsibilities and promises so unlimited and unspecified as to be eternal in both kind and duration. With this understanding, marriage is as permanent and unqualified as kinship or citizenship.

The ancient concept of status is also illustrated by the tradition that one or a few members of a clan could, by their individual action, bring a blessing or a curse to the entire group. The action of a group member could profoundly affect the glory or the shame of the group, because his or her personal action was always perceived as being on behalf of the group. The feuding Hatfields and McCoys illustrate this idea: if a McCoy injures one Hatfield, he has injured them all; hence, revenge by a Hatfield upon any McCoy is revenge upon the entire clan. Consider similarly the identification that some cities or schools establish with their athletic teams, or rivalries between neighboring towns or schools.

With this understanding of the general nature and meaning of *status,* let us further consider Sir Henry Maine's thesis that the gradual historical movement of Western society has moved *from status toward contract* as the basis for social cooperation and interactive human relationships.

Maine's work showed that the unit of which ancient societies took account for social, legal, or other reasons was the family, not the individual. This meant that individuals derived their identity from their role or place (their status) in the larger order. For example, in ancient societies real property was owned by tribal groups, not by individual owners. Thus, the Lord gave a promised land to Abraham and to Lehi not in their personal capacities but in their capacities as patriarchs for and in behalf of their extended families—their "seed," theoretically forever. Under this arrangement, the leader held the property essentially as a trustee, keeping it in trust for the clan—for the permanent benefit of his people and their descendants. If he then exploited the property for his personal benefit, he would be violating that trust.

The family trustee was not free to sell the property, because the very idea of selling land rather than passing it by inheritance did not develop in Western thought until after about A.D. 1100 in England. Until that time, the typical pattern of primogeniture dictated that when the patriarch died, the oldest living male family member who was otherwise qualified would assume responsibility to administer the collectively owned property for the good of the group. A similar pattern governed the transfer of property rights under the ancient laws of both Hebrew society and the Nephite society that derived its practices from the Hebrews.[8]

Since the time of antiquity, one of the clearest and most recent examples of a true status-based culture was the feudal society of the European middle ages. This historical period occurred toward the end of the domination of European society by the Catholic Church and the Roman Empire and before the rise of proud nationalism in France, Germany, England, and elsewhere in Europe. Feudal estates often became self-sufficient little kingdoms in which natural divisions of labor provided all that the feudal community needed for a stable existence. From the peasants to the lord and lady of the feudal manor, each community member knew and accepted his or her role.

As vividly illustrated by the players on a chess board, which is a direct reflection of the feudal era, all the members of a feudal manor had roles so fixed that their status determined how far and in what direction they could "move." The "knights" provided military protection, the "bishops" provided religious order, the "pawns" worked the land in large numbers, all through oaths of fealty to the "king" and "queen" of the manor.

Because the members of feudal society accepted these roles so fully, they lived in remarkable security made possible by the performance of their reciprocal understanding with one another. As a leading European historian said of medieval society:

> There was one major form of political relationship (feudalism), and a dominant economic arrangement (manorial agriculture). There was an all-embracing social structure, too, made up of clergy, nobility, and commoners, each with its assigned functions and legal status. . . . [This system produced] a strong sense of security, of "belonging." This does not mean physical security, of course, . . . but there was *psy-*

chological security for most men and women. They seldom had reason to feel isolated or rejected. Their Christian faith told them that their role in life . . . was divinely ordained, and all that was required of them was to live out their days according to approved custom.[9]

Whether in the ancient world or in feudal times, status and collective identity did not always guarantee individual happiness. Indeed, from the beginning of the ancient, status-based orders, individual members of a group were at times subjected to great abuse. As such abuses multiplied, the willingness of group members to continue thinking of themselves in terms of unalterable status was continually eroded. As long as tribal leaders and local kings observed the conditions that have always governed the legitimacy of patriarchal power (see D&C 121:36–46), individuals who derived their sense of identity from belonging to a larger order could be blessed with security, opportunity, and freedom. But the actual record of status-based systems increasingly proved the wisdom of Mosiah's counsel: "If it were possible that you could have just men to be your kings . . . who would do even as my father Benjamin did for this people . . . it would be expedient that ye should always have kings to rule over you." But "because all men are not just it is not expedient that ye should have a king or kings to rule over you. For behold, how much iniquity doth one wicked king cause to be committed." (Mosiah 29:13, 16–17.)

One vivid example of the arbitrariness of customary law in status-oriented systems comes from a Chinese film, *The Girl from Hunan*. Set in late nineteenth-century China, this film relates the story of a teenage girl in a village governed by the customs of patriarchal law. Early in the story, the girl witnesses the punishment the village patriarch directs against an older woman who was caught in the act of adultery. Without listening to any explanation she might have given, the village leaders bind her hand and foot, take her on a raft to the middle of a deep lake, then push her off into the water to drown. Not long after this incident, the teenage girl is raped by her uncle. She becomes pregnant—the obvious badge of adultery for an unmarried woman. The village system has no procedural protection for the falsely accused person: to be pregnant out of wedlock requires capital punishment, regardless of explanations, because upholding the rules and honor of the clan is more important than any individual's "rights." The girl's anguish in this system provides the drama for the remainder of the story.

Still, not all of the power conferred by status-based societies was abused. During much of feudal society, for example, "the upper classes enjoyed a good deal of independence, and authority was not exercised so thoroughly as to cripple freedom of mind and spirit. . . . Though living in a comparatively rigid society, people improvised, improved, and invented. This was as true in farming, commerce, and warfare as it was in law, education, literature, and the arts. . . . These admirable features have led some modern writers to adopt a nostalgic attitude toward the Age of Faith," despite the "famine, disease, and violence" that also characterized this era.[10]

The breakup of the feudal societies—and with it, the gradual breakup of status as an ordering concept—was caused by too many large-scale forces to recount here, but a brief sketch may illuminate the contrast between today's contractual society and the vestiges of ancient status that still shape and inform our ideas about marriage, family life, and religion.

At the relatively specific level of English legal history, the accelerating movement from status toward contract began at about A.D. 1200 with such ideas as wills and deeds. Property owners began finding ways to sell their property or to direct its disposition by a customized will rather than leaving such transfers to the sometimes arbitrary laws of inheritance. Marriage began to be seen as a matter of voluntary agreement rather than an arrangement between two families that predated and superseded the preferences of the parties to the marriage. The general concept of freedom of choice emerged as a major theme in these developments, emphasizing the idea that people should not be bound to relationships or obligations they did not voluntarily elect to enter.

At more general levels, European (and, eventually, American) history in the post-feudal era became a boiling cauldron of truly revolutionary developments, virtually all of which gave increasing priority to individual identity over group membership. The long-dominant power of the Roman Catholic Church was superseded by nationalistic forces that developed their own religious preferences, whether by the "divine right of kings" in France and England or by the individualistic flavor of the Protestant Reformation in Germany. Increases in trade, commerce, and personal mobility broke down traditional barriers of geography, language, and culture. Science and philosophy began to assert the individual's educated capacity to understand and control the forces to which people in earlier times felt almost helplessly subject. The arbitrary unfairness of certain class-based social, economic, and political patterns was increasingly exposed.

In all these movements, no idea was more powerful or more pervasive than the theme of the American Revolution in 1776: all men are created equal and are endowed with God-given individual rights. This philosophical assertion, which became entrenched in American soil more than in any other place, had originated in the minds of Europeans who advocated the ideas of liberty and equality to express their growing political discontent with the European aristocracy and other elements of status-like class systems. Actually, Sir Henry Maine documented his case for the status-to-contract theme in order to refute the claims of political revolutionaries that humankind had begun its history in a "state of nature" characterized by natural personal rights and political freedoms. Whatever had actually happened historically, however, the long-term momentum toward contractual individualism had made the Western societies ripe to hear the message of individual rights philosophy.

At the same time, as political scientist Walter Berns has pointed out, the U.S. Constitution was concerned primarily with the political world, not with the private sphere of family life. To that end, the Constitution rejected centuries of abuse under aristocratic status as a political and economic concept, stressing natural equality "as far as *political* right is concerned."[11] In the political and economic realms of what political philosophers called "the Social Contract," the framers of the Constitution assumed that people would be "calculating, fear-motivated . . . individuals" who act in their own interest rather than serving the interests of others.[12]

However, both during and after the Constitution's adoption, eighteenth- and nineteenth-century Americans regarded the status-based sphere of home and family life as resting on entirely different principles. The tradition of status sought to protect "the family as the place of love," based not on the ruthless self-interest of the political and economic worlds but on "self-forgetting" and the "willingness to care for others."[13] In more recent times, however, American society has gradually merged the individualistic assumptions of politics and economics with the family sphere, thereby accelerating the transfer from status-based to contract-based attitudes in all family and other personal interaction.

By the early nineteenth century, the excesses of contractual individualism in America were beginning to emerge, and by the late nineteenth century, those self-centered tendencies had reached such extremes as to become politically, economically, and socially destructive. For example, "freedom of contract" offered little support for personal equality when the contracting parties consisted of a large, monopolistic corporation and a few powerless laborers. As a result, the labor union movement was born as a way to give group power to otherwise ineffective and isolated individuals. In other words, society began looking for new forms of status to enhance individual influence through the greater economic power of collective organizations. The nation's first antitrust laws were passed in 1890 in an attempt to check the anticompetitive force of industrial powers that were exploiting the absence of state regulation of business activity, which had grown out of the concepts of unlimited freedom of contract and a free market economy.

Our society has witnessed in more recent times an ever-mounting accumulation of evidence that the movement from community-oriented status to individual-oriented contract has gone too far. Ours is the age of existential anxiety and cosmic loneliness. As the German philosopher Friedrich Nietzsche expressed that loneliness, "'Where is—my home?' For it do I ask and seek, and have sought but have not found it. O eternal everywhere, O eternal nowhere, O eternal—in-vain."[14]

One result of this general sense of anomie and disconnectedness is that individuals have begun searching, sometimes with great urgency, for new forms of status, new forms of belonging to groups that will restore their sense of identity and personal meaning. Most of these affiliations today are motivated by political and economic interests by which the individual seeks to achieve "clout" through the combined power of group membership. This phenomenon is at work in groups that have common financial interests or common political/social action causes, consumer groups, ethnic groups, groups of disadvantaged persons and political minorities, and the vicious youth gangs now emerging in U.S. cities. Group action in the legal arena—class action lawsuits—has also become one of the most significant developments in recent years, as the individual victims of governmental or other institutional action have banded together to allege collective rather than individual violations of their rights.

But these expressions of the "new status" differ fundamentally from the ancient concept of status, because they seek mutual *self-interest* in collective *contracts*, not the bonds of full belonging implied by kinship or citizenship. They are also oriented more toward rights than duties; hence, they lack the power of ancient status to induce people voluntarily and gladly to carry burdens of unlimited size on unlimited journeys. Their mutual commitments also flow from narrow political or economic causes, not from covenanting one's entire sense of self. For such reasons, the new forms of status are essentially group contracts rather than restorations of the highest ancient meaning of status.

CHAPTER SIXTEEN

The Familistic Life: Status and Contract in Modern America

In 1830, the celebrated French observer Alexis de Tocqueville visited the United States to study the phenomenon of democracy in action. In his book *Democracy in America,* Tocqueville observed with remarkable insight that democracy's strong individualistic tendencies could, if unrestrained, tear apart the very connections that hold a free nation together. The "every man for himself" attitudes generated by free political institutions and a free market encouraged greed and selfishness in ways not seen in other systems.

Tocqueville also saw, however, that Americans were heavily involved in such status-based "voluntary associations" as schools, churches, family groups, and village governments. Noting that "Americans . . . are forever forming associations,"[1] he took great interest in American approaches to schools, religion, and family life. He found that the "mores" formed in these settings (which he called "the habits of the heart") promised to be "one of the great general causes responsible for the maintenance of a democratic republic in the United States,"[2] because "there have never been free societies without mores."[3] He foresaw that the teaching of mores in freely chosen "intellectual and moral associations" would "combat the effects of individualism" by restraining individualism's destructive, acquisitive appetites and developing a sense of personal and civic virtue.[4]

These voluntary associations were—and are—not only the seedbeds of democratic cooperation; they are also the places where individuals develop a personal sense of responsibility and purpose for their own lives. Thus the idea of *belonging* to a family, a church organization, or some other status-oriented local group historically provided a natural base for moral education that mediated between the private, self-centered world of individual freedom and the abstract public world of huge megastructures, such as the national government or giant corporations.

In a democratic society, the national megastructures make no claim to providing meaning and purpose for individual lives—they function solely to support the political and economic infrastructure that makes personal choices about meaning possible. But unless true mediating agencies fill the resulting cultural void, individuals will necessarily inhabit a vacuum of meaning. Thus, smaller-scale intellectual and moral mediating associations are needed as the "value-generating and value-maintaining agencies in society," the "little platoons" within which people define the purpose and shape the direction of their lives.[5]

Today, however, the movement from status to contract has progressed to the point of undermining the informal authority of mediating institutions as well. Indeed, contemporary studies report Americans' concern that the excessive individualism of our day—the furious preoccupation with self—"may have grown cancerous," undercutting the influence of such institutions as family, church, and local community in ways that threaten "the survival of freedom itself."[6]

One modern scholar, Robert Nisbet, has warned against the effects of this problem by arguing that the institutional strength of status-based mediating institutions provides a crucial protection against totalitarian threats to the stability of democracies. The totalitarian cannot succeed, writes Nisbet, until "the social contexts of privacy—family, church, association—have been atomized. The political *enslavement* of man requires the *emancipation* of man from all the [intermediate] authorities and memberships . . . that serve . . . to insulate the individual from external political power."[7] Nisbet warns that reducing the authority of status-based institutions creates exactly the kind of "spiritual and cultural vacuum" that "the totalitarian must have for the realization of his design."[8]

In order to restore the meaning of status—and thereby the meaning of belonging—we must re-identify and reinforce the nature of status-based relationships, especially within such influential mediating structures as the family and the Church. This emphasis is necessary not merely to preserve group or institutional interests but also to develop and maintain truly meaningful individual fulfillment over the long run, because the values of belonging are indispensable to personal growth.[9]

Toward this end, how might we think of the ancient idea of status as we live in the modern era? What would it mean to think of contemporary marriage or family relationships, or perhaps Church membership, in terms of status? One of the most valuable responses to these questions is in the work of the distinguished Russian/American scholar Pitirim Sorokin. He once outlined three distinct types or systems of personal interaction that occur throughout human societies: *familistic, contractual,* and *compulsory* relationships. As will be seen from a brief summary of Sorokin's analysis, his "familistic" relationships draw on the root concept of status in ways that apply to today's world.[10] Moreover, his descriptions of "contractual" and "compulsory" relationships provide contrasts that sharpen our understanding of what familistic relationships mean. (Unless the context indicates otherwise, the quoted phrases in the following summary of Sorokin's thought are his language.)

First, for Sorokin, *familistic* relationships are not only intimate but very broad in scope: "Their whole lives [are] intermingled and organically united into one 'we.'" Despite differences in sex, age, or other characteristics, the members of a familistic system share commitments of mutual attachment and interdependence that by definition transcend self-interest. A relationship of this kind "yields, as a by-product, pleasure and utility; but it entails also sorrow and sacrifice. However, the sacrifice is regarded not as a disadvantage or as the personal loss of some value, but as a privilege freely and gladly bestowed." Because these relationships are based upon an "unlimited ethical motivation," detailed or legalistic lists of rights and duties among members can hardly describe the nature of the relationship, let alone prescribe it.

Because group welfare and the interests of other people take priority in familistic ties, "there is no formal domination and subordination, no master and servant." The Doctrine and Covenants describes this same pattern for the "order" of marriage or other relationships governed by the "order" of the priesthood: "The rights of the priesthood are inseparably connected with the powers of heaven, and . . . the powers of heaven cannot be controlled nor handled only upon the principles of righteousness." (D&C 121:36.) The larger order to which individual interests are subordinated in this model is (or is like) the family unit, which has its own institutional existence. That the family entity is comprised of more than a collection of merely individual interests is reinforced by society's interest in stable marriage, reflected in the traditional idea that the state is a party to each marriage.

To an outside observer, the spontaneous and extensive demands of familistic commitments may appear to be "a severe limitation of the freedom of the parties," even at times "a frightful slavery." However, experience demonstrates that

258

familism can yield in the lives of its participants a surprising blend of "discipline with freedom" and "sacrifice with liberty," even to the point of high personal fulfillment.

Sorokin's description portrays an ideal form that, in practice, occurs in "many gradations and degrees of purity." As the term *familistic* implies, family relationships represent the prototype for this social system: It approaches its "purest form . . . between the members of a . . . harmonious family," even though, obviously, not "all or even the majority of the social relationships among members of the family are familistic." Familistic relationships may also exist "[in] a more diluted form . . . between devoted friends, between the members of a religious organization," and in other deeply bonded associational and personal ties.

Second, *contractual* interaction, on the other hand, rests on different assumptions. In a democratic and market-oriented society like the United States, most organizations' operations and the conduct of most human relationships are contractual. This form mixes friendly and antagonistic elements, but it is distinguished from familistic ties especially by its defined scope—it is *always "limited* in its extensity." This clear distinction between unlimited and limited commitments marks a clear-cut boundary between familistic and contractual relationships. Even though a contractual relationship may have high intensity within the defined scope of its interaction, it never involves a contracting party's "whole life or even its greater part" and is of limited, usually quite specific, duration in time.

Contractual interaction is usually mutual, but its main motivation is "implicitly egoistic, utilitarian," and lacking in a "sense of sociocultural oneness of the parties." Each party typically enters the relationship "for his own sake, uniting with the other party only so far as this provides him with an advantage (profit, pleasure, or service)."

The egotism and self-protection inherent in this motiva-

tion do not allow the relationship to be "unlimited or unde-
fined"; therefore, its defined sphere remains "limited and
tends to be coldly legalistic" to the point of being "a lawyer's
paradise." In this environment, the parties cannot assume the
constant "good faith of the other party." (This suggests that
a purely contractual environment is not conducive to the fulfillment of *amae*, which depends on being able to trust completely in the good faith of others.[11]) Therefore, "the parties
feel quite virtuous . . . if they conform to the legal rule, no
matter how unfair, from a higher standpoint," their conduct
might be. Moreover, accepting self-centered assumptions
about the parties' expectations causes leadership within contractual relationships to be hierarchical, reflecting "formal
domination and subordination" based on defined privileges
rather than upon the service orientation of familism. In addition, the high value placed on personal choice in contractual
relationships emphasizes each party's opportunity to interpret the limits of the commitment according to his or her
own self-interest.

Because of the immense variety of contractual relationships, they may reflect numerous forms of cooperation, ranging from "benevolent neutrality" through "competitive cooperation" to "simultaneous love and hate."

Third, *compulsory* relationships, by contrast, have no
mixture of cooperation and antagonism. Rather, the parties
remain strangers who are exclusively antagonistic: "a hated
master and an inhumanly treated slave," an executioner and
victim, a despotic government and its subjects, a kidnapper
and the kidnapped. The subordinate party enjoys no freedom. Further, the parties do not share at all: "The inner
world of each is closed to the other." Thus, oppressors frequently develop "certain ideologies . . . to the effect that the
parties are fundamentally different in nature," such as pure
and impure races, masters and slaves, "caste and outcaste."
Coercion occurs in many forms, but "when it is applied

merely in the interests of the stronger party, the relationship becomes in part or in whole compulsory."

In an observation significant for family life, Sorokin notes that compulsory systems may at times take on a "pseudo-familistic" or "pseudo-contractual" appearance. This is the Machiavellian stance in which the stronger party coercively imposes his or her will on the weaker party while claiming that the coercion is not really forced. Such action can be made to appear legitimate by false claims that the action is benevolently motivated (pseudo-familistic) or that it results from the weaker party's free agreement (pseudo-contractual).

By combining Sorokin's thought with that of Henry Maine, we can now restate the status-to-contract thesis with more precision. We note first that both "familistic" and "compulsory" relationships are based on concepts of status. Western history reflects a long but steady decrease in the proportion of relationships that are either compulsory or familistic, and an increase in the proportion that are best described as contractual. This pattern has occurred in two very different ways, one more positive than the other. First and most positively, the liberating movements that have thrown off the yoke of totalitarian or aristocratic oppression over the past few centuries have freed millions of people from status-based compulsory relationships in favor of more freely chosen contractual interaction, both politically and economically. The American Revolution and its resulting Constitution powerfully illustrate this theme, as does the collapse of Soviet Communism in our own day.

The second and more negative variation is that the proportion of human relationships that are status-based but familistic has steadily been reduced, as institutions that were traditionally paternalistic and familistic have become more contractual. These institutions include, most notably, schools, churches, and families. Although this movement from familistic to contractual interaction has long been under way, it has greatly accelerated its pace in recent years.

In family life, for example, the past thirty years have witnessed the emergence of a legal, social, and often very personal emphasis on individual rights in family relationships, which has caused us to think of marriage in *contractual* more than *familistic* terms.

Recent research illustrates this trend, showing that today, men and women frequently enter marriage with the contractualist's assumption of "uniting with the other party only so far as this provides him with an advantage."[12] Therefore, modern marriage is "seen primarily in terms of psychological gratification," with partners often viewing their relationship with a self-focused "therapeutic attitude [that] denies all forms of obligation and commitment in relationships."[13] Today's marriage partners hold this view in part because they increasingly "think of [all] commitments—from marriage and work to political and religious involvement—as enhancements of the sense of individual well-being rather than as moral imperatives."[14] Many now think of the family as "a collection of individuals united temporarily for their mutual convenience and armed with rights against each other."[15]

In other words, the partners in a contractual marriage each expect to give 50 percent, while the partners in a familistic marriage each expect to give 100 percent.

In reviewing the recent shift from familistic to contractual assumptions about marriage, we should recall that our traditions regarding marriage did not derive from the same premises of self-interest that fueled the political and economic individualism of the nineteenth century.[16] But in recent years, Americans have extended the "rights" orientation that has come to pervade our society to a variety of social revolutions that tend to politicize whatever they touch. Thus, many people, often without consciously choosing contractual ideas over familistic ones, now rest their thinking about family relationships on notions of political and legal power, contract, and self-interest.

In addition, some critics actually interpret American marriage and family relationships as having originated not in familistic or contractual assumptions but in *compulsory* assumptions. These interpretations begin with the premise that all of our traditional social organizations, public or private, were established by men to protect their own positions of power over women. This generalization implies, of course, that there are no genuinely familistic relationships. It is hardly flattering to our traditional ideas about marriage to describe that relationship as falling within the same coercive category that is inhabited by masters and slaves or tyrannical kings and their subjects. But some modern scholarship has found enough evidence of "unrighteous dominion" by fathers and husbands to make a plausible argument that the husband/wife relationship—at least when it is not contractual in nature—belongs within Sorokin's compulsory category.

This interpretation sees traditional marriage as having a male oppressor and an oppressed female victim. In such a pseudo-familistic model, the male oppressor implicitly believes "that the parties are fundamentally different in nature"[17] (male and female) and deceitfully employs familistic terminology to justify his continuing domination. This deceit would, of course, excessively romanticize the domestic realm of marriage and motherhood.

If one accepts this picture, it is not difficult to conclude that recent moves toward a *contractual* understanding of marriage and family life are not backward steps away from relationships of enduring and genuine commitment; rather, they are steps forward from centuries of oppression toward legally assured protection. Because familistic commitments cannot be legally enforced (how can the law "make" one person treat the other with kindness and love?), a contractual version of marriage is clearly better than a pseudo-familistic version that is, in fact, coercive—such as when an abusive parent uses the private sanctuary of a seemingly familistic home to cover up his or her abuse.

Of course, the large and lingering question with the hypothesis that traditional marriage is a compulsory relationship is whether those who believe it think the contrasting familistic model never has and never could actually exist. If the entire idea of a marriage in which "their whole lives are intermingled and organically united into one 'we' "[18] is nothing but an idealized fabrication claimed by unrighteous men to justify their continued oppression, then a marriage based only on contractual commitments is clearly an improvement.

But if the familistic life really is attainable, and not just a myth, then excluding it from our aspirations will destroy the potential source of our most transcendent relationships—and we will never know what we have missed.

Whatever else it may be, this book is our combined testimony that Sorokin's description of familistic relationships is consistent with our experience. The status-based familistic life is not a myth. It is very hard to capture and maintain, so it often eludes us. But it is not a myth. Applying Sorokin's language to our experience, we have voluntarily mingled our lives into an organically united "we." We know firsthand about the "sorrow and sacrifice" required by commitments that almost daily ask more of us than we quite know how to give.

Yet our organic uniting is not only with each other but also with a family entity—a status-based unit, as in ancient times—that includes our children and is somehow a link in a great chain of family entities led by our parents and grandparents and followed by our grandchildren. We sense that, somehow, "we without them cannot be made perfect; neither can they without us be made perfect," and so we yearn for "a whole and complete and perfect union, and welding together of dispensations" through the spirit of Elijah and the blessings of the temple. (D&C 128:18.)

We frankly acknowledge that accepting our "status" in the "order" of our familistic entity at times imposes "a severe limitation of the freedom of the parties." But we have both found here a surprising blend of "discipline with freedom." We have found here the fulfillment of our *amae*—our *Freiheit in Geborgenheit*[19]—a freedom that bears fruits of personal fulness so rich with meaning that we can only describe them, in Ammon's words, as our "suffering," our "sorrow," and our "incomprehensible joy." (Alma 28:8.) We are satisfied that a contractual view of marriage does not have the power to bear such fruit.

We have learned that we are not two solos but two parts of a duet. And from three decades together, we know now that a duet is far richer than two solos.

Part IV

BELONGING FOR YOUNG SINGLE ADULTS

CHAPTER SEVENTEEN

Romantic Belonging

This chapter and the two following chapters are addressed especially to young single adults, for whom the future prospect of "belonging" to a person of the opposite sex often involves high stakes, high feelings, and high priority. Sometimes faithful young people are unsure whether it is all right for romantic feelings to be in their hearts at the same time as they may be having deep spiritual feelings. We bear witness in these chapters that a sense of romantic belonging toward another person and a sense of spiritual belonging toward the Lord can be not only compatible—they are often mutually reinforcing.

During our own days as single students at BYU, we heard Elder Boyd K. Packer teach:

> The powers awakened earlier in your life have been growing. You have been responding to them, probably clumsily, but they now form themselves into a restlessness that cannot be ignored. You are old enough now to fall in love—not the puppy love of the elementary years, not the confused love of the teens, but the full-blown love of eligible men and women, newly matured, ready for life. I mean romantic love, with all the full intense meaning of the word, with all of the power and turbulence and

frustration, the yearning, the restraining, and all of the peace and beauty and sublimity of love. No experience can be more beautiful, no power more compelling, more exquisite. Or, if misused, no suffering is more excruciating than that connected with love.[1]

We share Elder Packer's respect for romantic love to the point that even approaching the topic makes us feel we are walking on holy ground. This subject, delicate as it is, inspires our deepest reverence. The idea of romantic love, so commonplace that it is touched upon in almost every song or story, is also at the very center of the gospel of Jesus Christ. The Lord himself directed that a man shall "leave his father and his mother, and shall cleave unto his wife: and they shall be one flesh." (Genesis 2:24.) As Elder Packer put it, "Romantic love is not only a part of life, but literally a dominating influence of it. It is deeply and significantly religious. There is no abundant life without it. Indeed, the highest degree of the celestial kingdom is unobtainable in the absence of it."[2]

There is another side to this coin, of course, represented by what Alma told his wayward son, Corianton, who had become involved with the Lamanite harlot Isabel. Said he: "Know ye not . . . that these things are an abomination in the sight of the Lord; yea, most abominable above all sins save it be the shedding of innocent blood or denying the Holy Ghost?" (Alma 39:5.)

In this day of widespread sexual permissiveness, LDS young people understandably wonder why the Lord regards moral transgression as such a serious wrong. Sometimes we properly tell our children that God gave us the law of chastity to protect us against the risks of pregnancy, abortion, unwanted marriages, or sexually transmitted diseases, such as AIDS. In explaining the harm of adultery, we talk about the irreparable damage of destroying marriages and families.

Yet, as serious as these hazards are, there are even more fundamental reasons why the Lord has placed unchastity ahead of armed robbery and fraud in the seriousness of sins. These other reasons are less obvious than more tangible and immediate consequences, but they are rooted in both our human nature and our divine nature.

God has said that being unchaste is second in magnitude only to murder. Perhaps there is a common element in those two sins, unchastity and murder. Both have to do with *life*, which touches upon the highest of divine powers. Murder involves the wrongful *taking* of life, while moral transgressions may lead to the wrongful *giving* of life. At the least, sexual transgressions involve a wrongful tampering with the sacred fountains of life-giving power. Immorality rejects the God-given sanctity of life itself.

In addition, immorality is wrong because it betrays and undermines the longing to belong. Our inborn desire to draw close to other people, including especially the closeness of romantic intimacy, is a hunger for fulfillment that will, if properly nourished, lead to the fulness of eternal life. There is a clear connection, then, between our romantic longings and our feelings about losing someone we love, our homesickness for distant family members, and our homesickness for our eternal home. We should not trifle with such sacred things, lest we violate and eventually destroy the core sources of human happiness.

At this level, "the case for chastity" is less a series of reasons than it is an emotional—ultimately spiritual—appeal to the deepest and most positive intuitions of the soul. Our words can fail us here, as they often do when we try to plumb depths of joy or meaning that are too sacred, too significant, and even too mysterious to be quickly explainable. It is more at this level than the level of simple "thou shalt nots" that the Lord has said, time after time, over all the generations of man, "Thou shalt love thy wife with all thy heart, and shalt cleave unto her and none else" (D&C 42:22) and "Thou shalt not . . . commit adultery . . . nor do anything like unto it" (D&C 59:6).

To write or speak of this subject in today's world is to run the risk of sounding like a voice from a bygone era. But it is precisely because the topic of sexual purity seems old-fashioned that we need to explore it more deeply than we may have done in years past. We live in a culture so completely soaked through with wrong ideas about sex that our children must be *warned*—in love and kindness, but still warned—lest the moral sleeping sickness that is overcoming American society lull them into deadly slumber.

There were always violators of the moral code, but during the past generation, we have witnessed a major revolution in American attitudes about sex, not only among young people but also among many of their parents. As part of a broad revolution against tradition and authority, our cultural norms about sexual experience began to unravel among college students during the 1960s. In the decades that followed, the number of students who said they accepted the moral and social legitimacy of premarital sex grew from about 50 percent to nearly 90 percent.[3]

Premarital sex increased more among women during this period than it did among men, primarily because rates among men were much higher before the sexual revolution began.[4] To some degree, this change in women's sexual attitudes and experiences was associated with the larger scale women's liberation movement. Some voices in this movement, for example, loudly rejected society's "double standard," which had traditionally (and wrongly) tolerated sexual adventures among men while expecting women to adhere to higher moral principles.

Some research indicates that the most revolutionary changes have occurred not in actual sexual behavior but in the acceptance of sexual themes and actions in the public media. Many movie and TV producers now simply assume that it is as normal and natural to show people making love on the screen as it is to show them having dinner together. The amazing project of "taking sex public" has clearly been accelerated by two powerful forces that have paralleled the revolution in sexual values: a revolution in communications technology and fierce economic competition. Public TV channels, cable channels, video rentals, and movies have battled for public dollars in an audacious striptease game, with each step removing one more taboo than the last.

Unfortunately, American constitutional law has made all of this possible by categorizing this warfare as a First Amendment "freedom of speech" issue rather than what it is—essentially a business issue. If the Supreme Court's obscenity cases had been decided by the standards that apply to government regulation of business, rather than by free speech standards, our states and cities could have been far more aggressive in controlling the moral environment—as they have become in controlling other aspects of the environment that are affected by business interests.

Growing public fears about teenage pregnancy and sexually transmitted diseases, especially AIDS, have also hastened the movement of sex from the private realm to the public realm. Those who advocate the distribution of condoms in public schools, for example, usually argue not from the conviction that sexual permissiveness is a good thing for teenagers but from the belief that "safe sex" is better than unprotected sex. This belief simply (and, we believe, naively) assumes it is no longer realistic to ask young people to "just say no."

Ironically—and tragically—the best available research shows that safe-sex campaigns actually produce more teen *pregnancy*, not less. Those campaigns have sometimes reduced teen *births*, but only because there were concurrent increases in adolescent abortion.[5]

A change in society's sexual norms is also clearly evident in the attitudes that have developed among many professional therapists. For example, the American Psychiatric Association voted in the early 1980s to remove homosexuality from its list of disorders, even though reliable research shows that 50 percent of the male homosexuals surveyed in one American city had had at least 500 sexual partners, and 28 percent of them estimated they had had 1,000 partners.[6] If that is thought to be normal behavior, our definition of *normal* has changed beyond recognition.

In the past few years, homosexual behavior and other "alternative lifestyles" have come to seem increasingly legitimate, especially as they have been validated by the public acceptance implied in the high-level political appointments of openly gay men and women, a court decision allowing gay marriage,[7] and recent changes in U.S. policy on homosexuals in military service.

Some of the recent changes in public attitudes toward sex and sexual orientation are driven by a growing advocacy for more tolerant and more flexible attitudes about lifestyle choices generally. One therapist who claims to represent mainstream attitudes among psychotherapists wrote in a professional journal that most people in his field believe that "human disturbance is largely associated with and springs from absolutistic thinking," and that, therefore, being inflexible or extremely religious amounts to "essentially emotional disturbance."[8]

Whatever the causes and the detailed statistics, clearly the view of chastity taught in the scriptures has far less public, and private, support than was the case a generation ago. Society is now numbed, if not suffocated, by a dense fog of sensuality, which cannot help but influence our attitudes and dull our normal sensibilities. One writer has described this basic change in national attitude by reference to *Playboy* magazine:

While *Playboy* is much the same thing that it was during the 1950's, it is not *exactly* the same thing, and the difference is crucial. During the 50's, there was, of course, pornography. We used to get it at the newsstand from the old man with the black cigar who would produce it, literally, from "under-the-counter." Sometimes it would circulate through the boys' locker room—usually pictures of fat [women] with missing teeth. It was available, all right, but one came by it ["out behind the barn," so to speak].

But now that the *Playboy* philosophy has been declared innocent by the grand jury of public opinion, now that it "is involved in the mainstream of our culture and values," it is acquired, and consumed, as thoughtlessly as a pound of bologna. You pack Mildred and the kids in the station wagon, buzz down to the local drugstore, plunk your two bucks down on the counter, and bring home artful pictures of young women who have straight teeth, deep suntans, and college educations. Every one of them is a former cheerleader, a current jogger, concerned about ecology. Middle class. When you get home, you throw your copy on the coffee table promiscuously [alongside *Time* and *Newsweek*], a public pronouncement that *you* buy *Playboy* for the literature. It's true: the difference between the 50's and [today] is that we don't give pornography a second thought any more.[9]

And that is exactly what is going wrong—the public doesn't give a second thought these days to pornography and other evidence of an increasingly decadent culture. The willingness of people to accept these things is so widespread that there is really nothing to compare with it in many centuries of civilized society—not since Rome, not since Sodom and Gomorrah. The very scope of the attitudinal drift is what makes these times so treacherous. Even as we are surrounded by abnormality and evil, everything somehow seems so normal.

As the French writer Pascal stated: "When everything is moving at once, nothing appears to be moving, as on board ship. When everyone is moving towards depravity, no one seems to be moving, but if someone stops, he shows up the others who are rushing on, by acting as a fixed point."[10] Latter-day Saints, who know better, must be that fixed point.

It is not easy for the two of us to paint such an extreme picture, because we think of ourselves as restrained and reasonable people. But when we examine this problem for what it really is, we honestly believe that American society in the area of sexual morality is in the grip of the Evil One.

There is a reason why the scriptures record the word *devilish* after the words *carnal* and *sensual*. As early as the days of Adam's children, "Satan came among them . . . and they loved Satan more than God. And men began from that time forth to be carnal, sensual, and devilish." (Moses 5:13.) And when Cain took Abel's life, he said, "I am free." (Moses 5:33.) Cain was never more in bondage than when he said he was free. In the same way, the American people have never been in greater moral and spiritual bondage than in this time when so many glory in being "free" to pursue pleasure as if there will be no tomorrow.

We want to say to our children and to any young adults who will listen: We've moved into turbulent times. Fasten your spiritual seat belts. Please pray, fast, and "fast forward." You simply must resist the influence of the vulgar music, erotic media, and other products of the carnal environment that now surround us as water surrounds the fish of the sea. Remember: we're talking here about the sin next to murder, not about lesser laws and optional standards. This is a sin that can destroy not only bodies but also marriages, families, and spiritual lives.

If the H-bomb symbolizes our age, we are now playing not with fire but with the moral equivalent of nuclear power—and the Prince of Darkness has dragged out the heavy artillery. He is no longer limited to arrows and swords and BB guns. Now he is Darth Vader, with laser guns, light speed, and the death star. We are near the end of a fight to the finish, and no holds are barred.

Let us turn now to the positive dimensions of the law of chastity, because that is the most fundamental—and mean-ingful—perspective. Elder Boyd K. Packer has said, "Oh, youth, the requirements of the Church are the highway to love, with guardrails securely in place, with help along the way. How foolish is the youth who feels the Church is a fence around love to keep him out. How fortunate is the young person who follows the standards of the Church, even if just from sheer obedience or habit, for he will find rapture and a joy fulfilled."[11]

The English writer David H. Lawrence takes the high road in describing marital love as among humankind's most exquisite blessings, as ordained of God:

> There is a profound instinct of fidelity in man, which is deeper and more powerful than his instinct of faithless promiscuity. The instinct of fidelity is per-haps the deepest instinct in the great complex we call sex. Where there is real sex there is the underly-ing passion for fidelity. The prostitute knows this, because she can only keep men who want the coun-terfeit: and these men she despises.
>
> The [Chief Thinkers of our Generation] know nothing of [this]. To [them] all sex is infidelity and only infidelity is sex. Marriage is sexless, null. Sex is . . . a thing you don't have except to be naughty with.
>
> [However, the truth is that] the [Christian] Church created marriage by making it a sacrament . . . of man and woman united in communion, never to be parted, except by death. . . . Marriage, making one complete body out of two incomplete ones, and pro-viding for the complex development of the man's

soul and the woman's soul in unison, throughout a lifetime. . . .

This oneness, gradually accomplished through a lifetime of twoness, is [one of] the highest achievements of time or eternity. From it springs [the greatest of human creations]—children. It is the will of God [for] this oneness to take place, fulfilled over a life-time. The oneness of man and woman in marriage completes the universe, as far as humanity is concerned, completes the streaming of the sun and the flowing of the stars.[12]

Lawrence writes here of children, and of "oneness" through a "lifetime of twoness," as being among humankind's highest achievements. He senses, even if only on the level of intuition, how married love and parenthood respond to and fulfill our longing to belong and our inborn desire for *amae*.

Properly understood, the gospel teaches us to be virtuous not because romantic love is bad but precisely because romantic love is so good. It is not only good; it is pure, precious, even sacred and holy. For that reason, one of Satan's cheapest tricks is to make profane that which is sacred. It is as though Satan holds up to the world a degraded image of sexual love, suggested by the drunken, boisterous laughter of men in a brothel located on some crowded, dusty highway. Here the flower of virtue is jeered at, dirtied, and brutalized with unclean hands.

Meanwhile, far away from this teeming crowd, high up in the cool protected valleys of tall mountains, grows virtue's priceless flower. It waits as a sweet prize for those few wise enough to climb to its heights by paying the price of patience, obedience, and a lifetime of endless and unselfish loyalty—loyalty not only to God but also to a future companion.

With this warning about the modern carnal environment and with this general affirmation of romantic love, we offer

our children and other young single adults ten practical suggestions that may support their desire to find the fullness
promised by the hope of romantic belonging:

First, have reverence for the human body and its life-
giving powers. Your body is a sacred and holy temple. It
deserves the same reverence you should have for any temple
that seeks to be the dwelling place for the Lord's Spirit. It is
also the dwelling place of the seeds of human life, and the
nurturing of that life with your chosen companion, within the
bounds set by God, is lovely and of good report.

Second, during your time of courtship, please be emotionally honest in expressing affection. Sometimes you are
not as careful as you might be about when, how, and to
whom you show affection. The desire for that expression can
be motivated by forces and needs other than true love. In
addition, even when—or especially when—true love may be
present, that is only more reason to nourish love's integrity
as you look toward the genuine, lasting fulfillment of your
longing to belong. As Erich Fromm put it:

> *Desire* can be stimulated by the anxiety of alone-
> ness, by the wish to conquer or be conquered, by
> vanity, by the wish to hurt or even to destroy, as
> much as it can be stimulated by love. It seems that
> sexual desire can easily blend with and be stimulated
> by any strong emotion, of which love is only one.
> Because sexual desire is in the minds of most people
> coupled with the idea of love, they are easily misled
> to conclude that they love each other when they
> want each other physically. . . . [But] if [this] desire
> . . . is not stimulated by real love, . . . it . . . leaves
> strangers as far apart as they were before—some-
> times it makes them ashamed of each other, or even
> makes them hate each other, because when the illu-
> sion has gone, they feel their estrangement even
> more markedly than before.[13]

In short, save your kisses—you might need them some

day. Remember also that a kiss symbolizing love and respect is different from a kiss of self-centered passion. When you are given entrance to the heart of a trusting young friend, know that you stand on holy ground. In such a place you must be honest with yourself—and with your friend—about love and the expression of its symbols.

Third, be friends first and sweethearts second. Lowell Bennion once said that relationships between young men and women should be built like a pyramid. The base of the pyramid is friendship. The ascending layers are built of such dimensions as time, understanding, respect, and restraint. At the top of the pyramid is a glittering little mystery called romance. When weary travelers in the desert see that glitter on top of the pyramid from afar, they may not realize all that must lie beneath the jewel to give it such prominence and hold it so high. A pyramid won't stand up very long if you stand it on its point instead of its base. So: be friends first and sweethearts later, not the other way around.

Fourth, develop the power of self-restraint. Be like Joseph, not like David. When Potiphar's wife tried to seduce Joseph, he "fled, and got him out." (Genesis 39:12.) He knew that it is wiser to avoid temptation than to resist it. King David, by contrast, somehow developed too much confidence in his own ability to handle temptation. He was tragically willing to flirt with evil, and it destroyed him. Even when you feel that your courtship has a growing foundation of love, show your respect for that love and the possibilities of your life together by restraining your passion.

Please don't be deceived by the false idea that anything short of the sex act itself is acceptable conduct. That is not true, not only because one step overpoweringly leads to another, but also because touching another's body is, in an important sense, part of the sexual act that is kept holy by the sanctuary of chastity. If ever you are in doubt about where to draw the line between love and lust, draw it toward the side of love. Remember: nobody ever fell off a cliff who never went near one.

Fifth, as you search to fulfill your God-given romantic longings, live for the presence of the Holy Spirit as your constant guide. Don't date someone you already know you would not or should not ever want to marry. If you should fall in love with someone you shouldn't marry, you can't expect the Lord to guide you away from that person after you are already emotionally committed. It is difficult enough to tune your spiritual receiver to the whisperings of heaven without jamming up the channel with the loud thunder of romantic emotion.

The key to spiritual guidance is found in one word: worthiness. A comparison of D&C 63:16–17 with D&C 121:45–46 makes this point vividly: Those who look upon others with lustful hearts will not have the Spirit; they will experience fear; and they will deny the faith. In direct contrast, those who garnish their thoughts with virtue will have the Holy Ghost as a constant companion, they will feel confident in the Lord's presence, and the doctrine of the priesthood will distill upon their souls as the dews from heaven.

Sixth, avoid the habit of feeling sorry for yourself, and don't worry about seeming socially unsuccessful. Everybody in the world doesn't need to marry you—it only takes one. Seek opportunities for developing friendships, as distinguished from going on "dates." We discovered in our own courtship the natural growth and happiness of being friends first and sweethearts second—that sequence is worth waiting for.

Don't worry that you are not well known; seek to be worth knowing. The discouragement you may feel about your social life is often a form of the insecurity we all feel in trying to find ourselves. Without the apparent approval of your self-worth that comes through social success, you may experience feelings of self-doubt. That is not unusual—most of us wonder at times if the Lord loves us or if other people love us.

Some mistakenly seek the symbols of success—being popular or rich or famous—to prove their worth. Sometimes you may let someone take improper liberties with you, or you may indulge yourself in some practice that seems to bring temporary relief, but it only makes you feel worse in the long run. Some even make poor marriage choices, just to show the world that *somebody* will have them.

Ultimately, however, only the Lord's approval of our lives really matters. If you seek to be worth knowing and seek to do his will, the rest will take care of itself. Remember that all things work together for good for those who love God. (See Romans 8:28.) Your time for marriage may not come until the autumn of your life, and then it may be, in Elder Packer's phrase, "more precious for the waiting." Even if that time should not come in this life, the promises of eternal love are still yours in the Lord's view of time, if only you are faithful.

Seventh, avoid at all costs, no matter what the circumstances, participation in abortion or homosexual experiences. As serious as are fornication and adultery, abortion and homosexuality are equally wrong and may often be worse. Even people who only assist others, much less pressure them, to have an abortion, are in jeopardy of being denied the privilege of missionary service as well as other important Church privileges.

Eighth, know that there is repentance. If, through some unfortunate past experience, you have committed a serious moral transgression, there is a way by which you may receive full forgiveness: "Though your sins be as scarlet, they shall be as white as snow; though they be red like crimson, they shall be as wool." (Isaiah 1:18.)

The steps for repentance are best outlined in President Spencer W. Kimball's book *The Miracle of Forgiveness.* You must seek God's forgiveness, turn away from repeating your mistake, look for new ways to live faithfully, and seek to compensate for what has been lost—to the full extent of your powers. With truly serious errors, you will need to talk with your bishop. As frightening as that may seem, by this means you will find purpose and a peace of mind more hopeful and uplifting than you can imagine in advance. "By this ye may know if a man repenteth of his sins—behold, he will confess them and forsake them." (D&C 58:43.)

Ninth, don't sin while planning to repent. "Some people knowingly break God's commandments [even while] they *plan to repent* before they go on a mission or receive the sacred covenants and ordinances of the temple."[14] There is something especially perverse about "planning to repent" in the very act of transgression. This attitude twists the sublime source of our healing until it actually inflicts more sickness, like poisoning the medicine in the hospital for wounded soldiers, thereby wounding the soldiers twice.

This kind of thinking can begin early. We know a nine-year-old-boy who told his seven-year-old brother, "It's okay to steal things until you're eight years old. So, I say, live it up!" Sometimes young people preparing to attend a Church college, go on a mission, or be married in the temple will consciously "live it up," as if they can sin all they wish, so long as they "just repent" before the deadline. Paul described these foolish ones as wanting "to enjoy the pleasures of sin *for a season.*" (Hebrews 11:25; emphasis added.) Some even feel it is their right to romp in the mud of transgression right up to the moment they take their spiritual shower of repentance.

Sadly, those who frivolously engage in what they believe is a penalty-free romping time may discover too late that they cannot wash every stain from their clothes and hands. Of course repentance, when it is genuine and complete, can restore our spiritual standing before God. But even then, the entanglements of sin (see D&C 88:86)—the bent fenders and the broken hearts, the addictions and the lost opportunities, the unwanted children and the unfortunate marriages, the bills to pay and the fences to mend—these may never wash away.

Moreover, once sin's swift current carries us downstream, we can't always just turn around at will and swim back, against the current, to our point of beginning. We don't have that much control over our lives. One of the most exciting football games in BYU history was the "Miracle Bowl" in 1980 against SMU. The Cougars were behind four touchdowns with only minutes to play. Then, amazingly, they came roaring back to win the game with an onside kick and a "hail Mary" pass in the final seconds. The next year in an early game, BYU fell far behind against a very strong team. Our ten-year-old daughter said, "You know, this is a lot more fun for everybody—let the other team get way ahead, and then just pass them up like we did last year!" But it wasn't to be—the Cougars were soundly defeated, and our daughter had to rethink her philosophy about coming from behind.

The deadly AIDS epidemic illustrates the tragedy of ignoring the consequences of sin. For example, some American athletes and entertainment stars have been stunned to discover that, because of their sexual promiscuity, they are now infected with the AIDS virus. Magic Johnson is the most visible example of this trend. According to published estimates, some of these traveling celebrities have had sexual encounters with literally hundreds of different partners in city after city. Now they are discovering that their carefree lifestyles may cost them their lives. And beyond that, they may have unwittingly infected their spouses and children—those who mean the most to them. But now, even if they were to repent, they cannot possibly call back the seeds of destruction they have scattered in their past.

"Planning to repent" is also an affront to the Savior, because it assumes that we control our own forgiveness.

While we must do "all we can do" (2 Nephi 25:23) to accept Christ's grace, we cannot turn that miraculous power on and off like a water faucet. He *loves* us no matter what we do, but he *forgives* only the honest in heart, and on his terms, not ours. Because we lack the power to compensate fully for the effects of our sins, we are utterly dependent on Jesus Christ. Without his holy Atonement, no amount of agonizing repentance could return us to God's presence. We dare not trifle with so sacred a reality. But the Good News is, when we do fully repent in the honesty of a broken heart and a contrite spirit, he will do all the rest. Thank God, literally, *that* is under *his* control—not ours, for *only he* has enough power to make our scarlet sins become white as snow.

Tenth, let yourself "belong" to the natural order of God's laws. A critically important step on the path to maturity occurs when you realize that we keep the commandments not because parents and leaders insist, but because the natural consequence of our obedience is our own happiness. The gospel is simply the truth about "things as they really are." (Jacob 4:13.) Therefore, to live the gospel is to live in harmony with the natural laws of life, for there is a natural ecology in the spiritual world as well as in the physical world.

This principle is true because the universe is designed to produce human happiness. Living contrary to nature will make us miserable, while living harmoniously with nature is the pathway to everlasting happiness. Hence Alma's advice that "wickedness never was happiness." (Alma 41:10.) The wicked "have gone contrary to the nature of God; therefore, they are in a state contrary to the nature of happiness." (Alma 41:11.)

In certain sacred moments, we may sense the harmony of belonging to God's natural order, including the order of being friends, then sweethearts, then spouses, then parents.

At such times, the inborn yearning of our *amae*, our longing to belong, reaches out to touch its source of fulness.

A father we know recalls: On a bright fall day some years ago, my seven-year-old son and I drove off to try out a new fishing spot. As we splashed up the shallow stream looking for likely trout holes, he would jump up on my back as I waddled through the water in my rubber waders. He held his feet above the water and hugged me tight around the neck, laughing in my ear when I would stumble on the rocks.

As the peaceful afternoon wore on, I became more aware of the beauty of our surroundings. I looked up at the clear blue sky and could almost taste the crispness of the air. I saw early snow on a distant mountain peak. I drank in the sight of autumn-colored leaves moving gently in the back-lighting of the late afternoon sun. I glanced downstream and saw my boy skipping rocks across the stream, the small bursts of water glistening in the sunlight as he threw his little rocks. As the sun caught the pure whiteness of his blond hair, the outline of his boyish, agile form stood out brilliantly against the shadows of the wooded background.

I felt a sudden rush of feeling that I suppose only a father or mother can know. My heart reached out to touch him as the thought came to me: that is my son, my own little boy, and I am his father. We *belong* to each other. He is healthy and strong and filled with a child's love. I am responsible to God himself for my conduct as his father. We are sealed together, on condition of our faithfulness, for he was born under the same covenant that sealed his parents' vows of eternal marriage. As the fruit of their love, this child is the blessing of God's natural laws. He is growing up with a believing heart. The constancy of his mother's daily life is teaching him the way of truth and light. Perhaps that is why he is so strong, so secure, so mentally healthy. Thank God for such a child. What miracles are worked by the laws of nature and of nature's God.

In that moment, I felt in harmony with everything I saw. It was all a witness to me of God's holy love.

The commandments of God are designed for our ultimate happiness, and being sweethearts and parents in the way the Lord intended is worth waiting for.

CHAPTER EIGHTEEN

Celebrating Womanhood

As young people today think about the future, and especially as young couples wonder about a possible future together, their attitudes about "belonging" to each other are unavoidably influenced by their thinking about life priorities for women. What should be most important to a young woman's plans—education for a career? A liberal arts education? Marriage? Children?

Consider three familiar symbols—a diaper, a frying pan, and a boy's worn-out tennis shoe. How should we react to these objects? Are they symbols of joy and fulfillment? Or are they symbols of drudgery and submission?

Many people in today's world would be confused (perhaps some would be irritated) by these questions. Others would find the questions easy to dispose of, but only because they have avoided possible conflicts between plans for a marriage and plans for an education by choosing one and ignoring the other.

When I was growing up,* society placed great value on marriage and home and family. Since then, economic conditions have changed, social attitudes have changed, and on every side people are now questioning our traditional view of family life.

---

*Because Marie prepared this essay from her personal point of view, she writes here in first person singular.

Yet these three "homely" symbols introduce what is for me the surest place to stand in this bewildering cultural climate: the place called home. I want to say what being a wife and a mother means to me. Then I want to put those feelings into a larger context, because the choice between family life and education is not an either/or choice. For the sake of our own happiness and stability, for our families, for the Church, and for a better society, women need *both* domestic skills and a broader education; but they must develop, shape, and balance their commitments to obtaining them on the foundation of a gospel perspective.

My voice of celebration for women's possibilities is thus a voice of hope but also a voice of warning, because the confusion in modern society can unsettle all of us about the aspirations of women. Remember the Savior's words: "Behold, I send you forth as sheep in the midst of wolves: be ye therefore wise as serpents, and harmless as doves." (Matthew 10:16.) We need both wisdom and meekness to keep our balance in these times.

As my husband and I were first blessed with children, we soon discovered that, as someone said, "to believe in God is to know that the eternal rules are fair, and that there will be some wonderful surprises." One of those wonderful surprises was to learn what Lehi meant when he said that if Adam and Eve had remained in the Garden of Eden, "they would have had no children; . . . they would have remained in a state of innocence, having no joy, for they knew no misery." (2 Nephi 2:23.)

Astute parents will note here an apparent connection between having children and experiencing misery. But note also that without children and misery, Adam and Eve would have had no *joy.* Two verses later, Lehi tells us, "men *are,* that they might have [that very] joy." (2 Nephi 2:25; emphasis added.)

Now, after a house full of children and their not always

"wonderful" surprises for almost thirty years, *all* of Lehi's words have meaning for me. Of course there are days of drudgery. Dishes get dirty, children cry, and people get sick. There are bills to pay and cars to fix; too little time and not enough money. There is frustration and fatigue and disappointment. Yet somehow, amid this sometimes drab reality, there are moments of genuine joy and meaning so tender that all we can do is kneel to thank God through our tears for the gift of children and the bonds of married love.

One moment of that kind for me was the birth of our first grandchild, whose red hair is just the color of my mother's hair. During the first few months of her life, she slept in the same little white crib where, one by one, we had placed each of our seven babies. The crib, lovingly refurbished by great-grandparents and trimmed with fresh fabric and lace, is no ordinary crib, for this baby's father, grandfather, and great-grandmother each occupied it in the first months of their lives.

Is the white crib just a piece of antique furniture? Or does it, like the frying pan and the tennis shoe, represent the grandest cycle of life and love and hope?

Looking back a full generation now, I feel about raising children the way Ammon felt about missionary work when he and his brethren testified of "their journeyings in the land of Nephi, their *sufferings* in the land, their *sorrows,* and their *afflictions,* and their *incomprehensible joy."* (Alma 28:8; emphasis added.) Their joy was mixed with sorrow and affliction, for that is the very nature of joy.

As a core part of life's joy, I celebrate first of all the womanhood that is at the heart of life in a family home. I plead with both men and women—younger and older—to honor this womanhood and to cherish it in their own families and in their own lives.

Marriage and family come first, not only for women but also for men. So what should women think about education and careers? Remember, the issue is not marriage *or* education; the issue is marriage *and* education. But why—and how?

Let us consider seven variations on a theme I once heard expressed this way: "Before becoming somebody's wife, before becoming somebody's mother, *become somebody.*"

First, become somebody who can support herself. Young women should prepare for a career, but not because a career is more important than family life. A career isn't even *as* important as family life. As the prophets have counseled, mothers who have young children should avoid being outside the home whenever possible. Yet over many years the Church's leaders have also urged young women to seek education and to be prepared for careers and meaningful involvement in society.

Career-oriented education is important because women typically experience so many different phases of life—and because they can't always control when and what those phases will be. For example, at any given time, from 35 to 40 percent of the adult women in the Church are single, whether widowed, divorced, or not having married—with divorce being the greatest cause. The never married are the smallest group, since only 3 percent of LDS women never do marry. In addition, over 90 percent, including both married and single women, must work for some part of their adult lives. An LDS woman is now likely to work more than twenty-five years in one circumstance or another. And six out of ten LDS women who work are supporting not only themselves but also others in their families.[1]

What these statistics boil down to is that a young woman who believes she will always have a husband who will fully support her, making it unnecessary for her to work, is living in a dream world. Husbands die, or they can be disabled by accidents or illness. Children grow up, missionaries need financial support, and most mothers live healthy, vigorous lives for many years after their children leave home.

In addition, a young woman who finds herself living alone as a single adult cannot expect the Lord to keep her from experiencing life's natural adversities, even if she has lived righteously. A friend of mine tells of a woman who had expected someone else to support her at each step of her life. At first she thought her father would support her; then she expected her husband to support her; then she found herself looking primarily to her bishop and her divorce lawyer for support; and finally she realized that she also needed to support herself.

The gospel was given to us not to prevent all misery and sorrow but to heal us from—and teach us through—our misery and sorrow. The Lord often gives us friends and family members who are wondrous sources of unfailing support. He also gives us strength to deal with a world that can sometimes be lone and dreary. But in either case, we must also do "all we can do" (2 Nephi 25:23) to support ourselves.

Second, before becoming somebody's wife, please be careful about who that somebody is. Young people must obviously strike a sound balance between being too fussy and not fussy enough. Elder Boyd K. Packer once reminded us to "look for potential, not for perfection."[2] And one who has great potential may not be compatible as an eternal companion. Learning about a young man's potential or his compatibility will require the test of time.

It is therefore of great importance to become real friends before becoming romantically involved. Otherwise, a couple may discover, too late, that their philosophies of life are miles apart. I know a young couple who fell in love with the idea of love rather than with each other. Only after they were married did they start to discover real tensions between their attitudes on many basic issues. He was in school and thought she should work to support his education. She felt that she should stay home and be a full-time homemaker. Some women in her situation would have expected him to support *her* education. Then she became pregnant, which only complicated their unresolved differences. They should have become friends first.

This is not to imply, of course, that if people just become friends before becoming married that will solve all their problems. One result of becoming friends may be the friends' realization that they would not be suitable marriage partners at all. But that is just all the more reason for coming to know each other first at the level of friendship.

Third, before becoming somebody's mother, become capable of being a good mother. One of our teenage daughters once said to me in a moment of frustration about not having finished her assigned housework on time, "Look, Mom—I'm not *majoring* in homemaking!" Maybe not—but she aspires to motherhood someday, and part of being a good mother is to know how to make not only a bed but also a home.

I am distressed that the modern world's devaluation of motherhood is signaling to my daughter and her friends that preparing to be a homemaker, mother, and wife is "no big deal." This message implies that the recipe for successful parenting is too much like an instant mix: just add water, mix, and heat. I see too many marriages that consist mostly of mixed-up attitudes and heated feelings amid a watered-down home life.

In truth, learning to be a superb mother is a very big deal. Other than a desire for eternal life, I can't think of a more important aspiration for a young woman to have. There is no more meaningful career, no more divine calling, than being a person who truly *makes* a home. Such a task involves creating and maintaining a total environment of human warmth, intellectual stimulation, and spiritual strength by someone who sees the wellsprings of personal meaning that lie beyond a first glance at a diaper, a frying pan, and a worn tennis shoe.

Motherhood is above all an *educational* task, involving both teaching and learning of a very rich kind. A mother is the first and most important teacher in a child's life. G. K. Chesterton once compared a full-time specialist in a single discipline with a full-time mother who is a generalist in all the disciplines of life, noting that *the specialist is something to everyone, but a mother is everything to someone.*

The generalist and the specialist both contribute to the world; both require serious educational preparation. Many women play both general and specialized roles at one time or another. For me, the preparation required for the general role of motherhood is reason enough for all women to take education seriously, even if there were no other reasons.

I have enjoyed a lifelong love affair with literature, particularly the works of Shakespeare. After majoring in English while in college and graduate school, I taught freshman composition while my husband finished law school. Later, when our children were all old enough to be in school, I returned to some part-time teaching of Shakespeare and other writing courses at Ricks College and at BYU. Shakespeare is a master teacher, and he has been one means of helping me teach my children.

In recent years, I have accompanied each of our children into their own experiences with Shakespeare, through school assignments or otherwise. We have seen videos together, attended live plays, and read and talked together. These activities have helped me support their school projects, but that was only the beginning.

Beyond that practical level, what a delight it has been for me to interact in intellectually and spiritually stimulating ways with my own children as our study of Shakespeare has helped us confront essential questions about ourselves and about human nature. For example, I recall a conversation with my ten-year-old daughter as we watched *King Lear* on video. She asked, "He's old, but why are his children so mean to him? Isn't he their father?" These conversations have also helped us understand each other as we have explored our own individual nature as humans. Our visits have also opened the way for me to teach my children how to prepare for life in ways that provide a rich supplement to the lessons we draw from the scriptures.

Fourth, before becoming somebody's wife or somebody's mother, become somebody who can make her own life richer. Education not only prepares a woman for a possible career, it not only helps her teach and rear her children, it also enriches her own life. As Mr. Keating says in the movie *Dead Poets' Society,* "One reads poetry because he's a member of the human race. Poetry, romance, love, beauty—these are what we stay alive for!"

I love Emily Dickinson's description of the way education lifts our sights and liberates our spirits:

> She ate and drank the precious words,
> Her spirit grew robust;
> She knew no more that she was poor,
> Nor that her frame was dust.
> She danced along the dingy days
> And this bequest of wings
> Was but a book.
> What liberty a loosened spirit brings![3]

A friend I will call Marilyn is enjoying a far richer life today than might have been the case, because of the way the world of books and beauty opened her eyes and her mind. Marilyn grew up in a small town where the most important things in her friends' lives were being popular and being seen with handsome, high school athletes. She dated a rowdy young man who was a natural leader, but he had few serious aspirations for his life. Just as Marilyn was beginning to follow him in ways that would have hurt her in the long term, her family took her with them to pick up her brother after his mission.

For the first time in her life, Marilyn opened her eyes to the size and wonder and variety of the world: she saw art galleries and historic cathedrals; she saw the remnants of aristocracy and the grimness of urban poverty; she sang LDS hymns in a foreign tongue; she saw mountains and oceans she had never known existed.

When she returned, somehow her home town was not the same. She saw everything and everyone with new eyes. And from that perspective, she realized that she was far from ready to make serious commitments to her immature boyfriend. From that time on, her thirst for learning took her far beyond the days when the city limits of her home town had formed the limits of her aspirations.

Now Marilyn's continuing curiosity and broad vision of life enhance her well-developed religious faith. Her life is more full, her service to others is more meaningful, and her husband and her children are now blessed by her insights—because she stretched beyond the boundaries of an inward-looking, naive, teenage mind to touch the broader boundaries of an outward-looking, educated, adult mind.

Fifth, before becoming somebody's wife and somebody's mother, become somebody who is spiritually strong. King Benjamin spoke of the "happy state of those that keep the commandments of God. For behold, they are blessed in all things, both temporal and spiritual." (Mosiah 2:41.) Does this mean that if people keep the basic commandments, they won't have any problems?

If Adam and Eve had stayed in Eden, they would never have found genuine happiness. They would simply have remained innocent. There is literally a world—and a lifetime—of difference between innocence and joy. So when King Benjamin tells us of the blessed and happy state of those who keep God's commandments, he is not describing a Kingdom of Oz in which there are no witches. On the contrary, developing the strength that leads to authentic joy requires us to follow Adam and Eve into a world of thorns and sorrow.

Adam and Eve fell, and they were cast out from the Garden of Eden, that they might have joy. But they didn't skip merrily out of Eden singing and wishing each other a nice day. They walked in sorrow into a lone and dreary world, where they earned their bread by the sweat of their brow. There they learned about joy embedded in its larger context of misery and pain. Can you imagine how Eve felt when she learned that her son Cain had taken the life of her son Abel, and that God had banished Cain? The 1990s are not the first decade to see an increase in family violence and an increase in the crime rate.

How could Mother Eve have possibly found joy in the midst of such affliction? She found it by offering her trust and her heart to the Savior, allowing his Atonement to heal her pain and sanctify her experience. Indeed, her experience with sin and misery played a crucial role in preparing her for the joy she ultimately found.[4] Women in the modern world, like women in the ancient world, go forth as sheep in the midst of wolves. In such a world, we must be as faithful and as spiritually strong as was Mother Eve. She and Adam set a memorable example for all their children, men and women: "And Adam and Eve, his wife, ceased not to call upon God." (Moses 5:16.)

A young friend described her Eve-like experience in finding both God and true joy by serving a mission:

> When I left on my mission, faith was still just the first principle of the gospel. Now I need it and live by it more than food. I couldn't get through a day without it. . . . I know that I was born to be a missionary. I know that my spirit is a warrior, because it loves peace. I now know what it means to say that

my spirit rejoiceth. My spirit has found expression
and joy and finally been set free.

Another outcome of this mission that I didn't
expect at all is that I find myself wanting to get married and have a family. After seeing so much unhappiness I long to establish my own righteous fortress
on the earth. I have loved working so closely with
the priesthood and realize what an effect it has on
my life and attitudes. I also realize that a mission is
a priesthood-appointed calling. I understand that. At
the end of a great war even women and old people
have to fight. So here we are.

I also learn from Eve that applying the gospel to the
unhappiness and sorrow of life can awaken us to joys we
might otherwise fail to see, let alone appreciate. For
example, another young woman I know suffered the torment
of having committed a serious moral transgression. Then,
after searching her soul in much sorrow over many months,
she walked faithfully through the steps of repentance.
Suddenly she came to a moment of insight so overwhelming
that she felt like the first person to discover it: the Atonement
made Jesus Christ her *personal* Savior. She has never stopped
rejoicing since that day. She had found what Eve found:
were it not for her transgression and her complete repentance, she *never should have known* "the *joy* of her redemption, and the eternal life which God giveth unto all the obedient." (Moses 5:16; emphasis added.)

*Sixth, for young men as well as young women: take each
other seriously; encourage one another to reach the full range
of your intellectual and spiritual potential.* Opinion surveys
among LDS students have suggested that some men do not
understand why women attend college. The large majority of
women students reported that they attend college to gain a
serious education. But when men were asked why *they* think
women attend college, a number of them listed social rather
than educational reasons.

Perhaps some women hesitate to tell men their real motivations in seeking education because they don't want to be criticized. Of greater concern is the possibility that if male students and male faculty don't take women seriously as college students, they may (intentionally or unintentionally) discourage women students from pursuing educational goals. Anyone who uses Church teachings as an excuse for thinking that women should not wholeheartedly seek an education does not understand what the Church teaches.

In general, I find that increasing numbers of young men are taking more seriously the idea that young women have a wide range of genuine interests and abilities, from the educational and intellectual world to the world of athletics and politics. I also find that as men interact with women across the entire spectrum of personal and cultural experience, women also discover that men have a broader range of interests than the women might have suspected.

For example, I see more and more young men, married and unmarried, learning to share domestic and educational tasks with the women in their lives. This makes their present or eventual marriages become true partnerships in which a man and a woman stand side by side with one another, as did Adam and Eve, with neither one behind the other.

A married friend recently told me this story:

> Not long after we had a new baby, I was in a car accident in which my neck was broken. Because of that, I had to wear a big brace. Greg had to help me do almost everything. I couldn't bend over at all, so he had to change all of the baby's diapers. He helped me get dressed in the morning, tying my shoes, buttoning my buttons. He helped me wash my hair. I thought I loved him before we were married, but during this time I grew to love him much more for what he was willing to do for me.

I also see an increasing number of young LDS fathers

who are involved in the educational nurturing of their children. What a loss it would be, both to fathers and to society, if the bonds and blessings of child-nurturing belonged only to mothers. I agree with George Gilder, who said that one of the hallmarks of civilization is when men learn from their women to become interested in the education of their children.[5] From what I see, I am optimistic that men and women are becoming both more civil and more civilized toward each other and toward their children.

Finally, become somebody who understands that being a woman is worth celebrating. Women who are prepared for life can celebrate with confidence. Fully prepared women are not only needed—they are utterly indispensable, not only in the home but also in the church, in the local community, and throughout the larger society. A woman celebrates the diverse scenes of womanhood in many ways.

She watches her toddler look longingly at the stairs he doesn't yet know how to climb. When he looks back eagerly for approval, her answer must be no, and the little one bursts into tears. She is a teacher of tough love in the complex discipline of a loving but fully nurtured childhood.

She is a single-parent Primary teacher who tastes the magic of childhood when she greets one proud seven-year-old wearer of a CTR ring who thrusts his fist forward and exclaims with happy courage, "See this CTR ring? It throws out an invisible shield of protection all around me, and no evil force can break through!"

She is educated and able, sad that her day of marriage has not come but fully engaged in a professional world that needs the talent and training she offers. Added to these gifts, her caring touch can soothe and heal, for "charity never faileth" in a corporation, a government office, or a classroom, just as it never faileth in a neighborhood or in a home.

She watches as her teenage daughter is not asked to the prom, which brings back her own memories of not having been asked. Her heart aches, but she tells her daughter, "Not everyone needs to fall in love with you. It only takes one."

She works patiently as a volunteer committed to caring for the homeless; she cares lovingly over many years for an invalid mother-in-law; she accepts the confidence shown by friends and neighbors to run for the state legislature. "Look what you did for our school through the PTA," they say. "Our state needs you."

She watches her son kneel across the altar from his bride in a temple sealing room and thinks of her own marriage in such a room, celebrating the sealing of eternal love.

She walks into a hospital room to see her first daughter-in-law happily but gingerly lift up her own first baby to greet her: "Isn't she beautiful? Would you like to hold her—Grandma?"

She rejoices in the seasons of a woman's life, for each time and each season is worth its own celebration. Spread over a lifetime, celebrating womanhood is a celebration of life.

CHAPTER NINETEEN

Labor for That Which Satisfies

A mother once asked a wise old man, "What should I teach my son?" The man replied, "Teach him to deny himself."

Is self-denial wise because something is wrong with our passions, or because something is right with our passions? Alma taught his son: "See that ye bridle all your passions, *that ye may be filled with love*." (Alma 38:12; emphasis added.) He did not say eliminate or even suppress your passions, but *bridle* them—harness, channel, and focus them. Why? Because discipline makes possible a richer, deeper love.

The prophets have given both negative and positive reasons for obeying chastity's twin principles of abstinence before marriage and fidelity after marriage. The terrifying plague of AIDS amply illustrates the negative reasons: sexual promiscuity can literally kill us. And in addition to destroying the *body*, "whoso committeth adultery [also] destroyeth his own *soul*." (Proverbs 6:32; emphasis added.)

The positive blessings of chastity may be less familiar, but they deserve attention. For one thing, an affirmative view of chastity can be an appealing way to teach why an uncontaminated marriage is worth waiting for. Men and women should seek virtue not because romantic love is profane but because it is sacred. Indeed, the satisfying sacredness that is possible within marital intimacy illustrates one of the gospel's unique yet profoundly reassuring doctrines: the Lord seeks to fulfill, everlastingly, our deepest human longings. The longing for romantic love is thus only part of our larger longing to belong and to be deeply satisfied.

Jacob said, "Come, my brethren, every one that thirsteth, . . . do not spend money for that which is of no worth, nor your labor for that which *cannot* satisfy. . . . Come unto the Holy One of Israel, and feast upon that which perisheth not, neither can be corrupted, and *let your soul delight in fatness.*" (2 Nephi 9:50–51; emphasis added.)

Jacob's admonition to "feast" in some permanent way and not to labor for "that which cannot satisfy" suggests that we *should* labor for that which *can* satisfy. But isn't the religious life by definition a life of fasting, not feasting? The Savior told the rich young man to "sell whatsoever thou hast, and give to the poor, and . . . take up the cross, and follow me." (Mark 10:21.) And Peter told the Lord, "We have left all, and have followed thee." (Mark 10:28.) These passages seem to imply that to follow the Savior is to embrace a life of self-denial, in which we renounce the human urge to be satisfied in favor of strict obedience to heavenly laws. Isn't that what the Word of Wisdom and Fast Sunday and the Ten Commandments are all about? And what does coming unto the Holy One of Israel have to do with feasting and fatness?

Consider the doctrinal context for these questions. Traditional Catholic and Protestant teachings are rooted in the belief that, because of Adam's and Eve's original sin, all men and women have an inherently evil nature. This theology assumes that many of life's natural delights are evil reflections of a fallen world; hence the false medieval idea that the highest form of spiritual life is to reject marriage, deny other human passions, and withdraw monastically from the world.

Much of modern civilization rejects this dark view of human nature, having built on Greek humanism's confidence in man to believe now that man is by nature good.[1] In just the past generation, however, our society has also abandoned the strong sense of restraint that marked classical Greek thought. As a result, the world now presents us with two extreme, but false, choices about human intimacy: (1) the traditional "religious" choice is to believe that God is displeased when we find deep fulfillment in romantic relationships or natural beauties, and (2) the "worldly" alternative is to pursue our sexual urges wherever they take us.

The light of the restored gospel pierces through this dark confusion, illuminating the pathway to happiness and meaning. Ours is a revolutionary doctrine: children are born neither evil nor good by nature; rather, they are born innocent. (D&C 93:38.) They then encounter the free choices of mortality in order to develop the *capacity* to experience a fulness of joy. If they choose to follow Satan, they will ultimately become like him: evil by nature and eternally miserable. But if they, rather, accept the disciplined yoke of the gospel, they may one day become divine by nature. Their souls will then overflow with satisfactions "which perisheth not." (2 Nephi 9:51.)

The Lord ultimately seeks our self-fulfillment, not our self-denial. Yet our self-denial in the short run enables our self-fulfillment in the long run. God is the author of our passions. If we bridle them by the bounds *he* has set, our passions can be fulfilled. We submit ourselves to divinely ordered limits in order to find—not to deny—the abundant life. (See John 10:10.)

The human soul's universally recognized longing for fulness thus finds more expression and fulfillment in the gospel than in any other philosophy of life. Everlasting romantic love based on unqualified fidelity is both desirable and possible. In Parley P. Pratt's words, "Our natural affections are planted in us by the Spirit of God, and they are the very mainsprings of life and happiness. There is not a more pure and holy principle in existence than the affection which glows in the bosom of a virtuous man for his companion."[2] In its pure form, this yearning to love calls forth and satisfies our highest instincts. In its adulterated forms, it allures and dazzles, but finally, it only betrays.

So the problem with sexual license is not only that it *should* not satisfy but also that it *cannot* ultimately satisfy. To hunger for and pursue that which "cannot satisfy" is to starve the soul.

Sometimes the adversary tries to confuse us about the difference between lower and higher forms of satisfaction by blurring the relationship between the process of being satisfied and our concept of time. We once had a cat named Arthur. One day our daughter asked, "Do you think Arthur knows he's a cat?" Her dad said, "I don't think Arthur knows he is a cat—all he knows is that it is very nice when you live with someone who will love you, feed you, and keep you warm." Actually, quite a few people think the very same thing—their highest hope is just to have someone love them, feed them, and keep them warm. To them, as to Arthur, that's what it means to be "satisfied."

But people are different from cats and other animals. We not only have longer memories—our sense of time defines us. We derive the present meaning of our lives by reference to our past and to our future. Of course, some of our basic needs and feelings, such as hunger, thirst, and sleep, are similar to the needs of animals—and we must fill those needs before we can pursue our higher nature. Yet our unique ability to reason and our sense of time allow us to *delay* the fulfillment of even basic needs when that serves a higher purpose than simply giving in to an immediate urge.

We once watched the Cookie Monster from TV's "Sesame Street" win a quiz show. What a moment it was! The emcee congratulated the monster and his mother, offering them a choice among three big prizes: they could have a $200,000 dream home—next month; a $20,000 new car—next week; or a cookie—right now. The two monsters furrowed their furry brows and carefully weighed the pros and cons. As the timer buzzed, a big smile broke across Cookie Monster's face as he greedily announced their choice: "Cookie!"

Now nothing is wrong with a good cookie—the Cookie Monster's problem is not that the cookie is bad but that its satisfaction *cannot* last. Not *should* not but *cannot*. Jacob was right: do not spend money for that which is of no worth, nor your labor for that which cannot satisfy. Feast upon that which perisheth not.

The serious version of the Cookie Monster story is captured in the words of David Starr Jordan, inviting young men and women to think of their future selves:

> So live that the man [or woman] you ought to be may, in his time, be actual. Far away in the years he is waiting his turn. His body, his brain, his soul are in your [youthful] hands. He cannot help himself. What will you have for him? Will it be a brain unspoiled by lust or dissipation; a mind trained to think and act; a nervous system true as a dial in its response to the truth about you? Will you . . . let him come as a man among men in his time? Or will you throw away his inheritance before he has had the chance to touch it? Will you turn over to him a brain distorted, a mind diseased, a will untrained to action, a spinal cord grown through and through with "devil-grass" and "wild oats"? Will you let him come and take your place, gaining through your experience, happy in your friendship, hallowed through your joys, building on them as his own? Or will you fling it all away, decreeing wanton-like, that the man [or woman] you might have been shall never be? This is

your problem in life—the problem which is vastly more to you than any or all others. How will you meet it, as a man or as a fool? It comes before you today and every day. And the hour of your choice is the crisis in your destiny.[3]

Still, the younger we are, the harder it seems to think wisely about the future. In our high school days, we enjoyed hearing the song, "There's no tomorrow, when love is new./There's no tomorrow, for lovers true./So kiss me and hold me tight./There's no tomorrow, there's just tonight."

But because we have the gospel, we know there is a tomorrow. Thank God there is tomorrow. Tomorrow, like today, is everlastingly part of life. And because there is tomorrow, all our yesterdays have meaning and purpose. If we hold someone tight whom we really love, the *last* thing we want is no tomorrow. A shallow, impulsive infatuation that wants to shut out tomorrow is but a tiny flicker compared to the roaring blaze of genuine belonging in a commitment built to last literally forever.

There is an enormous difference between ephemeral, flash-in-the-pan, temporary pleasures and long-term, soul-stirring satisfactions. Yet, whether the subject is romantic belonging, education, or investments of scarce resources, one of Satan's cheapest and dirtiest tricks is that he deludes us into believing the cookie is more valuable than the dream home—partly because we can have it right now. His manipulation is deeply ironic, because *his* long-term intent with this delusion is that he "seeketh that all men might be miserable like unto himself." (2 Nephi 2:27.)

Once more: the problem is *not that worldly gratifications are too satisfying, but that they are not satisfying enough.* That was Jacob's point. The Lord wants us to be worthy and prepared to feel joy and satisfaction to the deepest regions of human capacity. It is Satan who seeks to numb our sense of well-being until we slowly become eternally miserable.

What kind of romantic belonging awaits those who patiently prepare for it? A friend told us that his teenage children were staying home one evening during a stake fireside. When he asked them why they chose to stay, one answered, "Oh, they've asked some seventy-year-old lady to talk about love. What does *she* know about love?" Consider what seasoned married couples know about love—even romantic love.

The *Odyssey*, one of history's memorable love stories, teaches symbolically that undefiled married love is not only worth waiting for; it is also the root of personal, family, and social stability. After twenty years of wandering, Odysseus yearns for his home in Ithaca, where his cherished wife, Penelope, waits for him. He is stranded on the island of a goddess, Kalypso, who promises him immortality if he will but remain to be her lover. But Odysseus looks daily across the sea toward Ithaca, until the gods order his freedom. He finally leaves the wild seas and traverses a series of boundaries bringing him ever closer to the center of his life: he moves across Ithaca to his own lands and his own house, which he must purify by ridding it of Penelope's tormenting suitors. Then he approaches his bedroom.

Despite—or perhaps because of—her long and patient waiting, Penelope is unsure of his identity. Her faithfulness prompts her to exact a test. In Odysseus' presence, she asks her maid to move their bed outside the bedroom. In response, Odysseus furiously objects, explaining that the bed cannot be moved without destroying it: he had originally built the bed by starting with the stump of a deeply rooted olive tree as the anchor bedpost. He laid out—and built—the bedroom, and then the house, from that point. Hearing this, Penelope no longer doubts his identity. She joyfully acknowledges him; then Odysseus "in his turn melted, and wept as he clasped his dear and faithful wife to his bosom."[4] The marriage bed, protected by their well-disciplined faithfulness, is the center that stabilizes their home. And the home's stability in turn reflects ripples of strength back through the boundaries Odysseus crossed, symbolically stabilizing all of society in Ithaca and beyond.

How, then, in the belonging of married love, do we "bridle all [our] passions, *that [we] may be filled with love"?* (Alma 38:12; emphasis added.) Consider three ways.

First, physical intimacy grows from and symbolizes a total relationship; like Odysseus and Penelope's bed, it cannot be detached from its intricate context, and it cannot flourish if the larger relationship is in disrepair. As Elder Jeffrey R. Holland has stated, the intimate dimension of marriage symbolizes a total bond that is

> the union of *all* they possess—their very hearts and minds, all their days and all their dreams. They work together, they cry together, they enjoy Brahms and Beethoven and breakfast together, they sacrifice and save and live together for all the abundance that such a totally intimate life provides. And the physical manifestation [only symbolizes] a far deeper spiritual and metaphysical bonding of eternal purposes and promise. [T]o give only [the physical] part [without also giving] the gift of your whole heart and your whole life and your whole self is its own form of emotional Russian roulette.[5]

Second, loving intimacy grows naturally from its bonds of interdependence and cannot be coerced. There may be the appearance of love—there may be surface-level cooperation and even physical manifestations. But if those expressions are not freely given, the relationship cannot meet the conditions that yield lasting satisfaction "in [the Lord's] own way." (D&C 104:16.) President Joseph F. Smith taught that God ordained sexual intimacy not only to perpetuate the race but also "for the development of the higher faculties and nobler traits of human nature, which the love-inspired companionship of man and woman alone can insure."[6] Perhaps this is partly because the desire to be freely and fully loved will motivate a marriage partner to be both lovable and worth loving.

A man and a woman can each be tempted to coerce the other. A man may be tempted to treat his wife as his subordinate or even his inferior, thereby subtly commanding her loyalty. She may be under covenant to honor him, just as he is under covenant to honor her. But if manipulated, those covenants can be forms of coercion. As D&C 121:37–39 makes clear, where there is unrighteous dominion, true priesthood powers are not operative.

A woman may be tempted to act "fascinating" for the primary purpose of manipulating a man's acquiescence or clouding his judgment by exploiting his desires. From Samson to Salome, the Bible recounts variations on this theme, as when Salome's dancing "pleased Herod" and he "promised with an oath to give her whatsoever she would ask. And she, being before instructed of her mother, said, give me here John Baptist's head." (Matthew 14:6–8.)

When men or women are true to the deepest instincts of their natures, they will nurture sensitivity and kindness as part of their marital fidelity. But when their motives darken toward betrayal or a quest for power, they cast away their human kindness in ways that deny the link between true sexuality and fidelity. When Shakespeare's Lady Macbeth was persuading her husband to seek the murderous capture of a king's crown, she cried out, "Come you spirits/That tend on mortal thoughts, *unsex* me here." She symbolically renounced her female nature in the raw pursuit of ambition: "Come to my woman's breasts/And take my milk for gall, you murdering ministers."[7] The contrasting inference here is that a person's true sexual nature will engender kindness and loyalty.

Third, the ecstasy of love's highest fulfillment weaves itself into a complex emotional fabric that includes the prosaic drudgery of daily responsibility. Lucifer, the enemy of our desire for fullness, tries to convince us that we must escape our dull routines and seek the dramatic gestures of "romance" outside the home, because he claims that life's petty burdens and chores impede the free movement of Eros. This viewpoint, continually portrayed by the popular media, has nothing but contempt for ordinary marriage, "which it finds hopelessly boring and middle-class." Thus one can hardly "imagine Romeo and Juliet routinely sitting down to breakfast."[8]

It is even more difficult to imagine Romeo and Juliet keeping their passion alive in the midst of household clutter, unpaid bills, the crying of children, and the sheer battle fatigue that often concludes our every day. But if two married lovers simply understand how natural is the untidiness of their lives, that understanding can nurture rather than smother the sparks of disciplined passion.

Jacob spoke of *laboring* for that which satisfies. And as Kahlil Gibran put it, "work is love made visible."[9] Tevye and Golde in *Fiddler on the Roof* discovered the meaning of Gibran's phrase when Tevye asked Golde in song, "Do you love me?" As Golde thought aloud in her response, they both realized that after twenty-five years of unreservedly supporting and living with each other, their mutual and unselfish sacrifices made their love quite visible.

President Rex E. Lee and his wife, Janet, once shared with the students of BYU the story of President Lee's traumatic struggle with cancer a few years earlier. They recounted the details and doubts of being hospitalized for five months of chemotherapy, during virtually every day of which Janet was by Rex's side. They described how the sterile loneliness of an urban hospital somehow had the effect of refining their love for one another. When Rex was so sick that he couldn't even read his favorite literature—Supreme Court cases—Janet read the cases aloud to him from the foot of his bed while tenderly rubbing his bare feet, hour after hour. In a multitude of such moments, the roots of their love, including their affection, grew ever deeper. President Lee said he knew Janet loved him before, but after their hospital stay, their love had a depth they could not otherwise have known.

In romantic love as in other meaning-laden experiences, we discover authentic joy in the mortal environment the way we discover gold within gold ore: the shiny particles of gold are embedded in and mixed with complex and sometimes dull-appearing surroundings. Our joy means more when we are fully conscious of the context that gives it meaning. As Arthur says in *Camelot*, our lives are like the water that forms the great waves of the sea. Occasionally a few drops sparkle through the sunlight; perhaps only for brief, shining moments, but they do sparkle. Those drops then plunge back into the darker seas of life, enriching all else that we experience.

In this mixture of sun and shadow, when we as couples have paid the high price required by temple covenants, true belonging, and a spirit of selfless compassion, we will taste the sweet joy of never-ending romantic love. And rather than leading us away from God, our yearning for such joy brings us closer to him, for this form of love awaits those who enter the highest degree of celestial life; in fact, such love distinguishes that life from all lesser degrees of glory.

In the long run, then, the gospel teaches self-denial not to stifle our passions, but, everlastingly, to fulfill them.

Consider a final question raised by Jacob's statement on laboring for that which satisfies: what does the fulfillment of romantic belonging have to do with the fulfillment of religious belonging? Jacob gave his injunction to "let your soul delight in fatness" in the context of his plea that we "come unto the Holy One of Israel, and feast upon that which perisheth not, neither can be corrupted, and let your soul delight in fatness." (2 Nephi 9:51.) Consider in this connection Joseph Smith's statement about the tie between our capacity for perfection and our capacity for joy:

> We consider that God has created man with a mind capable of instruction, and a faculty which may be enlarged in proportion to the heed and diligence given to the light communicated from heaven to the intellect; and the nearer a man approaches perfection, the clearer are his views, and the greater his enjoyments, till he has overcome the evils of life and lost every desire for sin; and like the ancients, arrives at that point of faith where he is wrapped in the power and glory of his Maker and is caught up to dwell with Him.[10]

There is here a link not only between joy and perfection but also between that state of joy and the state of being "wrapped" in God's glory and "caught up to *dwell with* him." Charles Wesley's lines from an old Christian hymn echo both the Prophet's language and the longing to belong: "Jesus, lover of my soul,/Let me to thy bosom fly. . . . Other refuge have I none;/Hangs my helpless soul on thee./Leave, oh, *leave me not alone;/*Still support and comfort me."[11]

When Jacob said, "Come, my brethren, every one that thirsteth, come ye to the waters; and he that hath no money, come buy and eat" (2 Nephi 9:50), he spoke of the Lord's free and atoning grace, which Alma called "the bread and the waters of life" (Alma 5:34). Elsewhere, Alma likened God's love and His Atonement to the tree of life, on whose fruit the Savior's followers may feast until they are *filled,* "that [they] hunger not, neither shall [they] thirst." (Alma 32:42.) The Savior makes this nourishment freely available to all who "come unto the Holy One of Israel," feasting "upon that which perisheth not" (2 Nephi 9:51)—"the word of Christ" (2 Nephi 31:20). And one of its blessings—charity—actually enlarges our capacity to love, making us capable not only of eternal life but also of eternal love.

The fulness we will know in returning to the Lord's presence to be "at one" with him comes to a husband and wife together, eternal companions who belong to one another as well as to the Savior. In fact, though we must be individually worthy of the blessings of exaltation, we cannot be exalted alone: we are exalted in a marriage of romantic belonging, or not at all.

Most of us have tasted the stirrings of pure and disciplined romantic love enough to yearn eternally for married companionship. Most of us have tasted the pure and disciplined spirit of the Lord enough to yearn for his companionship eternally. Those two yearnings are familiar to one another—each form of love, each form of belonging, helps us understand, and live for, the other.

Does the Lord want us to be satisfied? Yes—so much so that a central reason for his giving us the gospel is to make possible the everlasting fulfillment of our longing to belong, both to him and to each other. Thank God there is tomorrow.

Still, Still with Thee

T̲he gospel promises to fill all the spaces of our heart's longing for fulness, both here and hereafter. Consider, then, the prospects for hereafter, when "spirit and element inseparably connected, receive a fulness of joy." (D&C 93:33.)

If we are true and faithful, we will one day be welcomed permanently into the arms of the Atoning One. Then we, like the ancient Nephites, may "bow down at his feet, and . . . worship him; . . . and kiss his feet, insomuch that [we will] bathe his feet with [our] tears." (3 Nephi 17:10.) In that day, we will know, as they did, the height and breadth and depth of being fully *satisfied* in the Lord's own way: "So great was the joy of the multitude that they were overcome," and the Savior himself said, "Blessed are ye because of your faith. And now behold, my joy is full. And when he had said these words, he wept." (3 Nephi 17:18, 20, 21.)

He wept—he who had descended below all things, the Man of Sorrows, he who bore all our griefs. The height of his infinite capacity for joy is the inverse, mirror image of the depth of his capacity to bear our burdens. So it is with the enlarged caverns of feeling within our own hearts: as the sorrows of our lives carve and stretch those caverns, they expand our soul's capacity for joy. Then, when the Man of Sorrows turns our bitter tastes to sweet, our joy—and his— will fill the widened chambers of our hearts with what the scriptures call "fulness." That is when we have accepted his Atonement and love with such completeness that his purpose for us is fully satisfied. Then will we know that we were made for this. Then will we know where, and why, and to whom, we belong. "For he satisfieth the longing soul, and filleth the hungry soul with goodness." (Psalm 107:9.)

Because eternal marriage is a prerequisite to eternal life, all this is ours as we hold the hand of an eternal companion, to whom we also belong. We are then full unto overflowing. During mortality we taste and can therefore anticipate this fulness in the mortal stirrings of human love, or when we sense the movements of God's Spirit on our hearts. Our desire for fulness is directed both to loved ones and to God. For just as those worthy of celestial marriage are *sealed* in eternal bonds of love, so also, if we are "steadfast and immovable, always abounding in good works, . . . Christ, the Lord God Omnipotent, *may seal [us] his.*" (Mosiah 5:15.)

Both forms of sealing, both forms of belonging, are worth waiting for, worth trying and crying for, through all the days of life. This is the supernal fulfillment of which Jacob wrote, "Come, my brethren, every one that thirsteth, come ye to the waters; . . . wherefore, do not spend . . . your labor for that which cannot satisfy. . . . Come unto the Holy One of Israel, and feast upon that which perisheth not." (2 Nephi 9:50–51.) Then will we fully satisfy our longing to belong. Those "who dwell in his presence . . . see as they are seen, and know as they are known, having received of his fulness and of his grace." (D&C 76:94.)

Thus will we rise on resurrection morning *still with* that little circle of people whose existence gives meaning to our own existence. We will also find on that day that he whose

Spirit is promised always to be with us is *still with* us, as he was in mortality, but now with a fulness of eternal glory.

Harriet Beecher Stowe's hauntingly mellow lines about eternal belonging therefore speak not only of our relationship with God but also of our relationships with husbands, wives, children, parents, close friends, and other family members. All of them, those closest to us, could be included within the meaning of "Thee" here. What a day it will be!

Still, still with Thee, when purple morning breaketh,
    When the bird waketh and the shadows flee;
Fairer than morning, lovelier than the daylight,
    Dawns the sweet consciousness, I am with Thee!

Alone with Thee, amid the mystic shadows,
    The solemn hush of nature newly born;
Alone with Thee, in breathless adoration,
    In the calm dew and freshness of the morn.
. . . .
When sinks the soul, subdued by toil, to slumber
    Its closing eye looks up to Thee in prayer;
Sweet the repose beneath Thy wings o'ershading,
    But sweeter still to wake and find Thee there.

So shall it be at last, in that bright morning
    When the soul waketh and life's shadows flee;
Oh, in that hour, fairer than daylight dawning,
    Shall rise the glorious thought, I am with Thee![1]

Notes

PREFACE

1. Bruce C. Hafen, *The Believing Heart: Nourishing the Seed of Faith*, 2d ed. (Salt Lake City: Deseret Book Co., 1990), page ix.
2. Bruce C. Hafen, *The Broken Heart: Applying the Atonement to Life's Experiences* (Salt Lake City: Deseret Book Co., 1989), page 26.
3. See *Hymns of The Church of Jesus Christ of Latter-day Saints* (Salt Lake City: The Church of Jesus Christ of Latter-day Saints, 1985), no. 300.
4. "At the Baltimore session of the 1980 White House Conference on the Family, one delegate asked the conference to define the family as 'two or more persons who share resources, responsibility for decisions, values and goals, and have commitment to one another over time.' This proposal lost by only two votes among 761 delegates." (Bruce C. Hafen, "Marriage, Kinship, and Sexual Privacy," *Michigan Law Review* 81 (1983): 463–64.)
5. See chapter 10, "Hope," in Hafen, *The Broken Heart*.
6. Alan J. Hawkins, David C. Dollahite, and Clifford J. Rhoades, "Turning the Hearts of the Fathers to the Children: Nurturing the Next Generation," *BYU Studies*, 33 (1993): 280.
7. Erik H. Erikson, *The Life Cycle Completed: A Review* (New York: W. W. Norton & Co., 1982), page 59.
8. Hawkins et al., "Turning the Hearts of the Fathers to the Children," page 280.
9. Ibid.
10. Ibid. Erikson's own language refers not to Christian virtues but "to such major credal values as *hope, faith,* and *charity*." Erikson, *The Life Cycle Completed,* page 58.

CHAPTER ONE
The Longing to Belong

1. "People are usually surprised to learn that *atonement,* an accepted theological term, is neither from a Greek nor a Latin word, but is good old English and really does mean, when we write it out, at-*one*-ment, denoting both a state of being 'at one' with another and the process by which that end is achieved." (Hugh Nibley, "The Meaning of the Atonement," talk delivered November 10,

1988, in Riverton, Utah, as part of the Hugh Nibley Lecture Series sponsored by Deseret Book and F.A.R.M.S.)

2. See chapter 4, "Personal Identity, Individuality, and Belonging."

3. John Donne, "Meditation 17," quoted in Bruce B. Clark and Robert K. Thomas, eds., *Out of the Best Books* (Salt Lake City: Deseret Book Co., 1968), volume 4, pages 14–15.

4. Colleen McDannel and Bernhard Lang, *Heaven: A History* (New Haven: Yale University Press, 1988), page xiii.

5. Ibid., page 307.

6. Ibid., pages 309, 312.

7. Quoted in ibid., page 311.

8. Ibid., page 309.

9. Robert Browning, "Paracelsus."

10. Joseph Smith, *Teachings of the Prophet Joseph Smith,* selected by Joseph Fielding Smith (Salt Lake City: Deseret Book Co., 1938), page 255.

11. *Hymns,* 1985, no. 292.

12. *Hymns,* 1985, no. 301.

13. James Q. Wilson, *The Moral Sense* (New York: Free Press, 1993), page 226.

14. See Alex Haley, *Roots* (New York: Doubleday, 1976).

15. See Joseph Campbell, *The Power of Myth, with Bill Moyers,* edited by Betty Sue Flowers (New York: Doubleday, 1988). For a good summary of Jung's work, see Edward F. Edinger, *Ego and Archetype* (New York: Penguin Books, 1972).

16. See chapter 4, "Personal Identity, Individuality, and Belonging."

17. Bruce W. Young, "A Father's Perspective," unpublished manuscript.

18. Dion Boucicault, "The Corsican Brothers," in *The Magistrate and Other Nineteenth-Century Plays,* edited by Michael R. Booth, (Oxford: Oxford University Press, 1974), pages 199, 206.

19. See Campbell, *The Power of Myth,* pages 37–39.

20. Statement of the First Presidency, *Improvement Era,* March 1912, page 417.

21. See chapter 4, note 3.

22. First Presidency statement, "The Origin of Man," in Daniel H. Ludlow, ed., *Encyclopedia of Mormonism* (New York: Macmillan, 1992), page 478.

23. Elder Albert Choules of the Seventy told this story in a stake conference session for BYU students on February 14, 1993, in Provo, Utah.

24. *Hymns,* 1985, no. 219.

25. *Hymns,* 1985, no. 293.

26. *Hymns,* 1985, no. 300.

27. Spencer W. Kimball, "The Role of Righteous Women," *Ensign,* November 1979, pages 102–3.

CHAPTER TWO

Amae *and the Longing to Belong*

1. In addition to the thanks we expressed in the acknowledgments for this volume to Professor Morita and to Professor Van Gessel, we also thank Dr. Takeo Doi of Tokyo, Japan, for sharing with us his comments on this chapter through Professor Morita.

2. "Exploring Test Cases in Child Advocacy," *Harvard Law Review* 100 (1986): 435 (reviewing Robert Manookin et al., *In the Interest of Children,* 1985); "Children's Liberation and the New Egalitarianism: Some Reservations about Abandoning Youth to Their 'Rights,'" *Brigham Young University Law Review* 1976: 605.

3. "Individualism and Autonomy in Family Law: The Waning of Belonging,"

Brigham Young University Law Review 1991: 1; "The Family as an Entity," *University of California-Davis Law Review* 1988: 865; "The Constitutional Status of Marriage, Kinship, and Sexual Privacy—Balancing the Individual and Social Interests," *Michigan Law Review* 81 (1983): 463.

4. "Hazelwood School District and the Role of First Amendment Institutions," *Duke Law Journal* 188: 685; "Developing Student Expression through Institutional Authority: Public Schools as Mediating Structures," *Ohio State Law Journal* 48 (1987): 663.

5. Takeo Doi, *The Anatomy of Dependence,* translated by John Bester (New York: Kodansha International, 1982), page 169.

6. Ibid., page 167.

7. Takeo Doi, *The Anatomy of Self,* translated by Mark A. Harbison (New York: Kodansha International, 1985), page 160.

8. Ibid., page 138.

9. Doi, *The Anatomy of Self,* page 161.

10. Ibid.

11. Ibid., page 57.

12. Alexis de Tocqueville, *Democracy in America,* edited by Richard D. Heffner (New York: New American Library, 1956), page 194.

13. See chapter 3, note 13.

CHAPTER THREE

The Waning of Belonging

1. "Talk of the Town," *New Yorker,* August 30, 1776, pages 21–22, quoting an anonymous letter.

2. Jeffrey R. Holland, *However Long and Hard the Road* (Salt Lake City: Deseret Book Co., 1985), page 26.

3. *Hymns,* 1985, no. 166.

4. Robert Nisbet, *The Quest for Community* 75 (London: Oxford University Press, 1953).

5. See chapter 15, "From Status to Contract: Belonging and the Ancient Order."

6. One of the most widely read descriptions of the "counterculture" movement from the late 1960s was Charles Reich, *The Greening of America* (New York: Random House, 1970).

7. Robert B. Heilman, "The Great-Teacher Myth," *American Scholar,* 60 (1991): 420–21 (emphasis added).

8. Paul Adams, "The Infant, the Family, and Society," in Paul Adams et al., *Children's Rights: Toward the Liberation of the Child* (New York: Praeger, 1971), pages 51–52. See also Hafen, "The Constitutional Status of Marriage, Kinship, and Sexual Privacy," *Michigan Law Review* 81 (1983): 463, 465 n. 9.

9. See Bruce C. Hafen, "Public Schools as Mediating Structures," *Ohio State Law Journal* 48 (1987): 663, 679–88.

10. Diane Ravitch, *The Troubled Crusade: American Education, 1945–1980,* (New York: Basic Books, 1983), page 200.

11. Ibid., page 183.

12. Gerald Grant, "The Character of Education and the Education of Character," *American Education* 18 (1982): 41.

13. Olmstead v. United States, U.S. (1928) (Brandeis, J., dissenting opinion).

14. See Edinger, *Ego and Archetype.*

15. Viktor Frankl, *Man's Search for Meaning: An Introduction to Logotherapy* (New York: Pocket Books, 1963), page 168.

16. Thomas Greer, *A Brief History of the Western World*, 4th ed. (New York: Harcourt Brace Jovanovich, 1982), page 535.
17. Robert C. Solomon, *Continental Philosophy Since 1750: The Rise and Fall of the Self* (Oxford: Oxford University Press, 1988), page 194.
18. Quoted in ibid., page 174.
19. Ibid., page 178.
20. Ibid., page 196.
21. Ibid., page 195.
22. James Q. Wilson, "Private Acts Not Beyond Moral Scrutiny, Pope Says," *Deseret News*, November 28, 1993, page A 16.
23. Watterson, "Calvin and Hobbes," *Deseret News*, December 5, 1993, comics section.
24. Wilson, "Private Acts Not Beyond Moral Scrutiny."
25. R. V. Young, "The Old New Criticism and Its Critics," *First Things*, August/September 1993, pages 39, 41.
26. Ibid., page 40.

CHAPTER FOUR
Personal Identity, Individuality, and Belonging

1. Lisa Ramsey Adams, "Eternal Progression," in *Encyclopedia of Mormonism*, page 465.
2. See chapter 15, "From Status to Contract: Belonging and the Ancient Order."
3. It is not clear whether the use of "intelligence" in this passage refers to individual, conscious identity. Some Church authorities "hold that the terms 'intelligence' and 'intelligences' have reference to a form of prespirit conscious self-existence, which included individual identity, variety, and agency. . . . Others maintain that while these characteristics, attributes, and conditions are eternal, they essentially came together for each individual at the spirit birth," fathered by our Heavenly parents as their spirit children. (Paul Nolan Hyde, "Intelligences," in *Encyclopedia of Mormonism*, pages 692–93.)
4. See chapter 11, "Family Belonging: These Bonds Are Our Liberation."
5. See chapter 2, "*Amae* and the Longing to Belong."
6. Kahlil Gibran, *The Prophet* (New York: Alfred A. Knopf, 1923), pages 15–16.
7. Alan J. Hawkins, David C. Dollahite, and Clifford J. Rhoades, "Turning the Hearts of the Fathers to the Children: Nurturing the Next Generation," *BYU Studies*, 33 (1993): 273, 280.
8. Erik H. Erikson, *The Life Cycle Completed: A Review* (New York: W. W. Norton & Co., 1982), page 55.
9. Hawkins et al., "Turning the Hearts of the Fathers to the Children," page 280.
10. Ibid.
11. Erikson, *The Life Cycle Completed*, page 60.
12. Ibid.
13. Ibid.
14. Ibid., pages 55–67.
15. Ibid., page 65.
16. Robert N. Bellah, *Individualism, Community, and Ethics in the United States and Japan*, Fourth Annual Conference on Ethics and Education in the United States and Japan, unpublished manuscript presented in Tokyo on November 19, 1993, pages 7–8.
17. Hafen, *The Broken Heart*, pages 38–39.
18. Ibid., page 42.
19. Bellah, *Individualism, Community, and Ethics*, page 8.

20. *Ensign,* May 1982, page 46.
21. The Caroline Hemenway Harman Continuing Education Building was constructed at Brigham Young University in 1980. Each year since then, members and friends of the extended Harman family gather in this building on "Aunt Carrie's" birthday to remember and to celebrate her memory and her example.
22. Wendell Phillips, *National Anti-Slavery Standard,* April 27, 1867.

CHAPTER FIVE

Eve Heard All These Things and Was Glad:
A Developmental Perspective on the Atonement

1. See chapter 7, "Forgiveness and Christ Figures: The Atonement and Being Harmed by the Sins of Others."
2. T. S. Eliot, *Four Quartets* (London: The Folio Society, 1968), page 55.
3. John A. Widtsoe, *Evidences and Reconciliations,* 3 vols. in 1, arranged by G. Homer Durham (Salt Lake City: Bookcraft, 1960), page 193.
4. Arta Romney Ballif, *Lamentation and Other Poems* (private printing, 1989), pages 3–6.
5. *Hymns,* 1985, no. 85.
6. Gary Morson, "Prosaics," *American Scholar,* Autumn 1988, p. 523.
7. Ibid.
8. Ibid., page 522.
9. Ibid., page 524.

CHAPTER SIX

The Restored Doctrine of the Atonement:
The "Authentic Theology"

1. *Newsweek,* September 1, 1980, page 68.
2. McDannel and Lang, *Heaven: A History,* page xiii.
3. Sixty-nine percent of those polled in a national survey by *Time* magazine reported that they believe in angels. (Nancy Gibbs, "Angels among Us," *Time,* December 27, 1993, page 56.)
4. See chapter 1, note 8.
5. McDannel and Lang, *Heaven: A History,* page 308.
6. Ibid.
7. Ibid.
8. Ibid., page 320.
9. John Dillenberger, "Grace and Works in Martin Luther and Joseph Smith," in *Reflections on Mormonism: Judaeo-Christian Parallels,* edited by Truman G. Madsen., (Provo, Utah: BYU Religious Studies Center, 1978), page 179.
10. Stephen E. Robinson, *Are Mormons Christians?* (Salt Lake City: Bookcraft, 1991), page 38.
11. David L. Paulsen, "Early Christian Belief in a Corporeal Deity: Origen and Augustine as Reluctant Witnesses," *Harvard Theological Review* 83 (1990): 105.
12. Elaine Pagels, *Adam, Eve, and the Serpent* (New York: Random House, 1988), pages 99–100.
13. Ibid., page 117.
14. Ibid., page 99.
15. Ibid., page 126.
16. Ibid., pages 125–26.
17. Ibid., page 106. See also Heinrich Boehmer, *Martin Luther: Road to Reformation* (New York: Meridian Books, 1957), page 139.

18. Herbert W. Schneider, *The Puritan Mind* (Ann Arbor: University of Michigan Press, 1958), page 98.
19. Published in two parts in 1808 and 1832, *Faust* is a literary masterpiece in which the central character has a consuming desire to comprehend life's meaning. He agrees to yield his eternal soul to the devil, if the devil can give him such complete access to the depths of human experience and understanding that Faust feels content to cease his quest for further knowledge. Mephistopheles thus leads Faust through a lifetime of complicated experiences with love, sin, disappointment, guilt, beauty, intellectual comprehension, economic power, and finally a taste of service to others. After years of ceaseless striving, it is only when Faust finally contemplates the joy of offering his knowledge and power to benefit other people that he utters the phrase of ultimate satisfaction, "Linger awhile, thou art so fair." Faust then collapses into death and Mephisto comes for his soul. But in that moment, to the devil's tormented astonishment, angels sweep down to bear off Faust's soul to heaven. The angels later explain, "Whoever strives in ceaseless toil, him we may grant redemption. And when on high, transfigured love has added intercession, the blest will throng to him above with welcoming compassion."

Both Faust and his author, Goethe, embody the indomitable human confidence of the pre-Restoration era. The Enlightenment's "light" regarding human possibilities was in utter contrast to the "dark" of Augustine's dark ages. One intellectual historian described this optimistic spirit with words Augustine and Luther would not have accepted: "We are agents as well as observers; we are not just objects in the world, but we can change it." (Robert C. Solomon, *Continental Philosophy Since 1750* [New York: Oxford: Oxford University Press, 1988], page 36.) Thus, writes a noted Faust scholar, Faust "assumes symbolic significance as the extreme exemplar of the deepest drives of western civilization. Self-realization . . . is a program without inner or outer limits." (Hermann Weigand, "Goethe's *Faust*: An Introduction for Students and Teachers of General Literature," in Johann Wolfgang von Goethe, *Faust*, Norton Critical Edition, edited by Cyrus Hamlin, translated by Walter Arndt [New York: W. W. Norton & Co., 1976], page 448.)

Faust also carries religious overtones. For one thing, Faust's stirring quest for knowledge in an imperfect world suggests a positive view of Adam's fall that was articulated by Goethe's friend Schiller, who conceded the tragedy of the fall but argued that "the fall was also an absolutely necessary first step in the higher development of mankind. . . . Without [the fall], man would forever have remained a child of Nature, innocent but ignorant, unable to develop the faculties of distinguishing between good and evil." (Ibid., page 447.) This positive understanding of the fall is closer to the truth as taught by the Restoration than it is to the traditional Christian heritage.

Moreover, we read the speech by the angels to mean that heaven's mercy allowed Faust to rob Satan's claim to justice only because Faust had demonstrated honest repentance and growth in the relentless and self-initiated striving of his whole life. At the same time, neither his effort nor God's mercy alone would have sufficed by itself: he was finally rescued by mercy, but only because he had worked hard enough to prove himself worthy of it.

Goethe recognized the individual's capacity to improve himself or herself by learning from experience, but he also saw a need for higher powers. And although he still needed to know the place of Christ's Atonement and its attendant commandments and ordinances, Goethe did sense generally the relationship between justice, mercy, and repentance as taught by the Restoration. But, significantly, traditional Christian theology offered him little support for that understanding, because its Augustinian premises were so limiting and so inconsistent with obvious human experience.

In that sense, Goethe and the Western thought he represented at Joseph Smith's time illustrate what Dillenberger meant in describing Christian theology's "untenable problem"—"how to reconcile the new power of humanity with the negative inherited views of humanity, without abandoning the necessity of grace."

20. Ibid., page 448.
21. Harvey Cox, *The Secular City* (New York: Macmillan, 1965).
22. Notre Dame theology department chairman Lawrence Cunningham, in Nancy Gibbs, "Angels among Us," page 65. See note 3.
23. Philip Turner, "To Students of Divinity: A Convocation Address," *First Things,* October 1992, pages 25, 26.
24. Dillenberger, "Grace and Works in Martin Luther and Joseph Smith," page 104, note 9.
25. See chapter 9, "Belonging to Jesus Christ."
26. *Daily Universe,* November 22, 1991, page 1.

CHAPTER SEVEN

Forgiveness and Christ Figures:
The Atonement and Being Harmed by the Sins of Others

1. M. Catherine Thomas, "When Our Reaching Reaches His," in Dawn H. Anderson and Marie Cornwall, eds., *Women and the Power Within* (Salt Lake City: Deseret Book Co., 1991), pages 186–89.
2. Allen Bergin, in *Counseling and Values,* 33 (1988): 28–30.
3. Carri P. Jenkins, "Toward the Light of Hope: Victims of Abuse," *Brigham Young Magazine,* May 1993, page 35.
4. Bergin, in *Counseling and Values.*
5. Ibid.
6. *Hamlet,* act 3, scene 1, lines 57–60.
7. Jenkins, "Toward the Light of Hope," pages 33–34.
8. Ibid., page 36.
9. Ibid., pages 38–39.
10. Anne Horton, quoted in ibid., page 39.

CHAPTER EIGHT

Belonging to the Church of Christ

1. *Hymns of The Church of Jesus Christ of Latter-day Saints* (Salt Lake City: The Church of Jesus Christ of Latter-day Saints, 1948), no. 70.
2. See chapter 1, note 1.
3. See chapter 6, notes 17–18 and accompanying text.
4. See chapter 4, notes 1–3 and accompanying text.
5. Hugh Nibley, in *Sunstone,* December 1990, pages 10–11.
6. Jeffrey R. Holland, "Belonging: A View of Membership," *Ensign,* April 1980, page 27.
7. Ibid., quoting Elder Marion D. Hanks in "Freedom and Responsibility," *BYU Speeches of the Year, 1964* (Provo, Utah: Brigham Young University), page 9.
8. Eugene England, *Why the Church Is As True As the Gospel* (Salt Lake City: Bookcraft, 1986).
9. Bruce R. McConkie, "The Ten Blessings of the Priesthood," *Ensign,* November

1977, pages 33–35. See also the listing of these blessings in chapter 13, note 1 and accompanying text.
10. See chapters 1 and 2 of Hafen, *The Believing Heart.*

CHAPTER NINE
Belonging to Jesus Christ

1. See chapter 2, pages 30–31.
2. See chapter 2, pages 30–31 and chapter 5, pages 91–95. The Greek use of "comfortless" and "orphans" is noted in Catherine Thomas, BYU Devotional, December 7, 1993.
3. *Teachings of the Prophet Joseph Smith,* pages 150–51.
4. See page 1 of Hafen, *The Broken Heart.*
5. Bruce R. McConkie, "Our Relationship with the Lord," BYU Devotional, March 2, 1982.
6. See pages 154–55, this chapter.
7. See Hafen, *The Broken Heart,* chapter 8.
8. See ibid., chapter 10.
9. See ibid., chapter 11.
10. See ibid., chapter 1.
11. See "Lecture Sixth," *Lectures on Faith* (Salt Lake City: Deseret Book Co., 1985).
12. See chapter 6, *The Broken Heart.*
13. "Lecture Sixth," *Lectures on Faith.*
14. From "The King of Love My Shepherd Is," by Harry Rowe Shelley.
15. See chapter 16, "The Familistic Life: Status and Contract in Modern America."
16. "Lecture Sixth," *Lectures on Faith.*
17. See Hafen, *The Broken Heart,* chapter 11.

CHAPTER TEN
Ten Insights from King Benjamin About the Atonement

1. For a summary of the basic doctrines of the Atonement, see the introduction to Hafen, *The Broken Heart.*
2. See chapter 6, "The Restored Doctrine of the Atonement."
3. See chapter 5, "Eve Heard All These Things and Was Glad."
4. See chapter 9, "Belonging to Jesus Christ."
5. Dallin H. Oaks, "Another Testament of Jesus Christ," CES Telecast for College-Age Young Adults, June 6, 1993.

CHAPTER ELEVEN
Family Belonging: These Bonds Are Our Liberation

1. See note 13, chapter 3.
2. Bellah, *Individualism, Community, and Ethics,* page 6.
3. Mary A. Glendon, *Abortion and Divorce in Western Law* (Cambridge: Harvard University Press, 1987), page 63.
4. Ibid., page 105.
5. Carl Schneider, "Moral Discourse and the Transformation of American Family Law," *Michigan Law Review* 83 (1985): 1,803, 1,807–8.
6. Patricia Wald, "Making Sense Out of the Rights of Youth," *Human Rights* 4 (1974): 13, 15.
7. "Through the Eyes of Children," *Time,* August 8, 1988, page 32.
8. Albert Ellis, "Psychotherapy and Atheistic Values: A Response to A. E. Bergin's

'Psychotherapy and Religious Values,'" *Journal of Consulting and Clinical Psychology* 48 (1980): 635, 638 (table 2).

9. Martha Minow, "Forming Underneath Everything that Grows: Toward a History of Family Law," *Wisconsin Law Review* (1985): 819, 894.

10. Carl Schneider, "Moral Discourse and the Transformation of American Family Law," pages 1,803, 1,860.

11. Robert N. Bellah et al., *Habits of the Heart: Individualism and Commitment in American Life* (Berkeley: University of California Press, 1985), page 86.

12. Stanley Kunitz, "The Poet's Quest for the Father," *New York Times,* February 22, 1987, section 7, page 36.

13. Ibid.

14. "Father and Son," in *Divided Light: Father and Son Poems,* edited by Jason Shinder (New York: Sheep Meadow Press, 1983), pages 20–21.

15. Carl Schneider, note 10, above, at page 1,819, quoting letter from Max Weber to Edgar Jaffe, written in 1907.

16. "Lindbergh Nightmare," *Time,* February 5, 1973, page 35.

17. See Sorokin, *Society, Culture, and Personality,* 2d ed. (New York: Cooper Square Publishers, 1962), pages 99–108.

18. Michael Novak, "The Family Out of Favor," *Harper's,* April 1976, page 37; emphasis added.

19. See chapter 12, "Planting Promises in the Hearts of the Children."

CHAPTER TWELVE
Planting Promises in the Hearts of the Children

1. "Talk of the Town," *New Yorker,* August 30, 1976, pages 21–22, quoting an anonymous letter.

2. Alston Chase, *Group Memory* (Boston, Mass.: Little, Brown & Co., 1980), page 284.

3. Marie Winn, *Children without Childhood* (New York: Pantheon, 1983), page 5.

4. Neil Postman, *The Disappearance of Childhood* (New York: Delacorte Press, 1982), pages 74–80.

5. Gerald Grant, "The Character of Education and the Education of Character," in *American Education* 18 (1982): 135, 146.

6. Michael R. Gottfredson, *A General Theory of Crime* (Stanford: Stanford University Press, 1990), page 96 (emphasis added).

7. Arthur Kornhaber and Kenneth L. Woodward, *Grandparents, Grandchildren: The Vital Connection* (New Brunswick, N.J.: Transaction Books, 1984), page xii.

8. Ibid., page xx.

9. Melvin Zelnik, John F. Kantner, and Kathleen Ford, *Sex and Pregnancy in Adolescence* (Beverly Hills: Sage Publications, 1981), page 182.

10. Baehr vs. Lewin, 852 Pacific 2nd 44 (Hawaii 1993).

11. Christopher Lasch, *Haven in a Heartless World* (New York: Basic Books, 1977), page 123.

12. See Tocqueville, *Democracy in America,* page 194.

13. David H. Lawrence, *Apropos of Lady Chatterley's Lover* (Brooklyn: Haskell Booksellers, 1973), pages 35–36.

14. Camille S. Williams, "Sparrows and Lilies," *First Things,* August/September, 1993, pages 12–13 (emphasis added).

15. Letter from Sarah Hafen dated October 28, 1993.

16. Williams, "Sparrows and Lilies," page 197.

CHAPTER THIRTEEN
Sustaining—and Being Sustained by—the Priesthood

1. Bruce R. McConkie, "The Ten Blessings of the Priesthood," *Ensign,* November 1977, pages 33–35.
2. Dallin H. Oaks, "Spiritual Gifts," *Ensign,* September 1986, page 72.

CHAPTER FOURTEEN
Women, Feminism, and Gender

1. William H. Chafe, *Women and Equality: Changing Patterns in American Culture* (New York: Oxford University Press, 1977), page 139.
2. Betty Friedan, *The Feminine Mystique* (New York: W. W. Norton & Co., 1963).
3. Robert A. Nisbet, *Twilight of Authority* (Oxford: Oxford University Press, 1975), pages 82–83.
4. See Mary Ann Mason, *The Equality Trap* (New York: Simon & Schuster, 1988), page 23–25. A recent survey on America's national mood reported that 80 percent of the nation's workforce is paid by hourly wages. Those wages increased an average of 2.6 percent per year from 1948 to 1973, creating increasing prosperity as seen in such indicators as home ownership. However, "from 1974 to the present time, not only have hourly wages not kept pace with inflation, they have actually gone down. The number of skilled manufacturing jobs that were well paying steadily declined, exchanged for lower paying service jobs. Today we . . . are living at the 1965 level in terms of real wages. So you have a generation of downward mobility since 1974." (Daniel Yankelovich, "The New Mood and What It Means for Higher Education," 45 *American Association of Higher Education Bulletin* #10, June 1993, page 5.
5. First Presidency Reaffirmation on ERA, August 24, 1978 (pamphlet).
6. *Newsweek,* March 31, 1986, page 58.
7. Orania Papazoglou, "Despising Our Mothers, Despising Ourselves," *First Things,* January 1992, page 11. Similarly, *Newsweek* magazine reported in 1986 that "acknowledging the excesses of an earlier generation, whose emphasis on equality for women sometimes crossed the line into outright contempt for motherhood, a number of leaders believe the movement must openly embrace basic female values, longings and priorities." (*Newsweek,* "Feminism's Identity Crisis," March 31, 1986.)
8. Betty Friedan, *The Second Stage,* rev. ed. (New York: Summit Books, 1986).
9. Carol Gilligan, *In a Different Voice: Psychological Theory and Women's Development* (Cambridge, Mass.: Harvard University Press, 1982).
10. "The Eternity of Sex," *Young Women's Journal,* October 1914, page 600.
11. Papazoglou, "Despising Our Mothers," page 15.
12. Tocqueville, *Democracy in America,* pages 499, 501.
13. See chapter 15, "From Status to Contract: Belonging and the Ancient Order."
14. George Gilder, *Men and Marriage* (Gretna: Pelican, 1986).
15. *Ensign,* May 1978, page 10.
16. In Marilyn Warenski, *Patriarchs and Politics: The Plight of the Mormon Woman* (San Francisco: McGraw-Hill, 1978), page 1.
17. Mary Stovall Richards, "Feminism," in *Encyclopedia of Mormonism,* page 506.
18. See pages 232–38.
19. M. Russell Ballard, "Strength in Counsel," *Ensign,* November, 1993, page 76.
20. Cheryl Preston, "Feminism and Faith: Reflections on the Mormon Heavenly Mother," *Texas Journal of Women and the Law,* 2 (1993): 337–86.
21. For example, "Over the past decade and a half, feminist activists and scholars

have begun a revolutionary movement in thought and behavior so profound and so rooted in a transformed consciousness that it will not stop until all Western consciousness and civilizations are transformed. The main reason for this is that we are seeing a beginning transformation in the consciousness of the half of humanity who, as a whole, has had relatively little *real* (as contrasted with ideologically constituted) investment in or benefit from the dominant patriarchal social order." (Ruth Bleier, *Science and Gender: A Critique of Biology and Its Theories on Women* [New York: Pergamon Press, 1984], page 199.)

22. As explained in Mary Stovall Richards, "Feminism," page 507.
23. Judith Stacey, "Good Riddance to 'The Family'": A Response to David Popenoe," *Journal of Marriage and the Family* 55 (1993): 558, 560. Compare David Popenoe, "American Family Decline, 1960–1990: A Review and Appraisal," same journal, page 527.
24. Ruth Bleier, *Science and Gender,* note at pages 199–200.
25. Joyce A. Little, "Naming Good and Evil," in *First Things,* May 1992, page 28.
26. "The scriptures and the teachings of the Apostles and prophets speak of us in premortal life as sons and daughters, spirit children of God. See D&C 76:24; see also Num. 16:22; Heb. 12:9. Gender existed before and did not begin at mortal birth. See D&C 132:63; First Presidency, 'Origin of Man' (November 1909); in James R. Clark, comp., *Messages of the First Presidency of the Church of Jesus Christ of Latter-day Saints,* 6 vols. (Salt Lake City: Bookcraft, 1965–75), 4:203; see also Spencer W. Kimball, *Ensign,* March 1976, page 71; Gordon B. Hinckley, *Ensign,* November 1983, page 83." (*Ensign,* November 1993, pages 21–22.)
27. Ibid., page 72.
28. Dallin H. Oaks, *Ensign,* November 1993, page 73.
29. John A. Widtsoe, *Evidences and Reconciliations* (Salt Lake City: Bookcraft, 1960), page 171. "Informed by revelation, we celebrate Eve's act and honor her wisdom and courage in the great episode called the Fall." (Dallin H. Oaks, *Ensign,* November 1993, page 73. See also Bruce R. McConkie, "Eve and the Fall," in *Woman* [Salt Lake City: Deseret Book Co., 1979], pages 67–68.)
30. Widtsoe, *Evidences and Reconciliations,* page 193.
31. Bruce R. McConkie, "Our Sisters from the Beginning," *Ensign,* January 1979, page 63.
32. Ibid., page 61.
33. Quoted in Maureen U. Beecher et al., *The Latter-day Saints and Women's Rights, 1870–1920: A Brief Survey* (Task Papers in LDS History, 1979, #29, page 12.)
34. First Presidency Reaffirmation on ERA, August 24, 1978.
35. Boyd K. Packer, "For Time and All Eternity," *Ensign,* November 1993, page 22.
36. Dallin H. Oaks, "Statement on the Education of Women at BYU," BYU President's Assembly, September 9, 1975; emphasis added.
37. Maureen Ward, *From Adam's Rib to Women's Lib* (Salt Lake City: Bookcraft, 1981), page 107.
38. Packer, "For Time and All Eternity," page 21.
39. Papazoglou, "Despising Our Mothers," page 11, note 6.
40. The October 1993 General Conference included numerous warnings to men regarding the hazards of unrighteous dominion, which violates the oath and covenant of the priesthood. For example, see Packer, "For Time and All Eternity," page 22.
41. See Ballard, "Strength in Counsel," page 76.
42. Hugh Nibley, "Patriarchy and Matriarchy," in *Old Testament and Related*

Studies (Salt Lake City and Provo, Utah: Deseret Book Co. and Foundation for Ancient Research and Mormon Studies, 1986), pages 97, 95.

CHAPTER FIFTEEN
From Status to Contract: Belonging and the Ancient Order

1. Henry S. Maine, Sr., *Ancient Law* (1st American edition 1870) (New York: Dorset Press, 1987), pages 163–65.
2. *Hymns,* 1985, no. 29.
3. This story is retold with Ara Call's permission. The circumstances surrounding the church's challenges with the peculiar property laws required by the Mexican constitution are explained in F. Burton Howard, *Marion G. Romney: His Life and Faith* (Salt Lake City: Bookcraft, 1988), pages 206–11. In 1964 the Church adopted the bold new policy of donating legal title to its properties to the government of Mexico, with the request that the government then voluntarily allow the Church to use the buildings. This change became a major factor in the Church's subsequent growth in Mexico. (Ibid.)
4. "Lecture Sixth," *Lectures on Faith.*
5. In "The Death of the Hired Man," as quoted in John Bartlett, *Familiar Quotations,* 15th ed. (Boston: Little, Brown & Co., 1980), page 747.
6. Merlin S. Myers, "Kinship, Religion, and the Transformation of Society," BYU Forum Address delivered April 1, 1975.
7. Quoted in Leonard Arrington, *Great Basin Kingdom: An Economic History of the Latter-day Saints, 1830–1900* (Lincoln: University of Nebraska Press, 1966), page 25.
8. See John W. Welch, "Lehi's Last Will and Testament: A Legal Approach," in *The Book of Mormon: Second Nephi, the Doctrinal Structure* (Provo, Ut.: BYU Religious Studies Center, 1989).
9. Thomas Greer, *A Brief History of the Modern World,* page 232.
10. Ibid., page 233.
11. Address by Walter Berns to the Philadelphia Society 12 (April 11, 1981), unpublished manuscript.
12. Ibid. at 11.
13. Ibid. at 12–13.
14. Friedrich Nietzsche, *Thus Spake Zarathustra,* translated by Thomas Common (Westminster, Md.: Modern Library, 1951), page 306.

CHAPTER SIXTEEN
The Familistic Life: Status and Contract in Modern America

1. Alexis de Tocqueville, *Democracy in America,* edited by J. P. Mayer (Garden City, N.Y.: Doubleday & Co., 1969), page 513
2. Ibid., page 287.
3. Ibid., page 590.
4. Ibid., page 509.
5. Peter Berger and Richard Neuhaus, *To Empower People: The Role of Mediating Structures in Public Policy* (Washington, D.C.: American Enterprise Institute for Public Policy Research, 1977), pages 3–6.
6. Bellah et al., *Habits of the Heart,* page vii.
7. Nisbet, *The Quest for Community,* page 202.
8. Ibid., page 203.
9. See chapter 4, "Personal Identity, Individuality, and Belonging."
10. Sorokin, *Society, Culture, and Personality,* pages 99–107.

11. See chapter 2, "*Amae* and the Longing to Belong."
12. Sorokin, *Society, Culture, and Personality,* page 104.
13. Bellah et al., *Habits of the Heart,* pages 85, 101.
14. Ibid., page 47.
15. Carl Schneider, "Moral Discourse," *Michigan Law Review,* page 1,859.
16. See chapter 15, notes 11–13 and accompanying text.
17. Sorokin, *Society, Culture, and Personality,* page 108.
18. Ibid., page 99.
19. See chapter 2, "*Amae* and the Longing to Belong."

CHAPTER SEVENTEEN

Romantic Belonging

1. Boyd K. Packer, "Eternal Love," BYU Fireside, November 3, 1963.
2. Ibid.
3. Katz and Cronin, "Sexuality and College Life," *Change,* February-March, 1980, page 44.
4. See the summary of social science and legal literature in Hafen, "Marriage, Kinship, and Sexual Privacy," *Michigan Law Review* 81 (1983): 463, note 9.
5. Stan E. Weed, "Curbing Births, Not Pregnancies," *Wall Street Journal,* October 14, 1986, page 32, col. 4–6.
6. Allen Bergin, "Bringing the Restoration to the Academic World: Clinical Psychology as a Test Case," *BYU Studies* 19 (1979): 449, 464.
7. Baehr vs. Lewin, 852 Pacific 2nd 44 (Hawaii 1993).
8. Ellis, "Psychotherapy and Religious Values," *Journal of Consulting and Clinical Psychology* 48 (1980): 635.
9. Kenneth Kolson, *Chronicles of Culture,* September-October, 1979, page 18.
10. Blaise Pascal, *Pensees,* Great Books of the Western World, vol. 33 (Chicago: Encyclopedia Britannica, 1952).
11. Packer, "Eternal Love."
12. David H. Lawrence, *Essays on Sex Literature and Censorship* (New York: Twayne, 1953), page 89.
13. Erich Fromm, *The Art of Loving* (New York: Harper and Row, 1956), pages 45–46.
14. *For the Strength of Youth* (Salt Lake City: The Church of Jesus Christ of Latter-day Saints, 1992).

CHAPTER EIGHTEEN

Celebrating Womanhood

1. *Church News,* November 6, 1983.
2. "Eternal Love," BYU Fireside, 1963.
3. "A Book," *Favorite Poems of Emily Dickinson* (New York: Avenel Books, 1978), page 41.
4. See chapter 5, "Eve Heard All These Things and Was Glad."
5. See chapter 14, note 13.

CHAPTER NINETEEN

Labor for That Which Satisfies

1. See chapter 6, "The Restored Doctrine of the Atonement: The 'Authentic Theology.'"
2. Parley P. Pratt, *The Essential Parley P. Pratt* (Salt Lake City: Signature Books, 1990), page 124.

3. Quoted in Obert C. Tanner, *Christ's Ideals for Living* (Salt Lake City: Deseret Sunday School Union Board, 1955).

4. *The Iliad of Homer and The Odyssey* (Chicago: Encyclopedia Britannica, 1952), page 314.

5. "Souls, Symbols, and Sacraments," BYU Devotional, January 12, 1988.

6. *Improvement Era,* June 1917, page 739.

7. *Macbeth,* act 1, scene 5, line 44.

8. Gary S. Morson, "Prosaics," *American Scholar,* Autumn 1988, pages 523–34.

9. Gibran, *The Prophet,* page 28.

10. *Teachings of the Prophet Joseph Smith,* page 51; emphasis added.

11. *Hymns,* 1985, no. 102; emphasis added.

EPILOGUE
Still, Still with Thee

1. In James Dalton Morrison, ed., *Masterpieces of Religious Verse* (New York and London: Harper & Brothers, 1948), page 75.

Index

333